ADVANCE PRAISE

"The book provides a provocative view on the technology-driven reshaping of the financial sector. It helps the reader understand how disruptive models are reshaping global economies and consider strategies for effective response."

Ricky Knox
Founder, Tandem Bank

Published by
LID Publishing
An imprint of LID Business Media Ltd.
The Record Hall, Studio 304,
16-16a Baldwins Gardens,
London EC1N 7RJ, UK

info@lidpublishing.com
www.lidpublishing.com

A member of:

BPR

businesspublishersroundtable.com

© Arthur D Little, 2022
© LID Business Media Limited, 2022

Printed by Gutenberg, Malta

ISBN: 978-1-911671-48-0
ISBN: 978-1-911671-49-7 (ebook)

Cover and page design: Caroline Li

IGNACIO GARCIA ALVES
PHILIPPE DE BACKER
JUAN GONZALEZ

DISRUPTION

THE FUTURE OF BANKING
AND FINANCIAL SERVICES –
HOW TO NAVIGATE AND SEIZE
THE OPPORTUNITIES

MADRID | MEXICO CITY | LONDON
NEW YORK | BUENOS AIRES
BOGOTA | SHANGHAI | NEW DELHI

CONTENTS

FOREWORD

Writing any kind of book is a major undertaking. Not only is there the initial thinking through and testing out of your idea, but also the research needed to validate it. For a technical book like this, that preparation and legwork is not insignificant. Then there is the selection and organization of the material gathered – and all this before any actual writing has been done.

But while much of this work is done in 'solitary confinement,' *Disruption* has also been a collaborative project, and that has been particularly necessary given the fast-moving nature of the banking industry.

So, in addition to drawing from many contemporary sources of information, the book would not be what it is without the invaluable contributions of leaders of banking and financial organizations from around the globe.

They must make business-changing decisions based upon how they see the world around them, where it currently stands and what must be done to equip their institution – long-established or disruptive newcomer – for the journey ahead.

This means each of them has brought an individual perspective, based on their understanding of banking's 'point of arrival,' encompassing their own business model, degree of technological adoption, location, and the nature of their customer base.

Not all agreed with our assessment of the traditional banking industry. Indeed, some were robust in their defense of its long-term future and thought that we were in a period of transition, after which things would settle back to something not dissimilar to before.

While there were different thoughts on banking's point of arrival, there was universal agreement that times were difficult in general for banks.

And even when our contributors' thinking did not entirely align with our central thesis, their insights forced us to question our position and, in some instances, to change it.

Unfortunately, the structure of the book and the editorial process mean we have only been able to explicitly include a fraction of the material from our interviews.

Nevertheless, the insights we gained proved instrumental in helping shape our thoughts and ideas in ways we had not foreseen at the start of this journey. We're extremely grateful to everyone who has so generously given their valuable time to be interrogated by us and help inform our thinking.

We would especially like to thank:

Sheikh Waleed K. Al Hashar, CEO, Bank Muscat

H.E. Mr Abdulaziz Bin Nasser Al Khalifa, Former CEO, Qatar Development Bank

Sheikh Mohammed Bin Abdulla Al Thani, Deputy Group CEO and CEO, Ooredoo Qatar

Mr Hakan Binbaşgil, Board Member and CEO, Akbank

Mr Giuseppe Castagna, Group CEO, Banco BPM SpA

Mr Sandeep Chouhan, Acting CEO and Group COO, Abu Dhabi Islamic Bank

Mr Frédéric Debord, CEO, Orange Madagascar

Mr David Dew, Senior Advisor to the Board, The Saudi British Bank (SABB)

Mr Joris Dierckx, Regional Head of Southeast Asia, BNP Paribas

Ms Fabienne Dulac, CEO, Orange France

Mr Peter England, CEO, Rakbank

Mr Jean-François Fallacher, CEO, Orange España

Mr Nazzareno Gregori, General Manager, Credem

Mr Oliver Holle, Co-Founder and Managing Partner, Speedinvest

Ms Alice Holzman, CEO, Ma French Bank

Mr Radován Jelasity, CEO, Erste Bank Hungary Zrt

Mr Jan Juchelka, CEO, Komerční banka, a.s.

Mr Ricky Knox, Founder, Tandem

Mr Paul de Leusse, CEO, Orange Bank

Mr Bernd van Linder, CEO, Commercial Bank of Dubai

Ms Regina Ovesny-Straka, CEO, Volksbank Steiermark AG

Mr Roberto Parazzini, Chairman of the Management Board and CEO, Deutsche Bank SpA

Mr Thorsten Piesl, CEO, KALYP Technologies

Mr Tomáš Salomon, Chairman and CEO, Česká Spořitelna

Dr R. Seetharaman, CEO, Doha Bank

Mr Bahren Shaari, CEO, Bank of Singapore

Mr Jack Stack, Chair, Supervisory Board, Ceska Sporitelna (ret.), CEO, Ceska Sporitelna (ret.)

Dr Mário Vaz, CEO, Vodafone Portugal
Mr Robert Zadrazil, CEO, UniCredit Bank Austria

Mr Igor Žganjer, Managing Director, Global Payments SRO

Again, thank you all for your input. This book is better for it.

I would be remiss not to acknowledge the contribution of my colleagues at Arthur D Little, who have offered their expertise and guidance many times during the writing of *Disruption*. Given their work with financial clients, they are acutely aware of how the industry is evolving, so being able to draw upon their high-quality research has been of exceptional benefit. I would particularly like to single out Juan Gonzàlez for his involvement as a contributor of material, perceptive critic and much-needed cheerleader during the whole editorial process. Thank you, Juan.

Now all that is left is for me to introduce you to *Disruption*.

CHAPTER 1

THE FUTURE OF BANKING

This is a book about the future of banking.

More specifically, it is about what are generally termed 'universal banks' and how they must change if they're to survive an army of new competitors and a potential economic downturn the likes of which they've never seen before.

The ideas and insights contained here were developed through our work and research at the international consulting firm Arthur D Little, as well as through interviews with leaders in a wide range of financial institutions around the world.

This opening chapter is a microcosm of our thinking and, unlike an Agatha Christie mystery, we won't leave it until the last page to reveal the killer.

We hope this book can be read by anyone with an interest in finance, one of the underpinning forces of our world. However, we think it will particularly resonate with those in the financial services sector who already have a strong sense that traditional banking has fundamentally changed.

 If that is you, we hope what you read here has something to offer. But, let us be clear: you won't find a magic wand or a miracle prescription for putting things right. This is not a cookbook filled with 'by the numbers' recipes for taking you from where you are to where you need to be.

Banks are too unique and too complex for anything like that. So, how each needs to react will depend on their history, the competition, the nature and complexity of their products, the external influence exerted by third parties such as governments and regulators, as well as their own readiness and willingness to change into something else.

Instead, think of *Disruption* as a roadmap that can suggest promising courses of action and help guide you in the right direction. In other words, consider this book a 'thinking tool' to stimulate action. If our thesis is right – and we believe it is – you'll need to take action sooner rather than later. That urgency is necessary to prevent disruptive new organizations from pulling the rug from beneath your feet.

WHAT'S THE STATE OF PLAY?

We say this because we can only conclude from our research and analysis that the model of the traditional bank we've all grown up with is no longer fit for purpose.

Of course, you may not agree with such a radical statement and dismiss us as intellectual scoundrels who have no right to issue such a stark warning. That is your privilege.

However, we think that the evidence is incontrovertible. It's our hope that you'll stay with us to the end of this book, and perhaps reach the same conclusion as to what the future holds.

We should also point out, in our defense, that we are not saying that banks have *no* future. We aren't implying that traditional banks should slink away into a corner, curl up and wait to wither away. Rather, we'd suggest that they must accept that they'll have a *different* future.

The bottom line is that the sector's future looks dark indeed if bank leaders don't make radical changes.

In the first part of this book, we will set out why we believe the traditional 'universal bank' model is dead. We'll examine how it was killed off by a changing marketplace and the emergence of a new breed of financial players. These disruptors are light on their feet and armed with awesomely destructive technological power.

The arrival of these industry-changing players should be a wake-up call to banks, because if they're to survive the threat they need to move quickly. Unfortunately, banks are conservative organizations that tend to move very slowly, have a track record of failing to adapt, and are generally poor at anticipating change. This tradition-bound inertia – and outright resistance to change – means that the transformation of 'legacy banks' will involve major effort.

The rules of the game have changed so fundamentally that traditional banks have no option but to adopt a different model, one that's much better suited to the world as we now know it. But there is a major problem facing all traditional banks whose very survival rests on becoming *something different*. Institutional reinvention comes at a substantial cost, which begs the question: where will the money come from to do what needs to be done?

From a quick look at the numbers, it's clear whom the markets are betting on, and it's not the universal banks that are trading at a discount and whose value would be far greater if they were broken up into specialized, stand-alone businesses.

It is the new players – financial services technology firms (the so-called fintechs) and challenger banks that often have yet to turn a profit – that are being backed.

THE TRANSFORMATION IMPERATIVE

In part two of this book, we'll consider this conundrum in more detail and look at what traditional banks must do to fight back and ultimately survive. We will suggest that they do this by improving their performance in the short term to deliver better results, reflected in such metrics as return on capital. This will generate the funds needed to embark on a program of innovation, the transformative engine of future growth.

But banks will only achieve this if they see the transformation for what it is – a fundamental reconfiguration. It is not a gradual, incremental set of improvements, or fiddling around at the edges, or battening down of the hatches and waiting to see what happens. Instead, we're talking about visceral change at the very core of the organization. Anything else is just rearranging the deckchairs on a sinking Titanic.

The route forward for traditional banks is relatively obvious, but that doesn't mean it will be an easy undertaking. Finding ways to simultaneously pursue two seemingly incompatible objectives – short-term improvement and long-term innovation – is far from easy.

But yes, we believe there is a way forward. In fact, we've found numerous organizations that are successfully juggling these two imperatives. The best of them are truly ambidextrous, with a balanced left- and right-handed approach that reconciles the need to bring about change while surviving day-to-day.

They've managed to square the circle by consistently and stubbornly focusing on long-term targets while making their operations ever more efficient. They continuously reshape their organizations through innovation, positioning themselves to meet the needs of tomorrow's marketplace. They are the very definition of ambidexterity.

THE RIGHT LEADER
FOR NEW TIMES

Perhaps not surprisingly, putting this new kind of model in place also requires a special kind of leader – an equally ambidextrous CEO who's willing to think beyond traditional banking norms and boundaries, and make the big decisions that are needed. One of their most important roles will be to convince stakeholders that radical change is required and that 'business as usual' is no longer an option.

Unfortunately, if an organization's current CEO does not fully understand that they need to do more than just manage the status quo, any transformation is doomed before it starts.

The situation is made more complex because the current crop of CEOs is staring into unknown territory. It's been well over a decade since the last global economic downturn, when most current banking leaders weren't yet in leadership positions. This means they've never had to deal with anything like what is inevitably coming.

So, the traditional bank needs someone in charge who can boldly envision the new organization that's required, and what needs to be done to create it. If they're unable to clearly articulate this, others won't follow them on the journey.

The implication is that if the wrong person's in the job right now, they should stand aside for someone willing to countenance the disruption of their business in novel, innovative ways. What's needed is someone who is strategically bold, willing to think the unthinkable, and ready to rip up existing business, revenue and operating models that no longer work.

In so doing, they must be clairvoyant – able to see the world as it will be and envision products and services their customers will want in two and five and ten years. They must also have the ambition to create a customer journey of such excellence that it will ensure brand loyalty for years to come. In doing to, banks will need to learn lessons not from other banks, but from the likes of Amazon, Google and Facebook.

Of course, any transformation will ultimately come to nothing if the CEO is not supported by the entire C-suite and the board. If the board does not recognize what needs to be done, it's likely that the institution will continue to be led – either through inertia or poor recruitment – by a leader who's focused on yesterday rather than tomorrow.

If the board and all senior leaders are not acting as one, lack of agreement will make it difficult to eliminate the internal divisions that often lead to the failure of major transformations.

TRAPPED BY TECHNOLOGY

Later in this book, we'll look in detail at how legacy banks can boost their short-term performance through productivity and growth while they embark on their transformational journey.

Historically, many banks have thought of improving productivity as just a matter of aggressive generic cost-cutting. Though this may bring some short-term relief, it is not a satisfactory response. Instead, this kind of bloodletting just tends to weaken 'the patient,' rather than helping them bounce back to good health.

So, it is much better to improve productivity through targeted interventions, aimed at specific processes, and through the introduction of new technology that enables banks to do more with less. This 'digital problem solving,' as we call it, can help improve every aspect of the internal workings of a business.

Unfortunately, when it comes to embracing new technology, banks once again have a big problem.

For years they have kept ancient IT calcified in place, adding new bits as needed while haphazardly patching what doesn't work well. As a result, most are now sitting on an unholy mess of IT that slows their performance rather than enhancing it. This needs to be gotten rid of. But who wants to do that when it will lead to massive financial write-offs? Enter that brave, ambidextrous CEO who must step up and convince their board that the time to rebuild the infrastructure from the ground up is now. No more adding sticking plasters to rickety old tech.

You need only look at the challenges of customer acquisition to see that traditional banks must introduce things like robotic processing automation (RPA) to handle the many tasks that they still do manually. Or, set up new digital communication channels that can better engage customers. Or, implement artificial intelligence (AI) systems that allow dramatically better analysis of data.

Data is the new currency – the oil that powers business – and banks are sitting on a mountain of it. However, this is of little use if you don't have the means to turn it into the knowledge that helps create the kind of hyper-personalized offering your customers demand. That's absolutely critical to legacy banks' survival and future success.

One of the major challenges facing traditional financial institutions is that much of their data is inaccessible, imprisoned in different silos. This is the historical result of banks' tendency to divide themselves by vertical lines of business, such as retail, corporate, and investment banking.

When data doesn't flow smoothly between departments, it's impossible to have a 360-degree view of your customers. That panoramic view is necessary if you are to see the interdependencies and connections that enable you to deliver the most relevant products.

Streamlining IT and processes is important, but it's just an element in the drive to achieve greater productivity. Removing complexity should be another area of focus, and there's much that the traditional bank can do in this respect. For instance, they should get rid of the obsolete and underperforming old products that litter their portfolios.

Of course, we should acknowledge that the task of removing complexity is not made any easier for traditional banks by industry regulators and ever-tighter compliance requirements. Their oversight and enforcement will only become more onerous.

IS THERE A ROADMAP?

What needs to be done simply won't happen if banks lack a clear roadmap for moving forward, and sufficient control over the process. That's why many banks' digital efforts prove unsuccessful, despite significant investment. These often amount to random acts, rather than part of a cohesive, overarching productivity strategy that would allow banks to earn more from their people and use their capital more effectively by allocating it where it has the most impact.

It's easy to think of productivity improvement as being about getting the business in the right shape for a future fight. Yet, on its own, this isn't enough to put in place the short-term improvements that banks need. The effort also needs to be accompanied by growth. That's the fuel that makes things happen; without it there can be no transformation.

The overriding need to expand your revenue streams – which will add to the top line rather than the bottom line, as productivity does – is something we call the 'growth imperative.'

From our own research, we can see that growth is vitally important. In fact, over a ten-year period, 75% of the performance of those companies listed on the S&P Index can be attributed to their growth rate.

It's such sustainable growth that helps create a virtuous spiral, delivering funds that can be reinvested in the organization to feed its future transformation. This is what will enable banks to shift from their current labor-intensive model to a capital-based one consisting of more IT and fewer people.

GIVING UP TO GO FORWARD

Sadly, growth doesn't happen at the flick of a switch. You can't just wake up one morning and declare that everyone should 'go for growth.' As we will demonstrate, things tend to end badly for those who go down this path in pursuit of 'the wrong kind of growth.' If your growth plan is too risky, it is destined to fail. At the same time, you will also fail if it's not radical or innovative enough.

One of the key messages of this book is that all but the very largest of traditional banks will have to relinquish elements of their business simply because it is too costly and inefficient to try to be *all things to all people*.

This requires the ambidextrous CEO to make decisions about what areas to prioritize, because you cannot do everything at the same time. Try to fight a war on every front and you'll put yourself at a great disadvantage.

So, while there is a need for speed, it would be a mistake to try and push through everything simultaneously. That's a sure-fire recipe for getting bogged down. We have seen it happen all too often: banks try to tackle a half-a-dozen challenges at once and fail at all of them.

While there are some obvious open doors, based on historical competencies, many opportunities will lie outside what has been done in the past. This is the realm of 'market adjacencies' – the segments that ripple outward from the bank in concentric circles.

Those nearest to the center may be the most comfortable to move into, but probably aren't radical enough to deliver the change that's needed. Settling into these sectors would be akin to switching from a mechanical typewriter to an electric one in the age of laptops. This might improve things at a micro level, but it doesn't actually matter, because you'll still get left behind. On the other hand, move too far out and you'll find yourself in areas that are too disconnected from what the bank is all about. This will lead to greater unpredictability and the potential for unexpected issues.

As such, banks need to look at sectors in a Goldilocks zone, where they can have more of a 'cheese and biscuits' relationship than one that's 'chalk and cheese.'

Here, one phenomenon worthy of exploration is the whole concept of convergence: how different segments and industries with commonalities and synergies are inexorably drawn together over time.

Eventually, the boundaries between them dissolve, enabling players to bridge the gap with relative ease. The benefits of convergence are two-fold: it allows competitors to disrupt existing value chains to their advantage, and it creates opportunities for those ready to seize them.

INNOVATE OR DIE

If banks are to find and move into the zone that's right for them, they have to start doing things differently. More of the same just isn't going to work. And so, in the final part of the book, we consider how banks can help secure their long-term survival by reinventing themselves through innovation.

Innovation is something that banks were quite good at. For instance, the world's first ATM, located at a branch of Barclays in Enfield, north London, celebrated its 50th birthday back in 2017.[1] Of late, though, the traditional bank has lost its way and handed the innovation torch over to the fintechs.

Now, there can be a sense that innovation is something of an irregularly visited event rather than the continual process that it must be. Recognizing this is often one of the biggest challenges for traditional financial organizations, because their very foundations are built on the premise of maintaining stability rather than being at the center of any kind of radical change.

This can be a chilling realization. So, enter once again the ambidextrous CEO who has to make sure that innovation permeates every cell of an organization as part of the transformation process.

But how best to bring about the innovation that's required?

Instead of focusing on usual paths, traditional banks need to scour the universe for new ideas, including (*especially*) those outside the realm of financial services. They must then take the best, and through testing, trial and error, and rapid prototyping develop those that have the greatest potential.

This is when banks need to think about nurturing new projects, so they can be brought to fruition in a safe and controlled manner. And, although these are powerful tools, many banks and financial institutions have struggled to use them effectively. The biggest hurdle is often that they're unable to scale up their 'incubator baby' into a fully functioning entity that's able to cope and survive in the grown-up world. All too often, the new offspring is overwhelmed by its parent because it is too weak to become a core component of the organization. That's frequently due to underfunding or lack of the resources it needs to thrive.

But we believe there is a way to do this effectively, using what we call a 'breakthrough incubator.' This is a vehicle that helps ensure that a new project can be successfully scaled up and properly connected to the main organization. That allows it to become a proper member of the family, breathing the same air and eating at the same table. When this is done once, and done well, it can become the model for all future innovation.

WETWARE AS MUCH AS SOFTWARE

Of course, it doesn't matter how good the idea is if it isn't implemented well, and here there's often one final impediment: people.

Many banks are facing an internal competency challenge. Their teams lack the skills necessary to enable a successful transformation. This lack of capacity is often related to technology, and not just in terms of setting up and running a new cutting-edge technology infrastructure. There are also problems with tech's practical application for customer management, digital marketing and data analysis.

Often, such skill gaps go unnoticed until the organization is suddenly confronted with a situation for which it is ill-prepared.

This means that banks must now start thinking of themselves as tech companies and recruit the right talent accordingly, which isn't easy when many Millennials and Gen Zers would prefer to work for a 'more exciting' fintech instead.

So, creating an appropriate culture must also be a top priority for the CEO of any truly ambidextrous organization. This requires a change of mindset that not only encourages initiative but also a willingness to accept change and not punish failure. Again, this is in the hands of the ambidextrous leader who must be proactive in finding ways to create trust and engagement, not only within the organization but also among those outside it.

Can legacy banks fight back from what is a precarious market position? Yes, they can, if they embrace some of the lessons we set out in this book and equip themselves to make a voyage of transformation that will be uniquely theirs.

So, let's take the first step by finding out what's really going on.

CHAPTER 2

HOW WE GOT TO WHERE WE ARE

"In our view, there will probably be only 10 to 12 global banks because of the challenges of regulation and digitalization, which requires huge investment – you need size to amortize that investment over a sufficient volume and that requires you to commoditize. Four or five of these global banks will be American, with some in Europe, Deutsche, HSBC and Barclays, for instance, with the rest in Asia, Japan, and China. Each will have their own dynamics and will operate at different levels. Outside of this, there's probably room for niche banks in terms of clientele, product or geography. So, smaller banks aren't going to disappear, they will just be different."

JORIS DIERCKX
Regional Head, Southeast Asia/Singapore,
BNP Paribas, in conversation with Arthur D Little

The 27th of October 1986. The day of the Big Bang.[2] This is the moment when the City of London deregulated and became a financial center to rival New York. The move away from face-to-face dealing to electronic trading pushed London to the forefront in European financial services and immediately made it a go-to destination for international banks. The highly competitive, fast-moving and innovative environment this created flipped the previous bowler-hatted world of banker and broker on its head.

To the average bank customer on the street, this meant nothing. But behind the scenes, and to the delight of those who had lobbied for this for so long, the world of banking was being abruptly transformed.

For the banks and those that ran them, this was a moment for ecstatic celebration, not least because of the stratospheric salaries that could now be commanded, and not solely by those at the top.

Suddenly, bankers were given the green light to create new 'synthetic' products they could aggressively sell into new markets and to customers who didn't know they needed them.

This was a prospect bankers embraced with such relish and recklessness, for decades, that the result was a financial crisis that brought us to the brink. This meltdown changed not only the rules of the game, but the game itself, sowing the seeds of its own destruction.

Given the resultant mess, the regulators stepped in with new capital allocation and compliance requirements. This made banking more expensive for incumbents, while creating the conditions that would lead to the emergence of a new generation who disrupted the financial services value chain with their brash 'delinquency.' If this weren't enough, the shifting sands of consumer behaviors meant that traditional institutions could no longer rely on customer loyalty. That erosion fundamentally damaged the comprehensive laundry-list model that many banks relied on, encompassing a core savings or checking account and a range of private-label products and services. How could this work when your competitors can make the same offer at a lower cost, with less friction and better customer service at every point along the value chain?

THE UNIVERSAL BANKING MODEL IS BROKEN

With gross margins decreasing to around 200 'bips' (basis points), the quality of held assets declining and their capital needs ever higher, once-venerable banks are now at the end of their days, unsustainable relics of the past… and the markets know it.

So, while the equity performance of banks in Europe was in line with the overall market from 1986 to 2007, they've never really recovered from the 2008 financial crisis. In fact, they have significantly underperformed. Compared to their peak prior to the crisis, shares on the European bank stock index (FSTE Eurofirst 300) have lost almost two-thirds of their value.[3]

We can see what has happened if we consider return on equity (ROE), the preferred metric of banking investors for assessing market value and growth, which differs from the earnings per share (EPS) yardstick most corporations use. While the European equity market as a whole has risen at a rate even higher than before the financial crisis, as can be seen in the illustration below, European banks' ROE has stubbornly averaged 5–10%, moving only once above 11% since the first quarter of 2018.

EUROPEAN BANKS RETURN ON EQUITY HAS REMAINED STUBBORNLY LOW

Return on equity of European banks (%)

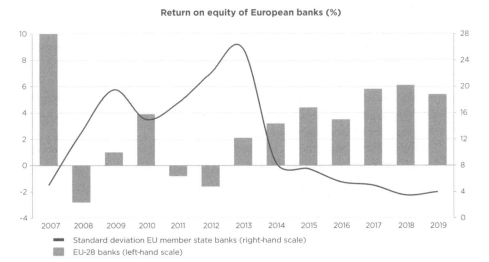

- ▬ Standard deviation EU member state banks (right-hand scale)
- ▪ EU-28 banks (left-hand scale)

Source: European Banking Federation

Such low profitability levels are simply not sustainable when 12% is often associated with banks' cost of capital. Adding a further depressing factor has been the Basel III directive, issued in 2009 by the banking governors of 20 top economies.[4] Among other things, the regulatory edict increased the minimum amount of capital that banks must keep in hand.

US banks have proven slightly more resilient and have expanded faster through both organic business growth and merger and acquisition activity, a pattern that's not been replicated in Europe. As a result, their average ROE is a most twice that reported by EU financial institutions, although many mega-banks, including Bank of America, Citibank and Wells Fargo, have had ROEs below the industry average.

PANIC AVOIDED,
BUT ALL IS NOT WELL

With advanced economies, particularly in Europe, facing years of low growth with little inflation and even deflation, many banks now face an uncertain future, as they're unable to earn the money they once did.

Banks traditionally make money from the fees they charge for products and services. Now, however, consumers are so conditioned to receiving more and more services for free that they balk at being charged for things they don't think they should pay for. Also drying up is banks' second predominant income stream: net interest income, the difference between the interest they pay out on credit balances and what they charge on loans. With the low interest rate economy that now seems the norm, there is not the margin to generate profits here, either.

In 2009, for instance, this spread stood at four percentage points in both the eurozone and the US; it's now just one point in the US and two points in Europe.[5] This could very well persist, replicating the situation in Japan, which has had a low-interest rate economy since the 1990s.

By the start of 2021, the world economy was still pretty fragile. Five of the big economies were at risk of recession, trade wars long brewing between nations showed no signs of easing, and on top of it all was a global pandemic that at the time of this writing was far from over.

For the first time since the Second World War, 2020 saw production around the world contract, creating the largest surge in deficits and government debt since the 1940s. In the month of March alone, global equity markets lost some $26 trillion in value.[6]

We've been here before, of course, with skyrocketing valuations and market indices going up and down like yo-yos.

This had all the makings of a financial crisis even more severe than that of 2008. The bond markets knew it, and continued to send out warning signals, with the yield on 30-year US Treasury bonds dropping below 2% for the first time.[7]

Given this rather gloomy picture, unless banks accept the continued erosion of their business, or think that in time there will be a return to some kind of normality, they have no alternative but to change their business model.

Fortunately, governments and global institutions like the International Monetary Fund (IMF) and central banks in Europe and the US did learn something from the 2008 financial crisis. To reassure increasingly jittery financial markets, central banks greatly eased the situation through interest rate cuts and a $6 trillion-plus balance sheet expansion through asset purchases, FX swap lines and credit and liquidity facilities.[8] The European Central Bank (ECB), for instance, bought more than €120 billion in additional assets from eurozone members.

And so, another global financial panic was averted. Precious credit – without which large parts of the world economy would have ground to a halt, as they had before – kept flowing.

Inevitably, the consequence has been a ballooning of the world's debt burden. In emerging markets, it was double what it was in 2010, at $72 trillion, mainly due to a $20 trillion surge in corporate debt.[9] Meanwhile, China's debt was approaching a colossal 310% of its GDP in 2019.[10]

In mature economies, total debt at the end of 2019 stood at $180 trillion, or 383% of these countries' combined GDP.[11] EU leaders signaled that they weren't shy about increasing that burden further when they agreed in July 2020 to set up a €750 billion recovery fund to guarantee the survival of the European Union project.[12]

There is still the risk that the protectionist measures of the US over the last four years will continue to have a negative impact on economic growth worldwide, even if they're reversed by the current president. And since what the US does affects the rest of the world, that matters. That's particularly true when rates in many geographies are likely to remain historically low – and for deposits, even negative – for some years to come.

Even without the presence of digital disruptors, such events would likely have deep structural consequences for the traditional banking sector, which still hasn't found its way back to sustainable profitability levels post-2008.

And so, with a big question mark hanging over their future, it's evident that legacy banks will have to find new money trees, and sooner rather than later. If they don't, they won't have the funds to reinvent themselves … and reinvent themselves they must.

FALLING OUT OF FAVOR
WITH THE MARKETS

Although some better-performing banks have managed to slow the erosion of their margins, they still aren't delivering the ROE that capital markets expect. That's why they remain unconvinced of the legacy banking model's long-term viability. And, those banks that continue to struggle are likely to be increasingly penalized by the capital markets.

As it is, banks in Europe are already trading below net tangible book value, making it ever more difficult for them to raise the capital they need to fund their much-needed transformation. When the market considers that tomorrow's value of a bank is less than it is today, that bank has a big problem: it can't raise capital without destroying its own market value.

And it's not just the institutions that are switching away from banks. Middle-class investors, for instance, are buying more products like stock index and exchange-traded funds, or fixed-income annuities, which they see as beneficial to them but offer banks lower margins.[13] Meanwhile, the more affluent still favor alternative assets and equities that are the natural preserve of non-banks.

Even worse, the disruptors are cherry-picking product battlegrounds where traditional banks can't compete with them on critical factors like price, the customer experience or scalability.

With 40–60% of retail banking customers now unprofitable,[14] and 20–40% bringing in 20% of the profits, the bulk of profits are being produced by just one in five customers. This makes them a vulnerable and risky asset, since they're the same fish the disruptors are going after. Without their contribution to balance the loss-making majority, traditional institutions in many segments are going to be left with high legacy costs and falling returns.

A TSUNAMI OF NPLS
SOON TO WASH UP

This is a paralyzing situation because it provides no opportunity to raise the short-term funds required to accelerate any kind of business transformation, or to gain scale, or to build the additional reserves needed to weather the likely tidal wave of non-performing loans (NPLs) resulting from the COVID-19 pandemic. This could wipe out the annual contribution of their retail and corporate divisions combined, as was the case with Royal Bank of Scotland (RBS), where provisions for bad loans wiped out the institution's annual profitability.

This will be a particular problem for those banks in southern Europe still recovering from a significant NPL hangover from the 2008 financial crisis.

These NPLs will eat into banks' capital reserves and mean that they're unable to maintain sufficient core tier-one equity (CET1), a position one would expect some 30% of the banks in the EU and UK to find themselves in.

The situation is only going to get worse, as prolonged lockdowns, sub-dued consumer demand, disrupted supply chains, and a sharp contraction of global trade bring about a wave of corporate insolvencies and Chapter 11 bankruptcies. Notable companies that have already reached the end of their road include Thomas Cook, Cirque du Soleil, Hertz, Advantage, Chesapeake, JCPenney, Neiman Marcus, Brooks Brothers, J Crew, and Virgin Atlantic Airways Ltd.

As more companies in a quest for short-term survival become over-leveraged and pile up debt, others in this line of dominoes will topple as those too fragile to keep going are taken out of the supply chain in every sector.

Worldwide, analysts are forecasting 2020–21 credit losses for banks approaching \$2.1 trillion;[15] the ECB expects European banks to experience more than €400 billion in credit losses.[16]

To handle the mountain of distressed assets – and if the NPL ratio in the eurozone does rise to the astounding 20% or so that some predict – a 'bad bank' like that created in 2011 to solve the subprime lending overhang may be required to bring some kind of stability to the situation.

The compounding effect of credit losses, NPLs and weaker banking revenues from both dwindling fees and interest will undoubtedly deplete bank earnings and balance sheets. This will drag down capital ratios and depress their market values even further. Those banks that manage to struggle on will likely continue to suffer from anemic returns of around 5% ROE, far below the cost of capital.

While the commercial and economic aftermath of the COVID-19 crisis has only added to bankers' woes, this alone won't be the root cause of any bank failures that are to come. It will have only played a part in exposing major fault lines that already exist and run deep.

PLAYING BY THE RULES

If this is the rock, then the hard place will be the ever-increasing costs of achiev-ing regulatory compliance, and the consequences of failing to do so. Banks have found it increasingly difficult to stay the right side of the law when it comes to meeting their regulatory obligations. As a result, since the 2008 crisis, banks have had to pay out \$100 billion in fines, and many of the culprits have been major players. These are just a few examples that have come to light over the years:

- In 2019, EU regulators imposed sanctions of \$1.2bn on Citigroup, JPMorgan Chase, Royal Bank of Scotland, Barclays, and Mitsubishi UFJ Financial Group for collusion over foreign-exchange trading.[17]
- Credit Suisse has admitted it helped its US clients avoid taxes in 2014 and were accordingly fined \$2.6bn.[18]
- In 2012, JP Morgan Chase was fined \$5.29bn for signing and notarizing doc-uments without verification.[19]

- Wells Fargo was among five banks targeted by the National Mortgage Settlement. It was fined $5.35bn.[20]
- In December 2016, $5.3bn was a similar amount that Credit Suisse agreed to pay over for wrongdoing.[21]
- In 2016, Deutsche Bank also agreed to pay $7.2bn for selling toxic residential mortgage-backed securities.[22]
- BNP Paribas, France's largest bank, pleaded guilty to two felony counts and agreed to pay $8.97bn in settlement because it had violated US sanctions by the processing thousands of transactions for clients in Iran, Sudan, and Cuba.[23]
- As part of the 2012 National Mortgage Settlement, the Bank of America was required to pay out $11.8bn for its part in selling subprime mortgages.[24]
- In another deal reached with the US Department of Justice in October 2013, between JPMorgan Chase made a $13bn payment to settle various number of lawsuits and investigations that largely related to the mis-selling of toxic mortgage debt to investors to Fannie Mae.[25]
- In 2014, the Bank of America agreed to pay a record $16.65bn to settle allegations that it had misled investors buying subprime mortgage-backed securities.[26]

SIZE ISN'T EVERYTHING

The need to meet increasingly robust compliance obligations is leading to market consolidation, as banks try to avoid being squeezed by adding muscle through mergers and acquisitions.

So, if we look back to 2018, we can see that there were 5,581 banks in the EU, a figure that was 30% down on what it was in 2008,[27] with over half of reduction occurring in just four member states (Germany, Poland, Austria and Italy). Something similar was also happening in the US, where number of FDIC insured banks has fallen by half,[28] from there being 8,315, in 2000 to around 4,519 two decades later. The picture is the same in Asia where bank numbers are shrinking rapidly as disruptors emerge and take over the markets, forcing incumbent players to consolidate.

Paradoxically, those looking for the economies of scale that size brings will actually find themselves less agile and responsive. This will leave them more exposed to the threat from capital-light competitors. These players' value propositions are reshaping the market and sucking away share and profits from those stuck in the traditional banking groove.

And while you can question the sustainability of some of the new digital players, fending them off will be an almost impossible challenge for many legacy banks, which don't have the weaponry to combat their aggressive pricing. How, for instance, can high-cost legacy banks win against someone who's offering what they do, but often for free? The only answer for traditional financial institutions is to learn how to fish in these new revenue pools before their depleted old ones run dry.

For the new players in the market, the world is a much rosier place. While banks may not be the flavor of the month with investors, their newly-emerged competitors certainly are. Their digitally-scalable business model gives them a marketplace advantage, and they're not constrained by the same regulatory oversight, which carries immense compliance costs. On top of this, the new-comers don't have the high labor and capital costs associated with maintaining and upgrading technology that's long past its sell-by date, and which requires endless unpicking whenever any change is required.

Because of all this, fintech firms can command much higher stock prices than banks, approaching levels not much below those of major tech firms.

While some European banks are continuing to dispose of non-core assets, contributing to a global trend that's seen assets fall, the growth of non-banks continues. Globally, in 2019, the non-bank financial intermediation (NBFI) sector grew by 8.9% to $200.2 trillion, which accounts for just under half (49.5%).[29] These entities now account for about 60% of global banking profits.

To get a sense of the magnitude of the challenge facing legacy banks, we need look no further than Ant, the financial arm of Chinese digital marketplace giant Alibaba. Ant's technology can handle 120,000 orders every second,[30] and reach a decision to grant a loan or not in just three minutes! This is the world's purest example of digital finance's tremendous potential.

But is there a sting in the tale? Are the increasing multiples and high valuation of many fintechs being driven by the strength of their underlying business models, or by a capital overhang created by low-interest rates and massive capital outflows from money market funds?

Regardless, at some point the current enthusiasm for tech stocks will translate into inevitable market consolidation, and there will be a bloodbath in an overcrowded space. This is likely to destroy shareholder value on a massive scale not seen since the dot.com bubble burst.

From this chaos will emerge new, even faster-moving giants. They'll dwarf the legacy banks of yesteryear and make it impossible for them to ever catch back up. So, where does that leave the beleaguered legacy banks?

In certain segments, larger banks will be able to use their market power to find a place at the table, though they may not be able to do so without irrevocably destroying value or denaturing the original business model. Recent history would suggest that both are likely outcomes.

WHAT IS THE INDUSTRY
POINT OF ARRIVAL?

Given the rapid development of e-commerce, deregulation and new types of competitors, what is going to be the industry *point of arrival*?

What will your vision be for effectively differentiating yourself in the marketplace if, as many believe, fintechs will become more 'client-facing,' further blurring what it means to be a bank? If people don't need banks, then how do banks stay relevant? Where will be the new market equilibrium? What will be the end game?

Should you simply try and manage the downturn? Go on a profit hunt? Cut costs through outsourcing and technology? Or, become a digital bank? If you want to be a player in tomorrow's financial services arena, what should you do?

Exploring questions like this is what this book is all about.

At this point, which is the better start point? Being a bank, or being a fintech that becomes a bank? Is it harder for a bank to be like a tech company or for a tech company to be like a bank? Certainly, having a bank charter would give a fintech the ability to build a long-term base and capture the net interest coming from loans that would normally go to the traditional bank. But while that makes theoretical sense, only a few fintechs, like Stripe, are ready to scale or have pockets deep enough to take on what will be an expensive exercise.

So, how long do we think legacy banks have to restructure?

Until recently, we might have said ten years. But there's no doubt that COVID has compressed the timelines. We have all seen how in 2020–2021 consumers made a dramatic switch to online shopping, a phenomenon that's spilled over into financial services. Although challenger banks may only have a tiny slice of US checking accounts, during the pandemic almost 60% of Americans downloaded an app to help them manage their finances.

Now we might say that legacy banks have a mere 3–5 years to remake themselves… if they still even have that runway.

CHAPTER 3

THE DISAPPEARING BANK

"I think the lessons of Glass-Steagall and its repeal suggest that the universal banking model is inherently unstable and unworkable. No amount of restructuring, management change or regulation is ever likely to change that."

JOHN REED
former Chairman and CEO, Citigroup

Over the three decades leading up to the 2008 crisis, the world's financial networks became increasingly interconnected. This was attributable to regulatory convergence, adoption of World Trade Organization rules and the creation of currency unions, such as the euro. These all fed into a surge in cross-border capital flows that led inexorably to the emergence of a single global marketplace.

In 1998, Sandford Weill, Co-Chairman of the newly-formed Citigroup, announced that this heralded the dawn of a new age of banking in which large institutions would be the financial supermarkets of the world. He trumpeted a set of activities so diverse that they'd be able to withstand the worst of any downturn. He was not alone in this view.

Major financial players, like RBS, Deutsche Bank, BNP Paribas, Barclays, HSBC, Crédit Agricole, UBS, Bank of America, Société Générale and JPMorgan Chase, sought to grow their international businesses on the back of this rising tide of global capital.

As we know, the financial crisis of 2008 brought an end to this dream. According to the McKinsey Global Institute, cross-border transfers that had risen from $500 billion in 1980 to a record $12.4 trillion in 2007 had by 2009 fallen by more than 80%.[31]

This trend continued as banks, having reassessed the risk associated with overseas business, offloaded the foreign assets they'd acquired during boom years and sought comfort in markets nearer home, where they had local knowledge and scale.

This withdrawal from both developed and emerging markets continued, with many of the world's biggest banks relinquishing the advances they'd made in the 1990s and 2000s to focus on their domestic bases, which lay largely in the US and Europe. Citibank, for example, announced in 2014 that it was leaving 11 markets,[32] including Egypt, the Czech Republic, and Japan, following earlier disengagement from consumer markets in Pakistan, Uruguay and Spain. This left the bank with a global footprint covering just 24 countries – half of what it had been just two years earlier. Others similarly curtailed their global operations. HSBC, for instance, has exited more than 20 markets since 2011, from 85[33] to just 64.[34]

In 2015, Deutsche Bank announced that it was closing operations in ten countries,[35] including Argentina, Chile, Mexico, Malta, and New Zealand, leading to the loss of 9,000 full-time jobs.

In continental Europe, Barclays sold its retail banking networks in Spain,[36] Italy,[37] and Portugal[38] before proceeding to do the same in Asia, Brazil, Russia, and Africa. The bank's departure from Egypt[39] ended a relationship that had endured with only occasional interruption since 1864.

By 2016 there was some reversal of the retreat, although international flows were still two-thirds or so lower than their high of 2007.

WHY THE INTERNATIONAL RETREAT?

When asked about their international retrenchment, multinational banks tend to offer up a litany of explanations. Some cite the need to improve their profitability. Others say they were looking to achieve a more efficient capital allocation, which would give them more income stability, or trying to avoid a volatile political environment.

Above all, though, two words lie at the heart of most responses: 'increasing regulation.'

A 2016 analysis by Spanish banking group BBVA found that regulatory pressure was the key driver behind banks in the US, Canada, the UK, Sweden, Germany, Austria, the Netherlands, France, Italy, Spain, and China pulling out of certain countries and business lines.[40]

Faced with the introduction of stricter capital and liquidity requirements, the fencing off of wholesale and investment banking from retail banking, and the speed at which particular countries were implementing banking reforms was cumulatively enough for them to close down their overseas operations.

Adding to this pressure were new reporting standards and a tougher stance by the world's major regulators on money laundering and other illegal activities, now a major concern of law enforcement agencies everywhere. As a consequence, banks doing business on a global scale have found it difficult to avoid being tainted by the estimated $2trn of 'dirty money' the United Nations Office on Drugs and Crimes estimates is being annually laundered.[41]

Inevitably, with all of this going on, global banks have become embroiled in various scandals that have led to multi-billion-dollar fines. With the US Department of Justice hovering above, warning banks about becoming involved with foreign ventures where there may be insufficient scrutiny, it's easy for shareholders to get the jitters.

All this means that the global reach that was once seen as a fundamental strength of large banking groups is now an increasing liability.

WHO'S FILLING THE GAP?

As global banks have stepped out of certain markets, others have stepped up to the mark. If we look at Asia, excluding Japan, domestic and cross-border loans rose from $7.8trn to $17.6trn between 2008 and 2018.[42] This came as banks from Taiwan, India, South Korea, Japan, and Australia ramped up their regional operations, as did lenders from smaller markets like Singapore and Malaysia.

However, it was Chinese financial institutions – like the Industrial and Commercial Bank of China, one of the world's largest banks by assets and an early entrant into the region – that really led the charge. This was driven in part by their willingness to take on more credit risk than their Western counterparts. One way they did this was by offering loans to private equity firms at up to eight times earnings before interest, tax, depreciation, and amortization (EBITDA). This was in stark contrast to the 4x earnings calculation most US and European banks would have used. By offering such favorable terms, Chinese banks were able to expand their lending portfolios at a compound annual rate of 17% over ten years.

In Latin America, essentially the same story was being played out. While some big banks with strong regional franchises, such as Santander and BBVA, remained there to do battle, many other multinationals – including HSBC, Citigroup and Credit Suisse – sold or reduced their operations. And once again, regional institutions moved in to fill the void.

In 2020, five of the 10 biggest banks in the region by asset size were headquartered in Brazil.[43] They included the state-owned Banco do Brazil and the private lender Itaú Unibanco, an organization that's on track to become a truly pan-Latin American institution, with a presence not just in Chile, Colombia, Paraguay, and Uruguay, but also in more developed markets like the UK, Spain, France and the US.

SO BIGGER WASN'T BETTER

Since the subprime crisis began in mid-2007, banks and insurers around the world have reported $1.1 trillion in losses.[44] Seventeen large universal banks account for more than half of these losses, nine of which have failed, been nationalized, or had to go on government-funded life support. That's made it necessary for central banks and governments in the US, the UK and Europe to inject $9 trillion to help prevent the collapse of global financial markets.[45]

Often these banks were large and complex financial institutions (LCFIs) that had grown through consolidation, conglomeration and mergers to dominate the international financial services landscape. They were, ironically, the very ones that were once deemed 'too big to fail.'

So, bigger was not better after all, and sheer size provided no defense against financial instability. If you look at the list of the world's safest banks, those at the top aren't the money centers or LCFIs, but mid-sized regional banks.

25 OF THE WORLD'S SAFEST BANKS[46]

RANK	BANK NAME	COUNTRY
1	KfW	GERMANY
2	Zuercher Kantonalbank	SWITZERLAND
3	BNG Bank	NETHERLANDS
4	Landwirstchaftliche Rentenbank	GERMANY
5	Nederlandse Waterschapsbank	NETHERLANDS
6	L-Bank	GERMANY
7	Kommunalbanken	NORWAY
8	NRW.BANK	GERMANY
9	Swedish Export Credit Corporation	SWEDEN
10	Caisse des Depots et Consignations	FRANCE
11	Royal Bank of Canada	CANADA
12	The Toronto-Dominion Bank	CANADA
13	DZ BANK	GERMANY
14	DBS Bank	SINGAPORE
15	Oversea-Chinese Banking Corporation	SINGAPORE
16	Svenska Handelsbanken	SWEDEN
17	United Overseas Bank	SINGAPORE
18	Korea Development Bank	SOUTH KOREA
19	The Export-Import Bank of Korea	SOUTH KOREA
20	Banque et Caisse d'Epargne de l'Etat	LUXEMBOURG
21	Banque Cantonale Vaudoise	SWITZERLAND
22	Industrial Bank of Korea	SOUTH KOREA
23	Deutsche Apotheker-und Aerztebank	GERMANY
24	DNB Bank	NORWAY
25	SFIL	FRANCE

A NEW ERA DAWNS

While the banking industry certainly has many issues to address, it would be overly simplistic to say that what we're witnessing is *the end of banking*. Banks have long been part of society, and the ongoing need to save, borrow and transfer money will ensure that they don't disappear en masse anytime soon.

Yet, it's all too obvious that some parts of the financial services sector are in less than ideal health and lack the immune system to handle a prolonged economic slowdown combined with a low or even negative interest rate environment. Inevitably, ongoing pressures will lead to a sharp and irrevocable division between banking's winners and losers. Among the biggest losers will be the all-purpose 'bells and whistles' banks that have long been the immutable cornerstones of the landscape, rarely changing except for the occasional flurry of M&A that came along every decade or so.

In this financial Jurassic Park, where there's been little differentiation in the marketplace, one bank looked much like another. And so, like a burger franchise, each has sold its own unfocused range of standardized products through branded distribution channels.

But what happens, as it has now, when your particular beef patty and relish no longer cuts the mustard because your customers want fish and chips, or a Thai green curry, or ramen noodles, or sushi? They'll simply leave you and go elsewhere, to someone who can offer something new and different. This is what happened with the arrival of the fintechs that we'll look at in more detail in the next chapter.

For now, just let's say they brought to the market faster, cheaper, more convenient ways of doing things. Rather than selling generic banking products, they offered solutions tailored to people's problems. This pressed the right buttons, and suddenly consumers became kids in a sweet shop, able to sort through suppliers until they found the one that gave them just what they wanted.

This has put traditional banks on the back foot – each time one of their customers bought elsewhere, it chipped away at the brand loyalty banks had worked so long to establish. That began to dilute the mental association consumers had between a bank and their money. It all amounted to a hammer blow to traditional banks that relied on the inherent 'stickiness' of their clientele to maintain long-term customer relationships.

Customers falling out of love with their banks also opened the door to not just fintechs, but other disruptors, like Amazon, who have made inroads into areas like virtual cash. With 'Amazon Cash,' for instance, you can load money from an Amazon account onto a card and use it to buy products at physical retailers, even if you don't have a payment card from a bank.

As consumers become more comfortable using the financial services provided by Amazon and Walmart, or a phone app like Apple Pay, at the supermarket, this dramatically weakens the mental association between making day-to-day financial transactions and traditional banks. After all, who's now making a purchase possible? Apple, or your bank?

This is all part of a move toward 'autonomous finance' as consumers look to take more control of their money, and seeing financial products not just as purchases, but as a means to greater personal empowerment. Increasingly, we will probably see consumers managing their 'personal balance sheet' using apps that are programmed to meet their financial goals with minimal involvement from them.

Of course, banking has always been about whom you trust with your money. That's why they go to such lengths to come across as solid and dependable. But when nearly two-thirds half of Generation Z still say they trust their primary financial institution (a bank) most with their money,[47] it seems like tomorrow's customers may no longer buying into that narrative.

But is that quite the case? A recent survey by Oracle suggests that younger banking customers are much more anxious and discerning than others when it comes to their finances. Having grown up during the last financial crisis, this is a more conservative generation financially. It's interesting to note that 56% of Gen Zers have spoken with their parents about savings.[48] One certainly can't imagine Baby Boomers having done that.

On top of this, another study shows that there is a deep desire in the Gen Z age group (10–25) to better understand and manage their money.[49] Many of them are doing this by turning to YouTube or Instagram.[50] This creates an excellent opportunity for established banks to play on their traditional, longstanding values.

So, traditional banks need to think about how they can best serve this group of new customers, and it won't be by requiring them to plough through paperwork, or speak with advisors in a marble and brass bank branch, to open accounts.

HOW AMAZON IS TAKING BANKING APART

Source: Amazon

As illustrated above, Amazon has become highly adept at unbundling traditional bank services. It's able to do this by capitalizing on its huge ecosystem, which consists of more than 310 million active customer accounts, 100 million Prime customers, 5 million sellers and 12 marketplaces (the USA, UK, Germany, France, Canada, Japan, India, Italy, Spain, Mexico, Brazil, and China). Two more, Amazon Australia and Singapore, will be launched soon.

Walmart is another large business that's offering money services to those who often aren't customers of traditional banks. In effect, their in-store money centers operate as quasi-banks by offering credit cards, prepaid debit cards that are said to have saved its customers more than $2 billion since 2017, as well as point-of-sale financing through the no-fee Affirm service. All of this helps Walmart grow in-store traffic. Meanwhile, this model is being adopted by others, like the Lazada e-commerce platform in Southeast Asia.

DISRUPTION'S NOTHING NEW

The developments we're seeing in banking right now may seem entirely new, but they're really just a duplication of what has gone before.

In 1982, the Maryland National Bank had the foresight to anticipate this market evolution and the courage to follow its instincts when it set up MBNA.[51] By focusing on check-clearing services, it became a dominant force in the US before repeating the exercise with bank card issuance. It eventually became the world's largest independent credit card issuer, with co-branded affinity cards as a specialty. Vanguard, Fidelity and disruptive brokers such as Schwab and TD Ameritrade did something similar in asset management.

Back in the day, there was also rapid expansion of virtual banks and credit cards in Europe. I In 1991, ING created ING Direct[52] while Midland Bank, now part of HSBC, set up First Direct. Seven years later, Prudential Insurance launched the Egg[53] card in the UK, which it then hatched in France in 2002, making it the first cross-border disruptive player. This credit card offered 0% interest on outstanding balances and balance transfers and was also the first to introduce innovative features like the Egg Money Manager, an aggregation tool and Egg Pay, which allowed you to make payments to e-mail addresses and move money between external financial accounts.

At its peak, Egg had more than four million customers, but the company eventually collapsed due to capital and funding constraints imposed on its parent company. The business was sold to Citigroup in January 2007, with the credit card accounts subsequently bought by Barclay's in July 2011.

Is Egg's fate indicative of the future for the new payment companies and digital non-banks? Will they also burn bright for a while and then fall to earth? Or, will the disruptors be able to develop profitably so they can stay in the game longer-term? These are questions traditional bankers are certainly asking themselves, and they're probably reaching different conclusions.

Of course, that doesn't mean it will be plain sailing for any disruptor trying to move into the financial services space. Facebook, for instance, failed to gain traction when it ambitiously attempted to mint its own cryptocurrency, Libra, despite having billions of users on its platform. There are no guarantees of success, even for Big Tech, especially when you throw regulation into the mix.

FRIEND OR FOE?
THE REGULATION CONUNDRUM

Paradoxically, market regulation has often offered a much-needed degree of protection for banks, even as they wailed about the constraints it imposes, while sheltering behind a steel ring of licensure laws, capital requirements, regulatory compliance and security that's almost impossible for outsiders to breach.

Of course, we know this is there because of what happened in 2008, when the world literally stopped because banks ran short of liquidity, and regulators' efforts to avert future crises ensured that balance sheets would be endangered by 'excessive competition.'

However, post-2008 governmental bailouts of banks that were deemed too big to fail' created precisely the conditions that led to the emergence of new market entrants who became the darlings of the capital markets.[54]

THE WALLS ARE TUMBLING DOWN

BANKING SPECIFICS		BARRIERS TO CHANGE …	… ARE VANISHING
CUSTOMERS	Personal relationships	Close relationship to personal advisor creates psychological barrier to switch	Product sales increasingly online with less opportunity for personal interaction
	Trust and need for security	Banks regarded as secure and most trustworthy partner in financial matters	Trust in non-bank FS providers steadily increasing, security weaker differentiator
PRODUCTS/ BANKS	Customer lock-in	Long maturity of banking products dampens impact of novel trends	Existing products expiring, with new customers possibly turning to disruptors
	Product complexity	Complex products requiring specific expertise and personal advice	Modularization enables automation and reduces need for personal advice
	Cultural inertia	Tradition and continuity seen as cornerstones of self image and brand	Leading brands focused on customer centricity and innovation
INDUSTRY	Scale economies/ technology	Substantial investments in (physical) infrastructure as barrier to entry	Virtualization and Internet enable rapid scaling based on versatile infrastructure
	Regulatory restrictions	Tight regulation raising barriers to new entrants and novel business models	Regulation increasingly aimed at promoting competition, also by non-banks

The regulatory requirements and other obstacles that once slowed the disruption of incumbents' business models are now rapidly vanishing, as illustrated above. In Europe, and particularly the UK, deregulation has moved ahead rapidly, primarily in payments, where the market has been more open to non-banks for a while. This means that the innate stickiness of a bank's customers can no longer be taken for granted.

THE HIGH COST OF COMPLIANCE

Some in the banking industry have questioned the motives of government and regulators in doing this. Are they trying to undermine the status of legacy banks to let the fintechs in? Or, as the regulators insist, are they pushing the start-ups to become even more disruptive, so they can create a more competitive financial marketplace filled with innovative products that benefit consumers?

Certainly, many regulators have been pushing for greater efficiency in the banking system and want to see more fees come into the revenue mix. But they're walking a tightrope, since they don't want to create a revolution. Rather, they aim to manage a market evolution that ensures that legacy banks remain financially resilient while opening the door to new, disruptive business models.

Traditional banks definitely have a view about this, which is why they vociferously denounce any further regulatory tightening as unfair. They argue that it puts them at a significant disadvantage against digital disruptors. For universal banks, compliance costs are especially high, since they must conform to multiple sets of regulations due to their wide range of business lines and geographies.

Compared to pre-financial crisis spending levels, compliance-related operating costs have increased by more than 60% for retail and corporate banks. Collectively, banks now spend $270bn per year on compliance.[55] This equates to average compliance cost per employee of approximately $10,000.[56] For most, 10% or more of their operating costs and at least 7% of non-interest or overheads expense can be attributed to ensuring regulatory compliance. Some believe these figures could double by 2022, given the acceleration in compliance complexity, with regulatory updates having increased by 500 percent since the global financial crisis.[57]

This obviously pushes up their prices and makes customer acquisition more difficult. Conversely, because they have more efficient systems and far fewer products, fintechs don't face the same problems.

WILL FINTECHS FEEL THE HARSH TOUCH OF REGULATION?

Going forward, banks will need to develop strategies that cut these costs, while still enabling them to maintain robust compliance programs. If there's a move to impose stricter regulation on the disruptors, they, too, will struggle. The impact could be even greater for the newcomers, as they'll generally lack the established compliance processes of banks.

This will be a major headache for the disruptors, because much of the viability and sustainability of new fintech start-ups is based on the assumption that they won't bear the same regulatory burden as banks. Ultimately, it's this belief that will continue to determine investors' appetite for fintechs.

So, what is likely to happen? The regulatory authorities do want to encourage competition and innovation, so that's a tick for the fintechs. But the more banks and these start-ups climb into bed together, the more the regulators will cast a quizzical eye over their activities, and that could raise the specter of wider oversight and greater scrutiny.

If regulators want to see more monitoring of fintechs in real time, rather than after the fact – and start demanding ongoing 'stress tests,' asset quality reviews, or enhanced reporting – that could disrupt the disruptors. After all, businesses that are largely based on rapid, frictionless processes aren't necessarily compatible with something like anti-money laundering (AML) rules. If they gain a reputation for non-compliance, it will be much harder for fintechs to secure funding or acquire a critical mass of customers.

Of course, banks won't be unhappy if that happens to a potential long-term competitor. Many already view fintechs as inherently risky because of their small size, and aren't keen to support them. That's why some banks are closing their accounts with fintechs, leaving them struggling to get the mainstream financial services they need to operate.

On the plus side for the fintechs, while they won't like having regulations imposed on them, they do have better technology than banks and more resources in the form of people and expertise, which will make it easier to meet compliance requirements. They're much better placed, for instance, to automate their monitoring of 'Know Your Customer' (KYC) ethics processes, AML, trade surveillance, reconciliations and other areas. That will appease the regulators, as long as they're satisfied that such tools are doing the job. If they aren't satisfied with the proposed technology solutions, that could lead to higher costs for the fintechs.

WHO ARE THE FINANCIAL SHERIFFS?

Many countries around the world are developing their own specific laws around how financial institutions within their jurisdiction must behave and process transactions for their customers. Implementation is then overseen by a wide range of regulatory organizations, like the ones listed below.

- In the US, the Consumer Financial Protection Bureau (CFPB) has invested heavily in analytics and digital technology, and created a set of e-regulations. And, the Securities and Exchange Commission's Office of Compliance Inspections and Examinations (OCIE) has put significant resources into enhancing its data mining and analysis capabilities. This led to the development of its National Exam Analytics Tool (NEAT), which combs through data looking for insider trading and other infractions.
- The UK's Financial Conduct Authority (FCA) is stepping up its game to ensure that there's no abuse of Big Data power. Similarly,

the EU is looking into whether current Big Data regulations and supervisory measures are up to the mark.

- The US Federal Trade Commission (FTC) is broadly empowered to bring enforcement action to protect consumers against unfair or deceptive practices. It has developed a sort of common law approach to regulatory expectations. The FTC has taken the position that a company's failure to comply with its privacy policy – by not implementing reasonable security measures to protect consumers' personal information – constitutes 'deceptive practices.'
- The CFPB also regulates certain financial services provided to consumers. The agency recently issued new policies intended to promote fintech innovation, but these remain untested. A key unresolved issue is whether federal regulations can preempt state laws or regulations in this area.
- In Europe, the General Data Protection Regulation (GDPR) lays out strict rules for companies that collect or process EU residents' data. This oversight has global reach, regulating any international company that collects or processes EU residents' data.
- The Telephone Consumer Protection Act imposes restrictions on US telemarketing.
- US State Data Breach Notification Laws, in force in all 50 states, require customer notification of security breaches involving personal information. Moreover, many states are establishing minimal 'reasonable standards' to protect consumer data.
- CAN-SPAM Laws place restrictions on email marketing.
- Federal and state laws, like the California Consumer Privacy Act of 2018, ensure GDPR-style rights for California residents around data ownership, transparency and control.
- The Gramm-Leach-Bliley Act, passed by Congress in 1999, imposes privacy and security obligations on insurance companies, banks and other financial institutions with respect to customer financial records.
- The New York Department of Financial Services' Cybersecurity Rules establish specific security requirements, including technical controls and reporting obligations, for licensed entities. The requirements are directed at the security of systems underlying the financial sector, not simply data.
- AML obligations apply to fintechs that handle, remit or transmit funds. These organizations may be required to comply with laws designed to prevent the 'cleaning' of dirty money by criminals and other illegal activities.

THE WIRECARD PROBLEM

It's too early to know how hard and in which direction the regulatory winds will blow. In the end, that may be decided by random events like the fall from grace of Wirecard.

This German payment firm was seen by many as the perfect example of how firms could make inroads into traditional, oligopolistic segments of the financial services market. Until 25 June 2020, that is. The company collapsed, owing creditors almost £3.2 billion. The black hole in its books was ultimately traced to the firm's auditor, EY, and blamed on a sophisticated global fraud. At the time of its failure, Wirecard was arguably the most established European fintech, worth more than €20bn.[58]

Wirecard was founded in 1999 off the back of the dot.com boom. It embraced the notion that as we became an increasingly cashless society, there would be growing demand for new payment services, with consumers switching to smart payment devices and online shopping. Wirecard was also the perfect platform for fintech start-ups like Revolut, Monzo and others who lacked the critical mass necessary to issue their own cards.

Unfortunately, reckless growth and a lack of regulatory oversight led to multiple allegations of fraud, which proved the undoing of what became known as 'Germany's Enron.' It was a clear example of how the capital markets can be blindsided by a lack of corporate governance and less-than-robust due diligence by institutional leadership.

Accordingly, the German regulator BaFin offered up a mea culpa. Its president, Felix Hufeld, admitted that "a whole range of private and public entities including my own have not been effective enough"[59] at preventing the "complete disaster at Wirecard." This prompted the European Commission to review current regulations and "act to improve the EU's regulatory framework where necessary."

It's uncertain how dark a cloud Wirecard's demise casts on the adoption of the more liberal approach being looked at by European regulators. However, it's likely that many deregulation measures initiated in the UK will be put into cold storage in Europe… at least for now.

In the US, regulators like The Federal Reserve, the Office of the Comptroller of the Currency (OCC) and others who oversee banks in each state seem unlikely to loosen their current administrative grip. Regulators have already used their legal authority to examine bank-fintech partnerships. Now, if a bank powers a fintech, the depository bank is ultimately responsible for any credit default or compliance risk.

The start-ups were thrown another curve in 2020 when a federal judge ruled that there would be no more 'fast passes' for fintechs wanting to become traditional banks.[60] They'd have to go through the same time-consuming approval process as everyone else.

This was a bit of good news for beleaguered legacy banks, as it may buy them a few more years of regulatory protection. Many bank leaders hope and pray they still have as much as a decade to transform their business model and supporting infrastructure. In fact, they don't.

Although they feel some pressure to transform because of continuing market losses and decreasing margins, they don't feel under duress, as they did after the 2008 crisis. Consequently, very few banks currently believe they're facing a critical turnaround imperative, and they're reluctant to embrace real change. That's why many still invoke the cost of transforming themselves, and the impact of inevitable accounting write-offs on financial returns, to justify inaction. A cynic might say this procrastination is rooted in bankers not wanting to damage the short-term financial returns on which their bonuses depend.

And there's another disincentive impeding such sweeping, fundamental change. When globally, the average tenure of a CEO in a large business like a bank is about five years[61] and a large bank's transformation takes around ten, it must be tempting for the incumbent to leave such a task to their successor. After all, when your bonuses are tied to delivering short-term results, why rock the boat when you can leave all that to someone else?

TECHNOLOGY IS SPEEDING UP TIME

So, how long do financial institutions have to put their house in order before the playing field definitively tips the new disruptors' way?

Perhaps we can get a hint from what happened to print media. Historically reliant on advertising for revenue, digital platforms and social media barely created a ripple at first. That changed when revenues fell off a cliff as advertisers switched wholesale to online channels. It was only because of indirect regulatory protection that much of the 'old media' sector survived. The same could very well be in store for traditional banking.

Although banks frequently complain they're held back by a straitjacket of regulations that don't apply to capital-light fintechs, they fail to see that these regulations are actually saving them from a brutal and bloody assault.

While the regulatory environment may give the old timers some breathing space, it also gives the disruptors time to look at the legacy banks' markets with envious eyes and draw up their plans. And they have a weapon in their armory against which the traditional legacy banks have little defense: technology.

Rapid tech adoption disrupts any information-driven sector, as we've seen play out in turbulent industries like media, telecom, automotive and airlines.

Tech-savvy entrants emerge with more innovative offerings and put the incumbents on the defensive, forcing them into a futile arms race as they try to reduce product lifecycles and squeeze the last bit of juice from their tired old products. In this game, they're never the winners.

If it weren't for cloud computing, AI, machine learning, predictive analytics, Big Data, the Internet of Things, robotic processing automation, and an ever-expanding list of other technologies, the digital disruptors wouldn't be nipping at the heels of traditional banks.

And in this turbulent space, it's the disruptors who truly know how to ride the wave of change. Banks, on the other hand, have the impossible challenge of trying to do business with processes and systems built around technology designed in the 1970s, when economies of scale were more important than agility. This fragile, inflexible legacy tech is now a millstone around banks' necks. It not only locks data away in historic silos, limiting accessibility and the insights that can be gleaned, but also ensures that the changes needed to launch new products are excruciatingly cumbersome and expensive.

This is a sure-fire recipe for disaster when victory hinges on the ability to quickly and effectively shift resources – including cash, talent, and managerial attention – out of less-promising units and into more attractive ones.

The requisite speed and agility just aren't there in the old legacy banking model, where rigid, arthritic processes are the norm. This is not a good sign when, in the world of 21st century financial services, the prize goes to the swiftest.

Google won the search engine war because it was able to consistently produce better results than its rivals. Apple won by creating its ecosystem of products and erecting barriers to entry that others couldn't penetrate. And Apple, because it had the first-mover advantage, was positioned to capture the lion's share of a vast array of customer segments. This creates a real economic barrier because those who want to follow must deeply discount their prices or increase their marketing spend to attract customers, which raises their break-even point and lowers returns.

Finding their way out of this disrupted landscape will mark another step in the banks' journey from being the all-encompassing financial provider in the '50s, to offering differentiated services to clusters of customers in the '70s, to the 'Noughties,' where their focus was more on affinity group marketing and brand association with specific interests, such as sport.

But doing so will require more than some short-term revenue fix to get through what will be one of the most difficult economic environments since the Great Depression. It will necessitate wholesale structural change. Those who don't recognize what's happening around them are likely to fail... and soon. Just think of all the typewriter manufacturers killed off by the word processor and the PC. The same will happen to the legacy banks, with their universal 'do it all' model.

To be an effective player in this new world, banks must accept that transformation isn't just about introducing new technology, but simultaneously embedding change into their organizational, managerial and cultural fabric in a way that touches every system and business process.

Not every traditional bank will recognize this. Even those that do will need to turn themselves into a very different type of organization, if they're to find a place in the new banking world. We will go there in the next chapter.

CHAPTER 4

WELCOME TO THE NOISY NEIGHBORS

"JPMorgan Chase should absolutely be scared shitless about fintech."[62]

JAMIE DIMON,
CEO, JPMorgan Chase

Growth hasn't come naturally to the banking sector of late. In 2018, the industry's return on assets (ROA), a key measure of profitability, was globally just 0.51 percent.[63] Similarly, the commercial banking sector grew at just 3.5% on average each year between 2015 and 2020. Banking's P/E ratio of 9.49 also looks decidedly peaky against an overall market average of 25.56, although this figure is skewed by a very small number of firms with P/E ratios of over 100.

While US and Asian banks have regained some strength since the 2008 crisis, the situation's more challenging in Europe. Here, structural deficiencies, over-capacity, low or even negative interest rates, and the absence of a pan-European banking regulatory agency have all contributed to persistent profitability problems.

Put all this together and it suggests that an already gloomy outlook is likely to get worse for legacy banks, especially with the arrival of their noisy new neighbors.

These are the financial disruptors – variously called fintechs, non-banks, neobanks or challenger banks – who have swarmed into the sector and like termites are attacking its very foundations. Whatever you choose to call them, they all do essentially the same thing: offer internet-only financial services. Powered by technology and with no physical branch structure, they're able to save on the cost of banking, which means they can offer lower fees for better products. And, because they generally work through mobile phone apps, they're particularly appealing to younger, tech-savvy consumers, although not exclusively so.

At present, these banking termites are extremely hungry. By 2022, it's predicted that the global value of the fintech market will hit $309.98bn, that's up from $127.66bn in 2018.[64] This is an annual growth rate of around 25%! The growth in the value of digital banking is expected to be similarly dramatic. By 2025 it's predicted value will be $1,610 billion[65] – three times what it was in 2015.

Statistics from the UK show the inroads that digital banks are making. At the start of 2021,14 million Brits had a digital-only bank account,[66] a figure predicted to rise to 23 million in the next five years that's more than a third of population and over three-quarters of the adult population had used mobile banking the year before. Over 80% of SMEs are now using mobile banking.

However, so far, most growth has been in North America,[67] where the market was value at $376.2bn in 2019 and is expected to reach $721.3bn by 2027. But there also a surge of interest in Asia,[68] and throughout Europe.[69]

Though they are the new kids on the block, digital banks certainly caught the attention of the markets. In fact, fintechs have become money magnets. While the financial sector overall continues to attract the levels of investment it historically has, investors and capital markets are rapidly switching from legacy banks to new disruptive players.

Consequently, tech firms have enjoyed a deluge of funding in recent years. According to a study by KPMG, global fintech investment was $105bn in 2020,[70] marking the third-highest year on record, despite a significant drop compared to $165 billion in 2019.

NEW BANKS TAKE OVER THE WORLD

NEOBANKS WORLDWIDE LAUNCHES

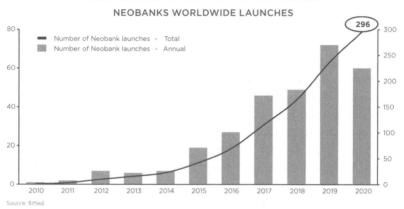

Source: Sifted

NEOBANKS GEOGRAPHICAL DISTRIBUTION

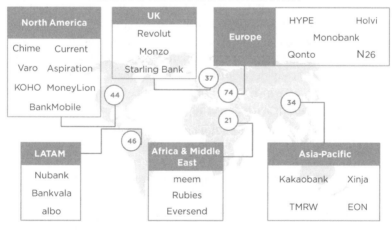

Source: ADL Research

The number of neobanks worldwide has tripled since 2017, climbing from 100 to nearly 300 over the last three years.[71] If you look at Fast Company's list of the most innovative financial companies,[72] eight of the top ten were started after 2010. A neobank is being launched somewhere in the world every five days. Europe is an active 'hotspot,' while UK has the highest number. About three-quarters of these newcomers are targeting personal banking and small companies.[73]

FINTECHS – THE EFFICIENT PREDATORS

The disruptors can make such inroads is because, unlike the large, bloated legacy banks, they are lean, mean moneymaking machines. In 2021, based on cost-income estimates, the four most-efficient European banks were DNB, Swedbank, SEB and Handelsbanken, all originating in digitally advanced Nordic countries.[74] In contrast, old warhorses like Deutsche Bank and Commerzbank were among the least-efficient financial institutions, with cost-income ratios of about 90% and 80%, respectively.

The efficiency gap becomes evident when you look at spending on customer acquisition. For the newcomer Monzo, in the UK, it costs about $8.37 (£6) to acquire a new customer. For a traditional retail bank it's around $200.[75] The writing is well and truly on the wall.

So, who's doing the disrupting?

One of the termites gnawing away at the foundations of traditional banking is actually an ant: Ant Financial, now the Ant Group and the world's most valuable unicorn with an IPO that stood at an historic £35bn.[76] The fact that its share allocation was oversubscribed 872 times just reinforces that this is one of the most spectacular individual success stories underpinning the powerful growth of the fintech sector.

By the middle of 2018, Ant was valued at around $150bn[77] making it at the time, just about as valuable as Goldman Sachs[78] and Morgan Stanley[79] combined. Ultimately, of course, this particular IPO failed as China's financial authorities, in an unprecedented move, suspended it citing "significant issues such as the changes of the financial technology regulatory environment."[80]

Ant Financial was created by the rebranding in October 2014 of Alipay, the payment tool specifically developed to facilitate transactions on China's equivalent of eBay, Taobao, which is part of the Alibaba Group.[81] When Alipay was spun off from Alibaba, it started offering a wider range of financial services that China's young and increasingly wealthy population embraced with enthusiasm. It's become so popular that Ant now has 1.2 billion customers worldwide, and there are plans to grow this base to 2 billion over the next decade.

Some 60–70% of Ant's revenues are coming from payments,[82] which is double that of a traditional retail bank. However, this percentage will drop as the company starts to offer higher-value products, like mortgages, credit cards and credit scoring. So, paradoxically, while most banks will need to escape the burden of having a far-flung lineup of products and services, Ant's future success will largely be based on being a complete, full-service bank.

What's really caught the attention of many investors has been the phenomenal pace at which Ant has developed from a pure-play payment provider into an integrated, full-range financial services company.

Of course, this is being driven by its technology, but also – as we'll discuss in more detail later – it's a reflection of Ant's willingness to innovate. As we've said, this is something that the broader financial services industry used to be quite good at. If we look back, we can see that in credit cards and internet banking, for instance.

And there are many others, of all shapes and sizes, carving out success in this space. In the UK, Chime, achieved $14 billion in market capitalization in November 2020, even though its earnings per share were close to zero.[83] This made it more valuable than many banks or publicly traded companies.

We can broadly characterize these disruptors as companies that develop technology-led innovations that result in new business models, applications, processes or products, which then significantly impact established financial markets and institutions. Despite their different characteristics, all possess one thing in common: their ability to capitalize on 'customer intelligence.' How well they do this will be the most important predictor of revenue growth and profitability. And their reach is growing; fintechs have even infiltrated the closed borders of North Korea![84]

Many of these new players have full banking licenses and offer the same services as their traditional rivals. In Europe, we find Monzo, N26 (acclaimed the World's Best Bank in 2021),[85] MyBank,[86] Starling Bank[87] and Revolut,[88] while in the US there are companies like Ally[89] and Axos.[90]

Neobanks, like WeBank, Yolt, Lunarway and Moven,[91] do not have a banking license themselves, but partner with financial institutions that do. Typically, they require a customer to have an account at an existing licensed bank. The fact that not all neobanks have a banking license makes many doubt their future profitability.

There are also beta banks. These are joint ventures or subsidiaries of existing banks, working under their parent company's license. Beta banks are often set up to offer limited services to consumers in a new market. AiBank, for instance, is a joint venture between China's CITIC Bank Corp and web-search giant Baidu.

However, you categorize them, these new players are growing fast. Europe's three largest digital banks – Revolut, N26 and Monzo – now have over 25 million registered users between them, a figure that is only likely to go up, particularly with Revolut driving things as it makes a move into the US.[92]

We can call these 'the usual suspects,' if you like, but there are increasing incursions into the market from those with business profiles very different from the traditional financial institution.

There's Google, for instance, which has launched a physical debit card linked to a Google Wallet account, and the coffee chain Starbucks, in whose bank account there $1.6 billion just sitting there,[93] all of which comes from customers pre-paid cards. This trend is being replicated across Europe, where supermarkets and high street brands have become post offices, banks and *bureaux de change*.

This is all part of a trend that is being replicated across Europe, where finance is becoming part of the mix, with supermarkets and high street brands, for instance, incorporating post offices, banks and bureau de change.

In fact, if they so wished, any large data processor – a telco, a utility, or a large tech firm, for example – could enter today's financial services space with relative ease, given their ability to innovate, scale and hold information securely.

Further confusing the picture is the crossover between financial services and other sectors. Consider JP Morgan, which is now offering Amazon and Airbnb customers virtual bank accounts.

On top of this, the gig economy is creating opportunities for non-banks like Uber Money to market aggressively to freelance workers and small businesses that are happy to shift allegiances if their current bank doesn't offer the financial tools they need for their work.

As more and more of these Non-Bank Financial Institutions (NBFIs) muscle in, they're forcing traditional banks to explore new revenue streams, like unsecured consumer lending. Goldman Sachs' 'Marcus' and HSBC's 'Amount' are digital channels set up specifically to tap into this new area of business.

Along the way, retail and large corporate banks are losing their grip as disruptors who are faster, cheaper and better move into product and service areas that were once the sole preserve of traditional banks. Monzo, N26 and Starling, for instance, have recently begun offering credit products to their customers, with mortgages, overdraft protection and an interest-paying savings offering all expected to follow.

Unsurprisingly, consumer banking, fund transfer and payments will continue to be disrupted over the next few years, as the business-to-consumer (B2C) space is where fintechs have differentiated themselves and shown their ability to rattle the traditional value chain. However, there's also been innovation in the lending sector, manifested in alternative credit models, the use of non-traditional data sources and powerful data analytics to price risks, accelerate customer-centric lending processes and lower operating costs.

The segments that will prove more challenging to disrupt are the banking models that are either relationship-driven, like corporate banking for large clients, or scale-driven operations, like trading that requires capital and technology investment that puts it out of fintech investors' reach.

Once the disruption starts, there can be an ongoing spillover effect that's hard to stop. In the payment industry, for instance, the newcomers have branched out from their starting point. PayPal is a good example.

When PayPal launched in 1999, taking online card payments was still a challenge for many merchants. Over time, PayPal broke through by making it easier for individuals and businesses to make and take online payments through a digital account rather than having to use physical cards.

Since then, PayPal has also moved into other areas of financial services, such as consumer credit, mobile card acceptance and even card issuance. According to Bloomberg, it now has around 250 million users worldwide[94] and processes some 30% of all e-commerce transactions outside of China.

Stripe is another payment company that has followed this path and is rumored to be applying for a bank license. This is in part due to regulatory convergence driven by the EU's second Payment Services Directive (PSD2), which significantly impacts multi-sided platforms, or marketplace businesses, in Europe.[95] Many of these are no longer exempt from requiring a license.

A NEW FINANCIAL ECOSYSTEM

This is creating a whole new, much more fluid ecosystem in which consumers move like bees from one financial flower to the next. If this trend toward an ever more dynamic and increasingly crowded marketplace continues – and there's no reason to think that it won't – banks could almost be entirely invisible to consumers by 2030. They'll be relegated to the role of behind-the-scenes enabler rather than up-front player. They'll essentially be the Intel processor of the banking world, not the flashy MacBook Pro.

So, if the traditional banks are disappearing, who are the new kids on the block that will be taking their place?

That's not an easy question to answer. In a marketplace that's moving faster than ever, it's not always clear who your competitors are, but we can say that they fall into three categories: aggregators, innovators and disruptors.

THE DIGITAL ATTACKERS

Source: ADL Research

The aggregator brings together data from multiple sources, giving customers the power to compare competing offers. By doing this, they put pressure on customer loyalty and force down prices in the market. This also means that banks lose direct contact with those who buy their products.

Innovators offer a range of integrated services that they deliver in novel ways, such as through 'super apps.' Included in this category are social investing apps that replace bank investment advice; payment players who offer more convenient ways to facilitate transactions; and lending platforms that use Big Data to speed up the financing process.

Finally, there are the pure disruptors. These are the non-banks that bypass historical banking processes. Here we have peer-to-peer platforms that cut out banks as the intermediary, as well as 'easy banks' that offer a wide range of mostly simple, value-added products.

WHERE ARE THE DISRUPTORS FISHING?

Inevitably, some areas of traditional banking are more attractive to disruptive competitors than others. In the illustration below, for instance, we can see that payments are the main point of focus for new entrants. Being in control of transactions opens the door to offering many other kinds of financial services, while interest in small- and medium-sized enterprises (SMEs) has to date been minimal. This is likely to change soon, since this is regarded as an under-exploited but lucrative segment.

WHERE BANKS ARE UNDER ATTACK

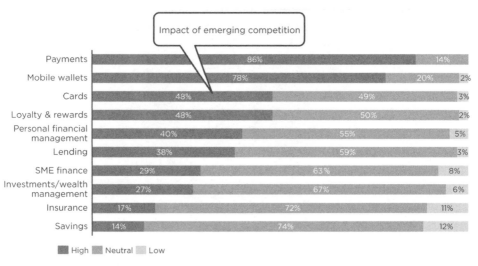

Impact of emerging competition

	High	Neutral	Low
Payments	86%		14%
Mobile wallets	78%	20%	2%
Cards	48%	49%	3%
Loyalty & rewards	48%	50%	2%
Personal financial management	40%	55%	5%
Lending	38%	59%	3%
SME finance	29%	63%	8%
Investments/wealth management	27%	67%	6%
Insurance	17%	72%	11%
Savings	14%	74%	12%

Source: Efma-Infosys (November 2016 the Financial Brand)

It makes sense for disruptive fintechs to target sectors that are the most profitable for them, or the easiest to enter. This illustration gives a good indication of the 'easiest to open' doors.

Each business line has its own set of competitive dynamics that are dependent on the relationship with the legacy banking model, whether new competitors have something different to offer and the nature of barriers to entry. Wealth management, for example, hasn't attracted much attention from fintechs because it tends to revolve around strong personal relationships. Yet, even this once solid bastion of traditional banking is being disrupted by the advent of social investing platforms, digital investment tools and robo-advisors that are empowering younger, affluent customers in particular, who want more control over their financial affairs. With nearly a quarter of younger investors saying they'd switch to a new provider solely to gain access to digital tools – things like portfolio simulation, scenario analysis, auto asset allocation and trade execution – this could spell trouble for their current banks, who don't provide any of these things.

Disruptors like Saxo Bank, Robinhood, Betterment and SoFi are beginning to challenge incumbents with unique integrated service offerings that have a clear value proposition: convenient investment at a low price. If banks can't now offer investment advice directly to consumers, that is yet another link broken.

Even an area like corporate lending, where you'd expect banks to maintain a competitive advantage, isn't exempt from incursions by the fintechs.

IS NOWHERE SAFE?

Global bank lending as % of total corporate financing

2006	2010	2014
39%	37%	32%

Source: FT.com, Capital IQ
Note: Aggregate of Belgium, France, Germany, Italy, Netherlands, Spain, UK and US

This illustration shows how even the large corporate banks are losing their grip as alternative providers lure away their traditional customers with cheaper, faster, more transparent payment services and superior deposit and lending platforms.

WINNERS AND LOSERS

While these new banks are increasingly popular, and continue to grow their customer base, many new digital players have struggled to make a profit. And so, they too are under pressure. One of the main players, Revolut, broke even for the first time in 2020, five years after its launch.[96]

There also are marked profitability differences between segments and geographies that can have a significant impact. Those majoring in digital payment, for instance, are doing well. Because more online shopping was being done during the pandemic, a company like PayPal saw its strongest ever performance, something that will continue in the short-term with the company expecting to add an additional 50 million more active users in 2021 and forecasting revenues of $25.5bn, far exceeding the previous estimate of $21.4bn.[97]

Not surprisingly, there's a strong investment appetite for these new models, which is reflected in their valuations. The US company Square, for instance, which was co-founded by Twitter creator Jack Dorsey and offers 'mom-and-pop' retailers and other small businesses easy credit card payment solutions via smartphones, is valued at around $122.71bn, making it the world's 125th most valuable company by market cap.[98] This makes it some five times higher than Deutsche Bank ($26bn)[99] numbers and 1.6 times that of one of Europe's largest banks, BNP Paribas ($75.5bn).[100]

Such enthusiasm for fintechs is reflected in a growing valuation gap between these digital disruptors and legacy banks. PayPal's $300bn valuation at the start of 2021 means that it is now the 17th largest company in the S&P 500 Index[101] and far more than that of traditional players like Citigroup ($140bn)[102] and Wells Fargo ($180bn)[103] in August 2021.

The valuation metrics for these capital-light models are fundamentally different, of course, from those applied to the incumbents. While for legacy banks the metric is a multiple of net tangible book value, this is often at a steep discount. The fintechs' capital-light model is based on multiple of earnings, or, if a business is not yet earning, on a multiple of the number of customers it has. As a rule of thumb, the new digital business model is valued at $1,000 per customer. Since many fintechs have yet to break even, the markets believe their model can at some point be monetized to generate significant profits.

And there's ample evidence to validate that thinking, given how the newcomers have collapsed banking's traditional value chain by offering innovative and convenient ways individuals and businesses can bypass traditional debit and credit card structures. Lending platforms do the same by leveraging the power of Big Data, giving borrowers greater access to funds at lower rates. Peer-to-peer platforms, for instance, are taking over what was once the sole preserve of traditional banking business by establishing themselves as 'easy banking' providers. With their fast application process and the wide range of mostly simple valued-added products, they're cutting banks out of the equation.

BIG TECH MOVES IN AS WELL

The fintechs aren't alone in wanting a piece of the banking action. We've already seen how a Big Tech player like Amazon is turning into a financial institution. Google is also working to develop financial services infrastructure and capitalize on the convergence in the payments and lending sectors, with plans to introduce consumer bank accounts[104] in collaboration with Citibank and a California-based credit union. This is somewhat similar to what Apple did in 2019 when it created a credit card[105] in partnership with Goldman Sachs. Apple left much of the financial legwork to its bank partner, as Google is doing now.

Google is also expanding through Google Plex, a partnership with banks and credit unions that not only gives users access to checking and savings accounts, but also plugs into Google Pay, the company's digital wallet platform, which isn't available elsewhere.[106]

Those financial institutions that become part of Plex hope to build new consumer relationships with technically-inclined consumers, particularly Millennials and Gen Zers, who value the simplicity of no-fee digital accounts. The company's pay-in-store capability is already pulling in merchants attracted by low credit and debit card transaction fees. If this particular ball gets rolling it could substantially cut into a $90 billion annual source of revenue for the traditional issuers and networks.[107]

But, while there would seem to be opportunities, so far Big Tech has been reticent about leaping feet-first into banking. That's largely because the capital required to run a traditional bank is a highly unattractive, alien proposition to this cash-rich, acquisitive, capital-light elite. They also worry about the compliance burden of operating a financial services provider, which is also anathema to firms used to working in loosely regulated, largely self-governed markets.

So, while Big Tech may actually like to get into banking, for the moment it's happy to just piggyback on existing bank customers in the market while continuing to provide infrastructure capabilities to financial services institutions.

If they ever got serious, Big Tech could possibly grab up to 40% of the $1.35 trillion in US financial services revenue from the incumbents.[108]

Big Tech will undoubtedly push deeper into finance over the coming years, but this will be "more of a slow creep than big strides," according to Sarah Kocianski, who heads up research at fintech consultancy 11:FS. "The headache of getting, and maintaining, a banking license would likely be considered too big a risk for these companies. Instead, they will continue to operate with licensed partners. So, the Big Tech firms will continue to add services that are peripheral to banking to their existing offerings without going full-stack banking."[109]

Meanwhile, the giant technology companies aren't the only ones taking an interest in financial services. In 2016, Ally Bank was born out of General Motors' consumer lending business (GMAC) with a view to creating a full-service online bank, with no physical branches, that could integrate all aspects of banking in a single platform.[110] After getting its banking license, Ally first acquired stockbroker TradeKing, followed up with the launch of Ally Home, a direct-to-consumer mortgage offering. GMAC developed this service in partnership with better.com and sold it through a dedicated digital platform.

HOW TO WIN AN IMPOSSIBLE BATTLE?

Faced with such levels of change, there is no question that many banks will be individually under threat, particularly if they can't find a way to combat one of their biggest challenges: how to compete against a rival who offers the same product as you, but for free!

Many of the new players are almost 'payment-free zones' because of the way they offer products and services at highly discounted prices, which, unsurprisingly, are quite attractive to their customers.

They can do this because they often have non-banking income sources to draw on, or through sharing infrastructure costs or product bundling with a partner. By bundling brokerage with banking, for instance, a stockbroker can offer free trades. Or, by working together, a telecom operator and an insurance company could conceivably cut other channels' car insurance rates by 30%.

One of the best examples of this 'triangular strategy' can be found in the mobile operating systems market. While Microsoft decided to sell its Windows OS to handset manufacturers, Google gave its Android software away so it could derive revenue by monetizing the data it collected. Microsoft obviously couldn't compete against free giveaways and was effectively locked out.

Properly applied, such a triangular strategy can lead to huge shifts in the profit pool and put entire banking segments under threat.

WHEN WILL FINTECHS BUY BANKS?

Banks buying start-ups isn't anything unusual. In fact, it's a quick and powerful way to tap into their technological expertise and keep more of the margin in-house, through the ownership of infrastructure.

For a financial tech start-ups looking to scale, buying a bank would also be an entirely rational move because it would allow them to acquire its banking license as well as gain access to an extensive customer base, which fintechs always struggle to build.

Unfortunately, the valuation disparity between fintech start-ups and banks can be a problem. How do you structure a deal when traditional banks are being valued based on their past earnings and tangible book value while, for fintechs, the yardstick is future growth measured in earnings multiples?

Despite such difficulties, we can expect more and more fintechs and technology firms to look at doing this. However, when they do 'attack,' it will not be so much about takeover, but *co-opetition* that sees both parties engaging though an ever-broader financial ecosystem.

And, of course, this sort of thing is already happening. The first transaction of this kind came in February 2021, when LendingClub was taken over by Radius Bank, a Boston-based digital bank with no branches and about $1.4 billion in assets.

By adopting a hybrid model where it continues to sell some 90% of its consumer loans through its platform, LendingClub hopes to retain the advantages of a loan platform while benefiting from the low-cost deposits and lower compliance costs that come from traditional banking.[111] In so doing, it will cut about $25 million from the annual fees it currently pays and a further $15 million a year on its funding costs, as Radius' lower-cost deposits give it access to cheaper money than it could previously obtain.

Having Radius' deposits will also allow LendingClub to hold more of its own loans on its balance sheet. This could generate a further $40 million in annual profit for every $1 billion held. That's significant when you consider that in 2019, LendingClub originated about $12.3 billion in consumer loans. In total, this adds up to about $80 million, which is a pretty remarkable return given that LendingClub only paid $185 to acquire Radius in the first place.

And LendingClub isn't the only one playing this game. In March 2020, German savings and deposits marketplace Raisin GmbH also flipped the script when it bought its service bank, MHB-Bank AG, and acquired its banking license, preempting the need to apply for one of its own.[112] Acquiring the bank's customers also means that Raisin will be able to expand and achieve scale faster.

In the US, you also have the prepaid debit card firm Green Dot, which acquired Utah-based Bonneville Bank and its $37 million in assets in 2011.[113] This purchase enabled Green Dot to grow and operate more efficiently, while collecting fees directly and introducing new products without the go-ahead from a bank. Since then, Green Dot it has been acquired by Google, closing the loop between fintech, traditional bank and Big Tech.

We can expect more fintechs and tech companies to go down this road and accelerate the convergence, which we'll talk about later.

AN ENDANGERED SPECIES

The only thing that will protect many legacy institutions from a direct onslaught from giants like Google and telecom providers is their banking license. While having such a license is no prerequisite for profitability, it does offer a generous degree of regulatory protection. However, it is something of a double-edged sword since annual license retention imposes a heavy cost burden on organizations.

Banks think this unfairly tilts the playing field in the direction of the fintechs, leaving them to capitalize on market opportunities and maximize profits because of their lower cost base.

This is why you find that many banks, rather than calling for the industry to be fully deregulated, want greater controls imposed on fintechs, so they're brought in line with traditional institutions.

DAVID VERSUS GOLIATH –
WHO WILL WIN?

You can think of all this as a David and Goliath battle for the very soul of banking. On one hand, we have the impudent, disruptive upstarts. On the other, there are the lumbering dinosaurs, albeit more like the herbivore brontosaurus than meat-eating velociraptor.

Isn't it David, with his slingshot 'technology', who's supposed to win? In this case, the battle isn't always going to be an easy win for the fintechs. One mustn't forget that most are minnows alongside the huge traditional banks, which means it can be difficult for them to gain a foothold or make headway. For instance, fintechs can never underestimate the huge spending power of high-visibility incumbents when it comes to something like direct consumer marketing to pull in new business.

As we've noted, acquiring new customers has always been something of problem for fintechs. For some, it will be their death knell. If they can't get enough customers quickly enough, they won't be able to attract the life-blood investment they need before they burn through their cash. Only a few manage this transition, and it is they who get the lion's share of investors' capital. Stripe, Robinhood, Ant Group and WeChat are among the select few. How this trend develops will depend on how the expectations of fintech investors begin to change as the market refocuses on results rather than growth.

AN INCREASINGLY
COMPLEX ENVIRONMENT

In this transformed landscape, legacy banks are likely to see revenue flowing to smaller institutions because they know how to create value and deliver a highly satisfying customer experience.

But while banks are certainly being challenged in this new environment, it's not all smooth sailing for the new entrants, who have to acquire capital and find ways to differentiate themselves with new customers in a marketplace that will continue to consolidate. And if that weren't enough, they're locked out of many markets by regulations and can be mistrusted by governments worried that they'll destabilize the financial markets.

This could leave the new players out in the cold, unable to gain the traction they're looking for. As Anne Boden, CEO of fintech unicorn Starling Bank, put it: "Something is wrong when 20 million potential customers carry on as they were, while we meet in conference venues and high-end coffee shops and agree how revolutionary we are."[114]

Going overseas is also no holiday for fintechs, given the high cost of expanding internationally. Annual licensing alone can run into hundreds of thousands of dollars per country. In the US, compliance is an especially huge barrier because fintechs require nationwide coverage. A neobank, for instance, would have to be regulated in all 50 states – an expensive and time-consuming process that makes it difficult for a financial start-up to achieve international growth. That's what led the German online bank N26 to pull out of the UK in 2020.

There is also the expense of having to make foreign exchange payments, which can be very draining if you don't have a strong local banking presence. That's why, when they can, fintechs often use banks to get access to 'For the Benefit Of' accounts (FBOs) and International Bank Account Numbers (IBANs).

THE FINTECHS' CHOICE

All told, the basic choice for fintechs is whether to be an unregulated digital platform or a depository. As an unregulated entity, a fintech could focus on a particular offer, product, service or customer segment to such an extent that they become a category killer. As an unregulated digital platform, though, they can't hold customer deposits and have no payment rails, which has profound capital and profitability consequences. They'd still be free of constraining capital adequacy requirements, which are increasingly difficult to fund. In any event, most investors now prefer businesses with a capital-light model.

Along the way, excessive AML controls, costly KYC compliance and the uneven application of rules mean that traditional banks can no longer justify a global presence, and have to 'go local' to redeploy their capital more effectively. Conversely, fintechs could focus on a single customer segment, product or service if they want to grow internationally.

The reality is that expanding abroad is challenging for both digital and legacy banks. However, the fintechs probably have a greater degree of the agility necessary to navigate different regulatory environments and meet a wider range of global customer needs.

BUT HERE'S THE
CONTRARIAN VIEW

While the disruptive fintechs undoubtedly hold a strong hand, that doesn't necessarily mean it's 'game over.' Perhaps what we're seeing is no more than a digital frenzy. After all, the rise of the disruptors hasn't fundamentally changed banking or its underlying revenue model. All that needs to happen is for banks to drive down theirs cost and increase their efficiency, and all would be well... would it not?

Might the capital markets have gotten it wrong with their valuation? At some point, could the tide turn back the way it has come? Will the fintechs ultimately eat each other for breakfast, trying to hang on to their bit of ground, as investors realize their mistake and turn back to tried and true 'real' banks for salvation?

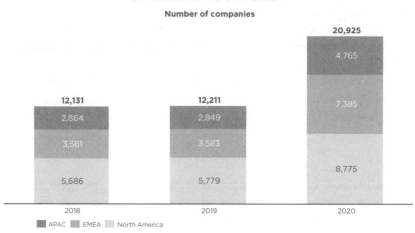

STANDING ROOM ONLY

Number of companies

	2018	2019	2020
Total	12,131	12,211	20,925
APAC	2,864	2,849	4,765
EMEA	3,581	3,583	7,385
North America	5,686	5,779	8,775

■ APAC ■ EMEA ■ North America

Source: Statista, ADL Research

After a spell of stability, more and more fintechs are now coming to market across all regions, each one hoping to take a little bit the banks' pie.

With so many fintechs in so many sub-segments, the space is becoming quite crowded. Eventually this will lead to a bloodbath as the market consolidates. So, analysts and investors are scrambling to discern which firms have the makings of champions, aligned business model economics, access to capital and a robust technology stack. One of the things investors will want to be reassured about is that a company's intellectual property, software and technology isn't easily replicable. If it is, the operation could lose any real competitive advantage. And then, having secured financing, they'll have to be careful not to burn through their newly acquired capital too fast.

Until that happens, most banks have sufficient funds to survive, because of their capital market capabilities, which enable them to make more 'money on money' than other market participants. This would be thanks to their treasury function, hedging practices and proprietary trading.

And all those 'open technologies' that are disrupting the market? Well, they too will eventually be regulated, stalling any possible convergence, as will the introduction of new privacy laws.

It's easy to get sucked into survival bias when we look at the fintech success stories, and start thinking that these new entrants are sure-fire bets. In fact, what we're actually seeing are just the few that have been able to fight their way out of the bear pit of start-ups.

The problem for the traditional banks is that those newcomers who make it out alive are efficient, tough and battle-hardened. They're more than equipped to put up a fight … and that spells trouble for mainstream banking.

But let's say for a moment that you aren't in denial and don't buy into the hopeful bedtime story, with the happy ending that traditional bankers are telling themselves. What do you have to do differently? In the next chapter, you'll start to find out.

NO FINTECH TAKEOVER... YET

Despite all the funding that has gone their way, there has been no sweeping market takeover by the fintechs. If we look at the new challenger banks' rate of market penetration, for instance, it's been relatively slow. This highlights in part customers' stickiness to financial brands they know, but probably more so the extreme cost of becoming a bank.

While technically it's now much easier to start a bank, as Monzo, N26 and Varo money have done, the cost associated with regulation compliance makes many blanch and walk away. This helps traditional organizations maintain their competitive advantage. Yet, banks cannot keep relying on this barrier to entry forever.

And the situation will inevitably change as the disruptors themselves mature and leverage trust in the marketplace, at which point we could see exponential growth in their rate of customer acquisition.

In the meantime, non-banks will have to pick their way through a post-pandemic downturn, something they have not experienced before. If they take a hit from this, it will have a disproportionate impact, given that non-banks have become such an important part of the industry, with a share in origination that had grown to 59% by 2019, up from just 9% in 2009.

On top of this, since the 2008 financial crisis, non-banks have acquired billions in mortgage servicing rights (MSRs) from banks.[115] This meant they were servicing 49% of the market in 2019, compared to just a 6% share in 2010.[116]

This is potentially bad news for the upstarts, with a spate of NPLs coming down the line, once the forbearance period ends. These will be at levels unseen since the 2008 crisis, which will create liquidity concerns that are bound to pose an existential risk to cash-strapped non-banks. Many may be forced to exit the mortgage industry, as their predecessors did a decade earlier. Once post-pandemic insolvencies start occurring on a large-scale, the banking sector – and new entrants in particular – will come under significant stress because of high credit losses.

CHAPTER 5

THE AMBIDEXTROUS ORGANIZATION

"Digital technologies are doing for society and business what the steam engine did for horsepower. Proof of innovation horsepower is the velocity of delivery of digital innovations commercialized in recent times."

FRED SWANEPOEL,
Chief Technology Officer, Nedbank[117]

If the universal banking model is dead after all, what's to replace it? Where will the new market equilibrium reside, and what impact will that have on the market structure? And, what will the retail bank of the future look like? In other words, what will be the industry point of arrival?

Some larger banks may of course decide that they can stay big and use their muscle to take on the tech giants, who they may come to see as their main competitors.

For the majority of traditional banks, however, this won't be a simple matter of cost reduction or adding more 'benefit-free' features to standard products and services. It will, instead, necessitate a total rethinking of how the bank will differentiate itself in a marketplace that's becoming increasingly commoditized.

Most banks will have to run a capital-light business model, like their digital rivals the fintechs, which are primarily online entities with few, if any, physical branches. And, instead of selling a wide range of one-size-fits-all products to meet the needs of the many, banks will have to be much more focused, cutting back on proprietary products and delivering a lean, hyper-personalized portfolio to individual customers.

They'll also have to look at becoming part of an entirely new ecosystem in which banks and fintechs will pursue mutual, complementary needs.

Lacking digital expertise, banks will become much more integrated with third parties – the digital disruptors – if they're to become the data-first organization they need to be, earning revenues from monetizing the wealth of customer information they hold. This shift will need to be driven by top-notch data analysis, algorithms and AI if banks are to provide a frictionless service for their customers, who will increasingly engage through technologies such as Augmented Reality (AR) and chatbots.

This will create a new industry point of arrival.

THE BANKING SECTOR'S NEW POINT OF ARRIVAL

A reshuffled market with new disruptors and transformed legacy banks

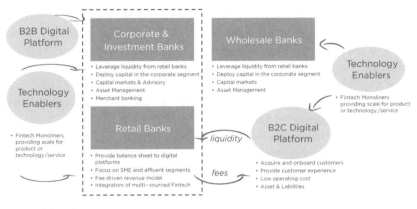

Source: ADL Research

The banking sector will reshape itself to meet the needs of a changing marketplace that's being upended by the incursion of fintechs. In this new world, retail banks, with their liquidity, will focus on higher added-value products and services in both retail and SME segments. Corporate banks will recycle that liquidity, focusing on large SMEs and mid-sized corporations as the traditional clients switch to issuing paper (debt and equity) directly to the market. Traditional business lines will be transformed and dismantled as different elements converge. Wholesale banks will focus on scaling businesses and where technology can create real barriers to market entry for others. They'll also provide 'white label' products that others then badge up as their own, gaining the benefit of a bank's brand equity or back-office capabilities, as well as co-investing in projects with their clients, as the old British merchant bank once did.

A NEW BANKING ORGANIZATION

All this will change how banks look and feel because, in this new environment, the universal banking model just doesn't work. That means legacy banks will need to find a way to move from where they are to where they need to be. So, what kind of organization do they need to become? Where do they need to go, and what will they look like when they get there?

For some years, Arthur D Little has been researching the capabilities of large companies. From this analysis, we can see that organizations fall into one of three broad groups.

Just over half of companies are what we call 'exploit-oriented.' Achieving scale and improving productivity is what matters most to them. They're all about execution, refinement and efficiency, so they look to get the most from what they have. This is what underpins legacy banks' M&A activity as they seek scale, and is reflected in their preference for spending time and resources refining historically successful business activities rather than venturing into new ground.

But, even if banks recognize that they have to make their operations slicker and more efficient, many are failing to do what needs to be done. This sub-par efficiency is something that's been worrying the ECB for a while, so much so that it developed a specific metric – Total Factor Productivity (TFP)[118] – to measure and compare growth between banks of different sizes, organizational structures, ownership types and specializations.

This revealed that across the EU between 2006 and 2017, a medium-sized bank could have produced the same output at just 84% of the cost. So, if you think your bank runs a tight ship, the reality is that it probably doesn't. And, if you want to achieve an adequate ROE, you'll need to cut your costs by a minimum of 15%. That's a big ask, especially if you've already been paring back.

Given this, if the world's 200 largest banks wanted to achieve a standard return on capital of 12%, they would collectively need to cut their costs by some $200 billion, based on our own research at Arthur D Little. The size of the challenge merely highlights how making incremental improvements to the status quo isn't good enough when times are fast changing. In effect, if you're not taking radical action, you're the very picture of Nero fiddling while Rome burns.

This is exactly what happens when you are too inward-looking. You just don't see the monsters lurking outside the gate. It's what happened in the 1990s to Kodak and Polaroid when, despite the many warning signs around them, they remained blissfully ignorant of the world's transition to digital photography. And then, of course, it was too late.

Perhaps the most famous example of an 'exploit' organization's failure to spot what's out there was Blockbuster, a brand that at one time had video rental franchise stores everywhere and now has just one (in the skis and sandals mountain town of Bend, Oregon).

Why did the once-ubiquitous Blockbuster crash so spectacularly? It fixated on trying to improve on what it had always done, while failing to innovate in response to emerging mail order and digital video-on-demand services. That's why you now watch your favorite movies on Netflix, and not on a DVD that comes in a big plastic box.

DON'T DO WHAT YOU'VE ALWAYS DONE

Scale and productivity will only take you so far. If banks are to take the necessary big step forward, they also need to learn important lessons from another kind of business – the 'explore-oriented' organizations that made up 8% of our study group.

Often smaller and less complex than those in the 'exploit' group, these guys are focused on experimentation, risk-taking, discovery and innovation. They're also far more flexible and comfortable in the presence of uncertainty. While these organizations still strive to be efficient, their *big thing* is the creation of a nurturing environment in which interesting innovations are far more likely to sprout. This is the world the fintechs inhabit, where speed and creativity are of utmost importance.

However, while these firms have the mentality of a start-up, they also have the problems of the start-up. Namely, a lack of visibility in the marketplace, insufficient mass to challenge entrenched incumbents, and difficulty replicating their early successes at scale. They also face the challenge confronting any early explorer: when entering unknown territory, they'll be the first to meet the hungry lions!

Of course, neither exploration nor exploitation is inherently good or bad in itself. They're both beneficial in their own way. The main issue here is getting the balance right so you can fully capitalize on the benefits of each approach. If you can do this, you will not only please your short-term stakeholders but also be able to explore innovative avenues that will lay the foundation for your future transformation and business success.

There's one special group of organizations that manages to do this exceedingly well. These are the 16% that are simultaneously exploit- and explore-oriented. In other words, they're continually experimental and curious, while at the same time looking to optimize the efficiency of what they're already doing. These are the ambidextrous organizations that legacy banks now need to become.

Amazon is one of the best ambidextrous performers, having managed to increase its valuation every time it raised capital without showing a true profit for 15 years.[119] Google and 3M are also among those who blend 'left and right brain' capabilities. However, there are few 'double-handers' in the financial services sector. One exception is Goldman Sachs, which is always developing new business models, exploring fresh partnerships and executing with agility. Santander has also segmented its businesses into 'tankers and speedboats,' reflecting the bank's ambidextrous nature. While one can argue whether JP Morgan is truly ambidextrous, it has been equally impressive in the way that it has reinvented its business and revenue models along these lines.

Obviously, becoming an ambidextrous organization is of immense value to any bank faced with delivering short-term results while still looking to future-proof itself by developing the structure, capabilities, technology and talent base required to remain competitive in a highly disrupted marketplace. This isn't possible when you're locked into an inflexible traditional banking model.

Although there are many academic frameworks for how organizations can create an advantage in an age of disruption, none offers any sustainable action plan for doing so. Trying to follow some generic, one-dimensional, off-the-shelf plan isn't going to work when every bank is uniquely challenged by volatility, uncertainty, complexity and ambiguity (the dreaded 'VUCA'). Simply seeking to replace old systems and processes with new 'agile' ones isn't the solution for most large complex companies, because of the disruption this causes and its impact on value-generating activities.

HOW TO BECOME AMBIDEXTROUS

Ambidextrous organizations are always looking to balance two elements – the Performance Space and Innovation Space – as the diagram below shows. Legacy banks must focus on both, if they are to gain the breathing space needed to generate the funds required to reinvent their business through innovation.

In the Performance Space, the focus is on improving productivity. This is something many legacy banks would say that they're pretty good at, although they're often pursuing generic cost-cutting rather than finding ways to get more from less. Growth should be sought at a rate that's viable and defensible, so that value is added rather than destroyed, as set out in the Sustainable Growth Rate Model (SGR).

BALANCING PERFORMANCE AND INNOVATION.

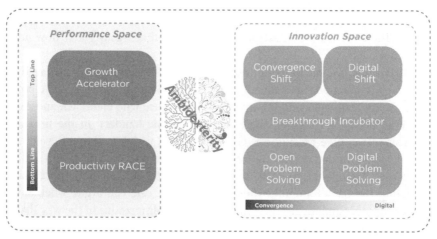

Source: ADL Research

Ambidextrous banks need to balance short-term performance improvements in productivity and growth with longer-term transformation. The latter requires them to innovate using digital technology to solve problems and create breakthrough opportunities that exploits the convergence of different sectors and industries.

The Innovation Space is the engine for change, the place where a new and rein-vented version of the bank is born. It's here that the organization will begin the process of shifting from its previous business model to a much more capi-tal-light approach, leveraging the best technological solutions. This is the only way that traditional banks will be able to stay within striking distance of the fast-moving fintech invading their backyard.

In other words, the focus here is not about just becoming 'digital,' which in itself is neither a strategy nor a business model. Rather, it's about seeing the world through new eyes to creatively solve problems and generate new oppor-tunities for differentiation. Later, we'll look at how this can be done using the 'breakthrough incubator' we mentioned earlier. This is essentially a nursery for new ideas, where novel new products and ventures can be tested out in safety.

Through it all, however, one important component must be in place if a bank is to transform itself. Without the right leader at the helm, none of this will be possible.

THE AMBIDEXTROUS LEADER

Of course, it's possible that a legacy bank may already have the right leader running the show... but that's unlikely. After all, if you aren't well down the road to transformation, why would you want to stick with the person who's overseen your current, misdirected journey to a place you don't want to be?

In their defense, the incumbents might say that in the midst of turbulence, now is not the time to embark upon any transformation initiatives. They'd argue that it will be too disruptive to any scrap of stability that comes with *business as usual*. But this is to miss the point because fundamental transformation is precisely what's needed. If they feel they can't, or don't want to, participate in this, they should get out of the kitchen and make room for someone who will do what needs to be done. Otherwise, they're going to find themselves losing customers and market share at a rapid clip.

If banks are to reach a new promised land, what's needed at the top is an inspirational and entrepreneurial leader who won't settle for more of the same. This journey requires a leader who understands the need for transformation and is willing to take risks and think differently to get there.

In other words, creating an ambidextrous organization requires an equally ambidextrous leader who can embrace a left-brain, right-brain approach. They must be *exploit-oriented* to achieve the short-term shareholder returns that ena-ble raising capital, while implementing an *explore-oriented* vision that reinvents the bank's future.

Not surprisingly, this requires a rather different kind of leader – one who doesn't come from the standard banking mold. For one thing, they aren't overly cautious or naturally averse to change. They have the courage to be a catalyst, not merely a copycat of what others are doing. They aren't satisfied with simply being on a par with their old-school peers. That outmoded thinking is just survival mode and nothing more.

If they are to develop a suitable survival, transformation and growth strategy, they can't just claim to be 'forward-looking,' acknowledge broad industry trends and sketch out possible options. Instead, they need a deep understanding of the banking world as it is now and how it could be, grasping what really matters through a blizzard of irrelevant information. The successful, ambidextrous CEO will know how to probe and cut through the complexity of others' opinions. He or she won't be immobilized by the fear of making a mistake, even if making decisions based on incomplete information.

All this means that the ambidextrous leader must be a mix of innovator and optimizer, someone who can resolve the exploration-exploitation dilemma we've set out above. It requires replicating in a large legacy bank the drive and innovative technology, risk-taking and experimentation of a digital start-up, while simultaneously squeezing the most from a traditional financial institution. This means that such a leader must be a true entrepreneur at heart.

They must be comfortable with technology, since they, rather than the Chief Information Officer (CIO), will actually be the ones who lead any digital transformation.

And, of course, they will need to be willing to take responsibility for an endless list of often-conflicting managerial tasks, initiatives and goals. This will require not just 'digital thinking,' but also traditional banking talents. That entails a high degree of proficiency in strategic prioritization and project management, which become especially important during times of change. If that weren't enough, they must also be on-the-spot firefighters, able to deal with unexpected flare-ups while keeping their organization aligned and on track.

Along the way, the potential for misunderstanding is immense in times of significant change. Honesty and transparency are key, so stakeholders don't feel uninformed or anxious. Nothing will diminish trust and faith faster than a failure to deliver on promised rewards.

Top management can never communicate enough when embarking on a bank transformation. Weak transformations can very often be traced to poor communication that fails to convey the reasoning behind – and sell the strategy, timeline and anticipated pain points involved – to jittery stakeholders. So, the CEO must be an exceptional storyteller, who can clearly articulate their vision through a powerful narrative that instills confidence while managing expectations.

The ambidextrous CEO will be able to inspire action across generations of employees, infusing excitement and pride into the journey by setting out an action plan that's ambitious but feels achievable, because it's grounded in day-to-day realities. If the leader can convey a real sense of opportunity, rather than a looming threat to jobs, they will have gone a long way to reassuring staff and fostering greater employee engagement.

As LinkedIn's Chief Operating Officer Dan Shapero said: "What makes a great leader in this new economy? In a way, it boils down to a few things. Do they build great teams? Do they understand the implications of technology on the business? Are they able to adapt to the speed at which business is happening? Can they operate at a high level and a low level simultaneously? And do they have the ability to build trust across the organization to get things done?"[120]

Unfortunately, finding someone who fits the bill on all these levels, and understands the banking industry, will be no easy task. This is especially true when many banking executives are less than confident about the prospects for change. A global study by professional services firm PwC found that while about 70% of these execs recognize the importance of having a clear vision for the industry's future point of arrival, only about half think large banks can come out as winners. They are almost preparing for failure before they start.

FINDING THE RIGHT LEADER

So, what specifically should banks look for in their new leader? An MIT-Sloane study[121] can give us some clues. It found that in a digital economy, highly effective leaders possess four distinct yet interrelated personas.

First, they must be 'producers' who can use analytics, digital savviness, execution and outcomes to accelerate innovation and improve the customer experience.

Second, they should be 'investors' who are dedicated to achieving longer-term sustainable growth, rather than short-term shareholder returns. They know the *why* behind their enterprise, and genuinely care about the communities in which they operate, as at BBVA, where employee welfare actually means something, and customers are more than mere revenue streams..

The third persona is that of the 'connector,' who's exceptional at building the partnerships and networks that are now so important in driving organizational effectiveness. Having this connector mindset helps a leader align many interests, individuals, functions, companies, geography and industries, often in a short period of time. Lori Beer, JPMorgan Chase's CIO, put it this way: "If leaders do not master collaborative relationships, inside and outside the company, it can limit production of the outcomes needed to win our customers' business."[122]

Finally, these new leaders must also be 'pioneers.' Curious and creative, they operate well in ambiguous situations, since they love continuous experimentation. Organizations with leaders who have an explorer mindset nurture tolerant cultures that encourage curiosity and are forgiving of creative failure. Explorers are intent on building amazing communities. One who exemplifies this persona is Piyush Gupta, CEO of Singapore's largest bank, DBS.[123] His mantra of "live more, bank less" has underpinned what is regarded as the most extensive transformation program of any.

Today's reimagined DBS is characterized by simple, effortless service delivery. How was this achieved? As Gupta explains, "I found that once you give people permission and some training, you unleash this tremendous energy to do things."

THE ROLE OF THE BOARD

A CEO dedicated to leading their bank through a significant transformation must first present a strong business case to the board. The rebirth will involve considerable disruption to all business lines, internal capabilities and organizational culture – it's never going to be some light undertaking.

This will be a multi-year effort that will put the entire bank under strain as it shifts from capital expenditure mode (major investment in physical assets) to operating expense mode (spending on business operations). The result will likely be a short-term dip in profits, so it's critical that leadership has the support of the bank's board, and possibly buy-in from anchor shareholders. If executives and directors aren't on the same page, it's difficult to see how a transformation can succeed.

Unfortunately, the board and C-suite are not always aligned, and when they aren't, that can be a real obstacle to any effective digital shift. A joint survey of more than 200 public company directors by Corporate Board Member, a board education group, showed that their thoughts on what digital transformation meant and involved could be significantly different.[124] Executives are more likely to say they're focused on evolving new capabilities that will modernize the brand, while directors say their focus is primarily on the need to transform the core business model and redefine the company. This means that boards are often much more 'switched on' than the person leading the bank. If that is the situation, the board may quickly determine that they need someone different at the top.

Boards have a central role to play in creating an ambidextrous bank, by choosing a CEO with the requisite transformational capabilities, even if this forces them to set aside old expectations of what leaders look like. That will only really happen on an industry-wide basis if boards recognize that they must change themselves to reflect the new environment.

The fact that the same kinds of people still tend to dominate banking's C-suite in many geographies stands in stark contrast with the profile of future employees and broader societal demographics. This is contrary to the fact that children of foreign-born mothers are on the increase in Europe,[125] for instance, and that and more and more new quality businesses are being started by women[126] and members of minority communities.[127]

The good news is that women, who constitute the majority of employees in many banks, are now beginning to take on more and more senior management roles in those organizations.

There is also a need to recruit tech-savvy directors from diverse backgrounds, and with different skills, as they are all too rare in today's boardrooms. Without their presence, it will be that much harder for a bank to shrug off its old way of doing things and reshape a board's appetite for risk.

If a board is to stimulate change, it must bring in new blood and become increasingly diverse. Research clearly shows that diverse teams with a greater mix of age, gender and ethnic profiles, as well as deeper technology skills and digital acumen perform better,[128] which makes them critically important in challenging traditional assumptions that hold a board back from change. This will help avoid the 'groupthink' that leaves many large organizations out of sync with both their business and their marketplace.

This can be a real problem in big corporations where, even if senior management agrees it would be beneficial to foster more innovation, rigid processes and legacy policies can get in the way of switching to exploration mode.

Does this mean that ambidextrous organizations require a new kind of governance? We believe so. While there's an obvious temptation to simply keep using what's in place, we believe that would be a mistake, as it's likely to put too much emphasis on control, rather than encouraging dynamic and free-thinking action from inventive, curious, digitally savvy and analytically minded leaders.

BECOMING TRANSFORMATION CHAMPIONS

To make the leap, every board member must ideally become a transformation champion, ready and willing to 'think the unthinkable' and facilitate the wholesale remaking of the organization.

Yet, even when they've adopted the right mindset, the board must ensure that sufficient time and resources are allocated. If they don't, the process will be stymied by under-investment, which is one of the biggest reasons transformations fail.

When BNP Paribas launched Hello Bank in May 2013, for instance, it had the stated ambition of acquiring 1.4 million customers by 2017. Two-thirds of those were to be new clients, on top of the existing account-holder base.[129] But the bank only invested €80 million over a two-year period in developing and launching the new entity, which wasn't nearly enough to make a difference.

CHANGE NEVER STOPS

Even with the CEO, senior leadership team and board in perfect harmony, bringing about any transformation – let alone a radical, game-changing shift – will take the bank on a highly disruptive journey, impacting its business model, financial structure, processes and employees. Even if you make all the right moves, getting where you need to be is never an overnight project. Get ready for a difficult, multi-year slog.

The Commonwealth Bank of Australia (CBA)[130] isn't big, but even so it took 15 years to go from starting its transformation to becoming a technology-led bank that holds a market-leading position.[131] To get there, CBA had to completely overhaul its revenue, distribution and technology models while revamping the entirety of its internal processes to ultimately deliver the desired customer journey.

Given the pressure a bank's going to come under, a good interdependent relationship is necessary across the leadership team to ensure understanding and continued alignment. As part of this, boards need to get properly involved in the strategic planning process. While regulators would say they should be driving this already, in most financial institutions a board member has likely never been to a substantive planning meeting, let alone dived deeply into operational matters or been involved in technology decisions.

This has to change, particularly when it comes to technology, since this is no longer solely a back-office consideration but a primary route to succeeding as a business. With new technologies emerging faster than ever, board members need to be knowledgeable and involved, here and now, or they won't be equipped to steer, monitor, measure and review what's going on. The better they understand this new environment, the better they'll be able to extract and comprehend the data they need and adjust their strategic thinking accordingly.

THE REWARDS OF SUCCESS

Mistakes will undoubtedly be made during this kind of transformation program, which will require real tolerance from the board. Directors must be willing to embrace and encourage some degree of risk-taking. For example, a CEO shouldn't be automatically penalized for going over budget, because moving the needle often requires more investment than initially anticipated.

Of course, there's still an obvious need for regulatory oversight by a board, which must ensure that the bank's audit, compensation and risk committees are ready, willing and able to put the brakes on any misguided initiatives. But, given that the whole nature of the CEO's role will change to one of embracing risk-taking, the board must reassess compensation plans, for instance, so that failure (within reason) isn't unduly penalized. If executive contracts remain based purely on short-term results, there's no incentive for a CEO to embark on a radical journey that could well involve writing off a major investment in legacy IT that will hit short-term returns, even when this is exactly what's needed.

Offering multiples of a bank's traditional bonus for achieving an effective transformation would be one way to incentivize, as would a generous equity stake in any new venture that's created. This has worked at companies like

PingAn, a $90 billion conglomerate that's currently one of the leaders in China's digital insurance sector.[132]

Whatever the incentive format, it should be based on tangible objectives and hard, measurable data rather than woolly aspirations. That way, the CEO's progress in particular can be monitored and judged against the right set of Key Performance Indicators (KPIs).

These metrics don't have to be complex or extensive. In fact, banks should avoid having too many, as they can lead to contradictory objectives. They do need to be quantifiable, accurate and relevant.

As such, they could focus on gauging user adoption: how quickly customers begin using new digital products and services, and how easy and efficient that is. Or, a performance measurement could be leadership engagement: the degree to which leaders in key functions embrace and successfully leverage digital transformation. There's also the net promoter score (NPS): a measure of the enthusiasm with which customers recommend or promote new digital products and services to others. And, of course, the all-important customer experience: whether new digital users complete their journey or take their business elsewhere, which may indicate lack of user-friendliness or poor customer support.

If all has gone well, such metrics will reflect favorably on the CEO. However, there's a good chance that they won't, since the failure rate for all large-scale business initiatives, not just technological ones, stands at 70%.[133] This, perhaps more than anything, is indicative that truly ambidextrous leaders are rare individuals.

Of course, even if a transformation is successful, it may still be time to bid *adieu* to the CEO who's taken you here. This is not an act of disloyalty, but simply recognition that the skills required to bring about radical change are probably not the ones needed to oversee a subsequent phase of stability and growth. The board needs to recognize that finding the right leaders for transformation is actually a sequential process, with one doing their bit before handing the baton to another with a different set of skills.

Great innovators are not always great managers. Those who establish and launch a new digital venture, and then take it through its initial stages, must often be replaced by someone more experienced. The tie-dyed computer whiz who creates a revolutionary new product in a California garage is rarely the seasoned business leader needed to shepherd it through to global market domination. When the academic Noam Wasserman analyzed 212 American start-ups, he found that half of all founders were no longer the CEO.[134]

THE CEO DIFFERENCE

Having the right leader in place can make all the difference. Research by the consultancy Deloitte suggests that who's at the helm can affect a bank's value by as much as 35%, depending on whether the leadership team is perceived as weak or progressive.

It's therefore critical that a CEO has a transformative vision that will take a bank to a new point of arrival without destroying it in the process.

Some CEOs of large-scale banks are better equipped than others for the challenge. One success story is that of Dave McKay, who reimagined leadership at Royal Bank of Canada (RBC).

When McKay became CEO of RBC in 2014, things were going well for the Toronto-based global financial institution. It was the world's 14th-largest bank by market capitalization and held top positions domestically in consumer lending, business loans, business deposits and long-term mutual funds.

However, McKay was worried that the institution's rich, 150-year legacy had made it complacent and too reliant on old business methods that wouldn't serve it well going forward.

With new technologies allowing traditional competitors to reinvent themselves and enabling well-capitalized upstarts, McKay knew he had to prepare for the future while still dealing with "a group of leaders who didn't want to set bold objectives for fear of failure. That wasn't the culture."

So, as he described it in an interview, the bank: "… introduced a new leadership model where we ask leaders in clear language to set and articulate more ambitious goals and to lead in a more ambitious way. We have encouraged them to be even more fallible, to say to their teams, 'We're not going to get it all right' and allow the space to fail. And what I'm maybe most proud of is that we used this opportunity to do a complete reset on diversity and inclusion in the organization. Of the senior roles that we replaced, 50% or more went to women. And for us, it was a tangible demonstration of a reset on diversity and inclusion. Our client satisfaction results have never been better. All our core metrics including TSR have benefited from this transformation."[135]

To help pivot from a tradition-bound focus on running a tight ship, McKay invited RBC's 80,000-plus employees worldwide to participate in an online 'vision and values jam.' The all-hands exercise, originally pioneered by IBM, guided the workforce through facilitated discussion and debate over the organization's guiding principles, core values and overall purpose.

Drawing on that, McKay then set out to align a new corporate culture with a freshly articulated vision. He did this by bringing together a core team who together could create a new leadership model focused on encouraging the behaviors that would be so critical to future success. Once new habits were established, a performance management and development system was set up to make sure they stayed in place.

McKay was acutely aware that much of the change at RBC had to come from C-suite executives, who acted as role models. As he described it, they turned themselves into "leaders who set bolder aspirations for their teams and are willing to fail publicly and take some personal risk."

RBC's leadership model encouraged people to be open to new ways of creating value, reducing complexity and accelerating decision-making.

It also aimed to make the bank less hierarchical. Employees were invited to share ideas with their boss's boss, a recognition that in a digital ecosystem, leaders don't have all the answers. "You have to move to a culture of openness, partnership-building and authenticity," said McKay, "because the idea of the strong, confident, authoritarian CEO, which worked to a large degree over the last 40 years, doesn't work anymore."

By reimagining its hierarchical structure, RBC became much more inclusive, diverse and team-based, which made it more agile and able to discover value in places it hadn't thought to look.

In the process of transforming RBC into a nimble, purpose-driven company, the initiative ignited the passion of its employees.

"So, no longer is it just about your product and service and winning and losing," McKay said. "They are engaged by the mission of helping the community. We're only as strong as our clients, and our clients are only as strong as the communities where they live and work. Therefore, we have a vested interest in the health and success of that community."

By all measures, RBC's revamped leadership model has been a success. It has created the conditions for sustainable growth, while also generating above-average shareholder returns. Employee engagement is at an all-time high, and RBC is registering high marks for customer satisfaction and loyalty.

The bank's transformation holds lessons for today's corporate leaders, who acknowledge not feeling that their companies are prepared or equipped to overcome these complex hurdles.

McKay's leadership team exemplifies all four of our desired leadership mindsets: investing in employees, customers and communities (the investor); becoming less rigid, more open and curious (the explorer); encouraging greater collaboration, inviting participation in strategic decisions from a wide array of workers (the connector); and improving their digital skills while paying close attention to results (the producer).

RBS RIP

Let's contrast that with an epic failure, that of RBS and its CEO, Fred Goodwin. This spectacular car crash of a collapse involved the 294-year-old Scottish institution's retreat from investment banking worldwide.

The seeds of its demise were sown in an internal culture that set selling dubious financial products far above any concerns about customer interests and stability. Even as RBS sped forward on a wave of reckless growth, it was undermining itself by overpaying for the acquisition of other banks in pursuit of the belief that only big (and bigger still) was beautiful. And so it was that the banks' balance sheet inflated to a spectacular $2.4 trillion, as big as the Germany economy in 2008.[136]

That this could be allowed to happen was due one thing: the appallingly bad leadership of two CEOs – Goodwin and his predecessor, George Mathewson – who sought growth with megalomaniacal zeal.

When the credit crunch hit in 2007, the bank's plethora of risky investments imploded, leaving the British government (the British taxpayer) to put their hand into their pocket to the tune of £45.5 billion, bailout money that it is not likely to get back.[137]

The UK Financial Services Authority said with a degree of understatement that the "RBS management and board undoubtedly made many decisions which, at least in retrospect, were poor."[138] Given that neither CEO had any direct, hands-on experience in banking, this shouldn't have come as much of a shock.

If a non-bank like those we've been discussing had taken similar risks, they probably wouldn't have been hit with similar regulatory sanctions. And, the impact of their poor decisions would have fallen primarily on capital providers and the workforce, and much less on the wider taxpaying society.

Having looked at the difference a good and a bad CEO can make in a bank's fortunes, it's time to consider the first challenge any new ambidextrous leader should endeavor to tackle. That challenge how to improve productivity.

CHAPTER 6

IMPROVING YOUR PERFORMANCE

"The previous banking model of figuring out what the opportunities are after setting up the business is no longer viable because the price of mistakes is very expensive, and the consequent damage to reputation is not something banks can afford to bear. So, to be everywhere and in every business, I think that is over. Of course, size still matters in terms of the ability to compete and to be able to capture the market opportunities, but banks now need to focus on areas where they want to compete and can really create value, while taking into account the regulatory environment of the region or country. This means that banks now need to decide which are the right industries, markets, and opportunities to invest in and scale, so they can allocate capital accordingly."

BAHREN SHAARI,
CEO, Bank of Singapore, in conversation with Arthur D Little

So, let's remind ourselves of the situation.

The conundrum facing legacy banks goes something like this: to service the short-term reality of satisfying stakeholders and remain afloat, legacy banks have to generate revenue. At the same time, they must take measures to transform themselves into an organization that can compete against disruptive fintechs.

However, the funds they need to do this aren't forthcoming from the capital markets, and they can no longer rely on economic growth or interest rate differentials to pull them out of the proverbial economic doo-doo. And that muck's only going to get deeper with the tsunami of NPL defaults coming post-COVID pandemic. The threat of more bad debt will undoubtedly increase banks' need for capital to cover the accompanying losses, which will turn the markets off even further.

If this weren't enough, new players are disrupting the marketplace. Alongside this, there's the increasing cost of regulatory compliance. And with regulators like the ECB not offering a hand of encouragement when they tell banks to stop dividend payments and refrain from share buybacks and other forms of shareholder remuneration, this is only going to further depress bank valuations.

Against this backdrop, banks worldwide need to at least maintain their profitability – and preferably increase it – over the next 5–10 years. That's critically important, because if they don't find ways to bolster their balance sheet, they'll struggle to find investors or funds to carry out their digital transformation.

CUTTING COSTS THE RIGHT WAY

If building the bottom line is an immediate priority, one way to do this is by improving productivity. As a first step, banks should look to cut costs. Many have already been doing this over the last decade. If we look to the US, total bank overheads (or 'non-interest expenses,' as they're known), have been steadily decreasing as a percentage of asset size. Since 2013, there's been a fall of 36 basis points in larger community banks, with assets of $1–10 billion, and a similar 37 basis-point drop for those with assets of more than $10 billion.[139]

However, attempts at bringing business overheads under control are often blunted by the increasing costs of regulatory compliance, which actually pushed up the operating costs of banks in Europe and the US by 6–8% between 2010 and 2018.

Faced with these ballooning numbers, the instinctive reaction of many legacy banks has been to embrace generic cost-cutting as the go-to solution. While this may provide some temporary comfort and allow executives to pat themselves on the back, such a 'slash and burn' approach ultimately just weakens an organization long-term. What's more, it simply doesn't work, as, all too soon, those underlying costs will inexorably creep back up.

With that said, it's a certainty that many banks will need to engage in some wholesale retrenchment. In fact, if they want to remain competitively priced, some will need to have cut their costs in half by 2022, based on the research that we have done.

And the pressure to do this is growing, as the fintechs' strategy is based on ramping up quickly, using predatory pricing to grow their customer base, to which they then sell proprietary or third-party products. This is how the native digital bank N26 and the non-bank Revolut work.

Of course, many banks will say that they're on the case when it comes to productivity improvement. Unfortunately, their efficiency measures are hampered by the 800-pound gorilla in the room: their legacy technology.

GETTING RID OF THE FREELOADERS

So, if generic cost-cutting isn't the right answer, what is?

Perhaps a better starting point is to think about reducing complexity within the organization, as this not only drives up internal costs but also diminishes the quality of service delivery. Banks are of course complicated businesses by their very nature, but they make things much worse for themselves by creating staggeringly complex and costly operating models. They're burdened with multiple business lines and too many products aimed at different customer segments and geographies, which are then distributed through a tangle of ineffective delivery channels.

And as banks unveil new products – often rolled out with too little thought given to how they actually add value for the customer – they rarely phase out the old, outdated offerings. This inability to prune means it's not uncommon for banks to have in their portfolio hundreds of largely redundant or obsolete products they've stockpiled over the years.

Having a long list of legacy products wouldn't matter so much if there were little attached cost. Unfortunately, such unbridled comprehensiveness comes at a price.

All these product combinations require multiple administrative processes and risk-scoring models to handle the kaleidoscopic array of features, credit terms, interest rates, payment methods, prices, discounts and bundles that inevitably force up costs.

Front office staff have to spend much more time on customer interactions and transaction processing, while middle- and back-office teams are forced to maintain the bloated portfolio indefinitely. Much of their bandwidth will be expended on maintaining regulatory compliance, which can become unmanageable.

All of this is just wasted effort, and a drain on the balance sheet, which legacy banks instead need to strengthen in preparation for post-pandemic fallout, including a sharp rise in bad loans.

As it is, very few of these products are worth keeping because they often don't generate substantial sales. In 2020, a survey by PwC found that more than 80% of revenues – and an even greater percentage of profits – came from just 5% of banking products.

It makes sense on so many levels to revamp product portfolios to weed out the poor performers. 'Less is more' – the very antithesis of their existing business model – should be the guiding principle for legacy banks.

A stripped-down, more standardized portfolio of offerings would trim costs and accelerate time-to-market, while providing greater transparency and better day-to-day operational control. Product rationalization in itself may not always bring about significant savings, but the lowering of technology costs that go with an out-of-control portfolio can be considerable.

By reshaping its product portfolio, a bank can better balance interest income and fee generation, helping it shift from a labor-intensive stance to the more capital-focused model it requires to take on the disruptors.

But while there's real merit in focusing on a 'core' portfolio rather than the 'nice to haves,' this can be difficult for banks used to producing endless streams of products. Some bankers argue that such product complexity is a good thing, as it creates a barrier to entry that strategically prevents competitive pressure. Well, it's certainly a barrier to entry for the many customers who are confused by such random complexity, and it doesn't seem to be doing much to keep the fintechs at bay.

The case is clear: if legacy banks are to reinvent themselves so they can compete against digital disruptors, the importance of simplifying cannot be overstated.

CAN BANKS EVER BE LEAN ORGANIZATIONS?

Based on all this, you might be thinking that if banks are to do more with less, they should become lean organizations focused on providing perfect value to their customers through zero-waste processes. That's absolutely true. Because a bank is no more than an amalgamation of processes, there's no reason why this approach shouldn't work.[140]

Those financial institutions using lean operations report a 20–30% cost reduction within 12–18 months of adoption, and have cost-efficiency ratios below the industry average. Perhaps that's not too surprising, since in financial services at least 40% of costs result from wasteful activities that provide no added value to the customer.[141]

The good news is that, unlike other banking process-improvement methodologies, lean banking does not require a significant capital investment. The lean principles can feed into a continuous improvement culture,[142] which can be developed using defect-elimination techniques like 6 Sigma.

Taking a leaner approach forces banks to think more about customer value and how it can be incorporated across all areas of the operating model. By focusing on customer value, those activities that don't deliver end-user benefits are simply waste. If these are for some reason still necessary, they should be automated as completely as possible.

If banks are to respond to customer pull, instead of pushing products onto the market, their internal systems must have maximum flexibility and deliver minimum response time. Top-down command-and-control structures don't work well in large banks with multiple lines of business. So, value-based performance metrics enable managers to make better decisions.

TAKING A SAW TO OLD TECH

There is a further knock-on effect from getting rid of underperforming products, and that's the impact on IT costs. This is reflected in the time a bank's IT team must spend ensuring that old software languages are kept updated, to avoid issues when legacy product data is migrated. This is bad enough in itself, but becomes more difficult as fewer 'techies' coming through the ranks will understand how to use clunky programs from the 1980s or '90s. Beyond the obvious cost issues, maintaining legacy software designed in-house has the hidden cost of having to depend on system designers who are now fast approaching retirement age.

More broadly, legacy banks are increasingly encumbered by outdated IT infrastructures, some of which are nearly a half-century old. Such venerability confers no benefits; it just brings the pain of having to keep a raft of decentralized, unintegrated systems continually patched and mended.

While there's a need to consign these old systems to the dustbin of history, many bank leaders are reluctant to open this can of worms, given the massive disruption that will entail.

In any event, why bother biting this bullet if you have only a few years left on your contract and would rather pass the buck to your successor? In the interim, you can always cite the exorbitant cost of upgrading as a reason not to go there.

This is a flimsy excuse that simply doesn't stand up to scrutiny, given that banking's IT costs have grown at a 4% compound annual rate since 2013. This could be costing a tier-one bank more than $3 billion a year, wiping out any cost reductions in people or real estate.

While this level of spending is high, it still pales compared to the outlay large tech companies are making. Even the biggest-spending bank, JP Morgan, forks out less than half the amount of Big Tech. There's also significant international differentiation here, with US banks spending perhaps three times more on IT than the average large European bank.[143]

Technology obsolescence runs rampant in today's banking environment, and has now reached a tipping point.

This is a real issue for traditional banks. How can they go head-to-head against a disruptor with a best-in-class offering when they're locked into an old 'full-stack' model that requires them to maintain competitive advantage across every business line? They can't.

While it may be human nature for an incumbent CEO to procrastinate over this, it really doesn't help the bank. At some point, someone will have to tackle the issue of replacing steam-powered IT.

Those not paying attention to antiquated hardware and software that will soon drop dead are going to find themselves staring into a funding abyss. And banks won't have much choice but to address this, as many regulators have woken up to the reality that too many don't have sustainable technology. And so, regulators are likely to demand a review of a bank's end-of-life management plans for its geriatric IT.

Trying to keep inefficient old systems running on fumes can be a money pit, and opens the door to cyber breaches and the expensive penalties that go with them. As it is, our research shows that 15–20% of the banks' annual costs are allocated to IT – more than in any other sector. This is surprising, since technology is the backbone of almost every banking and finance process. Meanwhile, banks are leaning heavily on technology to replace what was their previous big spending target: their far-flung networks of physical branches.

YOUR TECH STACK OR MINE?

Mutualization – a structural reorganization in which customers become profit-sharing owners – is one way for institutions to deal with ever-increasing IT costs, It allows banks to share the risks of technology innovation and legacy migration with others. For instance, a significant percentage of bank IT costs are devoted to very basic activities, like transaction recording and regulatory compliance, which can be performed better and more cheaply when done at scale. The diagram below shows where the relative IT costs lie.

A BREAKDOWN OF IT COSTS SHOWING OPPORTUNITIES FOR MUTUALIZATION

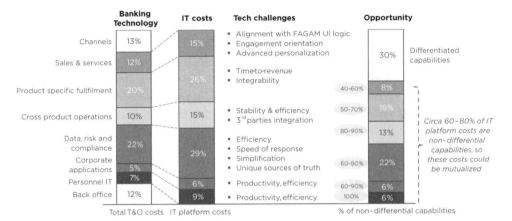

% of non-differential capabilities over total business area cost

Source: ADL Research

In traditional banks, 60–80% of IT costs are related to non-differentiated capabilities. Mutualizing tech costs could produce significant savings, and add to the bottom line, without limiting the opportunities for differentiation. The above illustration shows some of the areas where banks could look to mutualize.

Small and mid-size banks would probably benefit most from this, by outsourcing to a Managed Service Provider (MSP). Such mutualization is even encouraged by some regulators. The Monetary Authority of Singapore, for example, is working with several banks to build a national KYC utility that can be used by financial institutions to cut the costs for all.

GET YOUR HEAD IN THE CLOUDS

Moving to cloud architecture is the only way banks can achieve real cost and efficiency savings while effectively meeting customer expectations. They really have no choice but to make the switch away from their old location-based systems, even though this is complex and costly.

If banks were to invest in the appropriate cloud-based architecture, they would gain greater functionality while lowering back-office costs that are a constant drain. Not doing this seems like commercial madness. If cutting IT costs by some three-quarters by moving data and applications to the cloud isn't sufficient incentive to trigger a technology revamp, then what is?

Cloud computing is essential for building 'knowledge-driven' banking, which is far superior to what's known as 'customer-focused' banking. The latter is actually little better than conventional 'product-based' banking.

One way for a bank to wean itself from feeding old, decrepit systems is to introduce 'starve-legacy' initiatives into its annual and multi-year plans. This gradually diminishes support for old IT, with those resources then redeployed to the bank's transformation.

Of course, IT isn't just about the cloud. If a bank really wants to make progress, it has to look at many other areas of technology. AI, for one, holds promise for an unparalleled set of new capabilities. *Fast Company* magazine suggests that banks could save as much as $1 trillion by 2030 if they adopted AI more widely.[144]

AI would be a fundamental element in helping financial institutions move from a labor-heavy position to a more capital-focused model. Citigroup CEO Mike Corbat states the obvious in noting that tens of thousands of call center jobs could be replaced by AI technology.[145]

And, of course, AI systems will generally improve the efficiency of a bank's back office by creating better workflow documentation and process automation.

Process mapping will give you a good sense of the business critical elements, help identify key metadata systems and establish essential tasks for both individuals and departments. When you know what processes to keep, you'll be able to perform a cost analysis of each, to get a sense of the pain or gain associated with any redesign. You can then either remove what's unnecessary, and doesn't add value, or automate it if it still seems to be useful.

RPA automations tools, which we mentioned earlier, are another highly effective technology that's perfect for performing repetitively manual, high-volume, rules-based tasks, like capturing important metadata. This is particularly the case with unstructured data from scanned documents, handwritten notes and images.

RPA is often used in regulatory compliance, to achieve lower costs and greater efficiency. JP Morgan's compliance department employs 13,000 people and burns through more than $1.6 billion annually. It's all aimed at avoiding regulatory breaches, which cost the bank $16 billion in legal penalties in 2015. Specialized regulatory technology (regtech) that reduces human error in KYC and AML checks can help banks save millions of dollars a year.

DIGITAL PROBLEM SOLVING DELIVERS BIG BENEFITS

Old IT is dragging legacy banks backwards. Embracing and leveraging digital technology is critical because it brings about much-needed improvement in so many areas. These include:

- Faster task completion. This is one of technology's greatest benefits. Performing often-complex tasks in seconds rather than minutes or hours is the best way to inject ever-higher levels of productivity into an organization. More is done in less time.

- Improved customer relationships. By using AI systems, banks can enrich the customer experience to make it more engaging, ensuring that they have the information they need at the moment they need it. AI-driven chatbots and platforms such as Salesforce Desk[146] and ZenDesk[147] can also help banks engage with their customers more effectively. If you can use AI to create a seamless customer journey, you'll be rewarded with people's loyalty. AR could also be used to add a new dimension to online shopping, transforming the customer experience as never before. And, video and live streaming can help give customers the information they need in the way that they want it.

- Deeper personalization. Creating a highly personalized customer experience is something fintechs are good at, but legacy banks aren't. Through the use of powerful analytics, banks can use the data they capture to provide better user-centered services. This is important because, according to Oracle, 86% of customers are ready to pay more for a better user experience.[148]

- Greater security. Newer technologies like blockchain can help ensure the safe exchange of data. This can be enhanced with biometrics – touch, face or voice ID capabilities – when additional layers of authorization are required.

- More precise marketing. Digital marketing can now be highly targeted to reach specific customers who use particular channels or media. Or, it can be based on previous product searches and views. Banks need to be talking to the right person at the right time, not all the people all the time, and using technology is the only way to do that.

INTRODUCING AI IS
THE BRIGHT THING TO DO

In addition to all the customer service benefits, banks should also be introducing technologies like AI and machine learning into every area of their front-, mid- and back-office operations, to achieve better regulatory compliance.

AI is perfect for evaluating inherent risk in operational processes, and it delivers far greater predictive power than the usual logistic regression techniques for understanding the complex relationships within high volumes of data. This raises warning signs much earlier. There are obvious advantages to using it instead of the sub-optimal heuristic ('hands-on learning') techniques that have been developed over time through approximation, trial and error and educated guesswork by human experts.

The challenge here is that credit risk is heavily regulated, and regulators aren't keen on allowing opaque 'black box' algorithms to run the show when no one knows quite how they arrive at a solution.

But while these tech capabilities deliver tangible benefits, they won't dramatically reduce overall operational costs if they're confined to just a few isolated areas. For instance, achieving 20% efficiency improvement in account-closure processes is a good result in itself for a bank, but if that process constitutes less than 1% of total operations cost it's not going to move the needle much. Similarly, you could use smart workflow tools to automate corporate credit assessments, and improve productivity by 80% in doing this, but if this is only done *where it doesn't matter*, a bank's aggregated costs will hardly fall a jot.

PUTTING CUSTOMERS ON
THE ANALYST'S COUCH

AI's real value can be seen in its ability to analyze complex customer data, to pull out hidden insights. As we've seen, traditional banks must get good at that if they're to provide the right products to the right customers at the right time.

At a more sophisticated level, an AI Assistant can anticipate and respond to the needs of customers by providing them with more 'strategic' financial knowledge. This might address maternity grants if users are pregnant; appropriate mortgages if they register to view properties; travel insurance if they've booked a flight; or car warranties if their current coverage is coming to the end. These are all small services that banks could provide to their customers by using AI to create the frictionless experience people are looking for from their financial providers. The more of these 'quality touchpoints' you can give them, the more they'll value you and not someone else.

AI also has a role to play when it comes to security. KYC diligence, for instance, is a constant challenge for all banks. That's increasingly the case as fraud has become more sophisticated and intricate, as the technology employed by the bad guys has evolved.

And now, as regulators layer on obligations, banks are being forced to invest more and more in their KYC systems. They're compelled to expand their infrastructure to store increasing amounts of customer data that can be combed by sophisticated analytics to spot fraudsters and avoid false positives. Processing technologies like biometrics and technology-enabled, behavioral-based security tools are going to become increasingly important.

At the moment, though, most banks' IT systems and architecture aren't sufficiently scalable or flexible enough to do the data collection, mining and analysis that's needed. A report by the European Banking Authority (EBA) noted that the application of predictive and prescriptive analytics remains at "an early stage," with only one in ten banks making use of them, and one in four still using basic historical reporting data.[149]

Fortunately, this isn't an insurmountable problem, since appropriate software can be readily acquired. The real issues don't lie so much with the technology but with how data is kept. Most resides in an architecture of disconnected silos, because banks organize their business units around fenced-off product areas like lending, savings accounts and mortgages.

This means it's not easy to adapt, since new applications must be created for new products, which creates additional processes and costs. Meanwhile, trapping data in different places like this makes it unusable for Big Data tools, which require unfettered access to drill into the detail if you're to really personalize your offerings to customers. So, banks must get sharper with their internal content management, to ensure that information flows in a timely fashion to where it's needed and doesn't become stuck in departmental silos.

This is why progressive banks now have internal teams responsible for analyzing business processes to determine which have value and which do not. Some large commercial banks, like Citi and Wells Fargo, have centers of excellence entirely devoted to this.

Those banks that have already embedded AI into their consumer and wholesale offerings are reaping the benefits of being able to provide much more personalized and relevant solutions.

RUBBISH IN, RUBBISH OUT

Any bank not making the best use of analytics and data is putting itself at a real disadvantage.

While data is important, its quality is also critically important, as this will have a major impact on what comes out of any analytical model. No matter how good your AI systems are, if the data is poor, the negative implications can be significant, especially when issues of regulatory compliance are involved.

One of the major causes of data inaccuracy is, of course, human error, which rears its ugly head whenever information is entered, or transferred between systems, manually.

There is also the issue of sheer data volume. In a large bank this can be particularly overwhelming, with many thousands of interlocking data sets making it difficult to extract relevant insights. Banks also tend to suffer from an inability to effectively use the data they have, or how to measure and integrate data from third-party platforms or technologies such as the Internet of Things (IoT), robotics and Virtual Reality (VR).

On top of that, if you aren't sure that your data is current, decision-makers can't be confident that they're acting on the most complete and accurate information. This can be a problem when information is siloed in disconnected systems, applications and devices. What is required instead is a centralized repository of all information from across the organization.

Of course, banks also need people with the analytical competence to make sense of the data. Unfortunately, this is often the kind of talent they struggle to recruit. We'll look at in more detail later. At the end of the day, those with the best algorithms become king of the hill. And right now, it's the disruptors who have the best tech stories to tell.

Many banks are only just beginning to wake up to this fact, perhaps because they don't have the time or resources to develop the systems. It's all they can do to redevelop their 'normal' Advanced Internal Ratings Based (AIRB) risk-assessment models. This is a place where they might want to draw on the expertise of fintechs to help fill the gap, which we'll also touch on later.

LEGACY TECH IS RUNNING OUT OF STEAM

A bank that's spent years building and maintaining outdated technologies will at some point find itself with a smorgasbord of functionalities and interfaces that's being made more complex by the pace of technological change. Just look at operating systems. Major patches or new versions used to happen once every 3–5 years. Now, they're yearly occurrences.

Under the covers there will be a vast, impenetrable, untestable mass of flawed 'spaghetti code' that's built up with every addition of new software and random patch to the old.[150] It's a salutary thought that 43% of US banks still use COBOL,[151] a programming language that dates from 1959, a report shows. Given all these extra layers, it's not surprising that there are innumerable outages. This is a major reason why some 80% of IT spending goes into keeping archaic legacy middle- and back-office systems running, rather than being spent on technology that optimizes a bank's data-driven capabilities. The illustration below shows the pressure banks are under when it comes to managing their IT costs.

BANKS' RISING COST OF IT

Inflationary IT costs compared to income growth

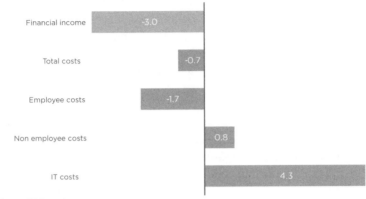

Spanish Banking Sector CAGR 2013-18 (%)

Source: ADL Research

IT costs poised to grow as banks become more technology dependent

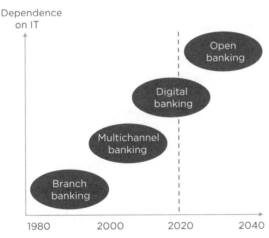

Source: ADL Research

Legacy banks' IT costs are on the rise, and they can be expected to keep growing. In the short-term, at least, they'll still have the cost of maintaining legacy 'run-the-shop' systems, while simultaneously needing to invest in the latest technology, to move from the mix of branch-based, online, mobile and voice systems that comprise traditional multichannel banking. The pressures of open banking will only add to the costs. If banks are to minimize the consequent pain of moving to a new digital model, which will allow them to compete against disruptive fintechs, they must accept the need to write off the cost of older IT and swiftly adopt new technology. It's imperative that the transition period be as short as possible.

This is why adopting next-generation banking architectures is absolutely mandatory for any legacy bank wanting to compete. A new technological stack will allow them to lower costs by 30–60%, reduce the time-to-delivery of functionality changes by up to ten times, and achieve much greater flexibility.[152]

Next-gen platforms are more efficient because they leverage the cost-saving advantages of the cloud. They allow greater automation of systems and help eliminate the contractors needed to maintain legacy applications. Look up into the cloud and you'll see the new services launching almost every week.

MAKING THINGS FIT

The pace of change in IT systems is exponentially, and that's having a dramatic impact on tech-dependent organizations like banks.

With the rapid growth in personal devices and technologies, your employees expect you to give them the applications they need to do their job. This has, of course, been heightened by wholesale switchover to remote working brought on by the COVID pandemic.

IT systems require ever-greater flexibility if they are to meet the needs of a post-pandemic future. And so, investing in the right parts of the technology stack will be more important than ever for businesses of every stripe. That requires a balance between continual tweaking of front-end, customer-facing systems, to ensure optimal service delivery, and sufficient care and feeding of less visible back-end systems. Even one outdated element can prove detrimental, as it can prevent other IT processes from functioning properly and evolving.

Poorly integrated legacy IT systems are inherently inefficient, which limits potential productivity gains, and they're also the biggest impediment to the development of digital banking capabilities.

So, one of the biggest challenges remains how to make old systems work with the new. While 80% of a cloud migration may be relatively simple, the difficulty of pulling old legacy systems into the cloud can make the last 20% quite difficult and time-consuming.

Until all applications are in the cloud and properly integrated, banks won't be in a position to fully benefit from the flexibility and efficiency of updated and automated processes.

As a result, migration is generally a long and costly process. The course and speed will depend on the characteristics of each individual bank. Our research shows that this can involve anywhere from 85,000-250,000 working hours, spread over a period of nine months to two years.

Financial organizations that balk at such a commitment, and don't take this final step wholeheartedly, will find themselves with a mixed bag of systems that will only put them in a worse position.

They have to understand the inherent weaknesses of their current IT systems, which many banks don't even realize need addressing. Gaining a real understanding of potential risks and benefits must be a priority for anyone committed to becoming a true ambidextrous leader. Only then will they be able to introduce new technology that does that most important of things: improve the experience for customers by making their lives better.

Without grasping how new IT underpinnings can ultimately deliver the highest quality, most personalized service possible, they'll fail to make their customers believe they actually care about them. If you aren't dedicated to constantly meeting and adapting to their changing needs, they will surely take their business elsewhere.

This is about much more than just enabling customers to see their most recent account transactions. It's about giving them the fullest picture of their financial world by going the extra mile, and recommending how they can live their financial lives better. That may take the form of advising them about possible savings and investment products, reminding them to pay bills, alerting them if they're likely to overdraw accounts when out shopping, or sending them push notifications on the location of nearby ATMs in case they're in need of cash.

With that, in the next chapter we'll look at that increasingly endangered creature: the traditional bank customer.

CHAPTER 7

GROWING YOUR CUSTOMERS

"In my view, the situation is unclear about what will be the banking industry's point of arrival, particularly because of the consequences of the coronavirus, which will hit banks' capital structure. In Austria, for instance, not a lot of our clients are having problems at the moment, so I'm not immediately seeing a big insolvency problem. But if support from state institutions goes down, this might have an effect. But it's difficult to predict. What will come from the corona pandemic is a lot more digitalization, because it's clear banks must become more efficient to save costs. So, more electronic services and fewer personnel. However, because banks' IT development is not the best, if I can put it like that, they cannot create platforms that are better than fintechs. This means, I think, that they will have to concentrate on creating a really good advice model based around empathetic advisers who really analyze clients' needs to find out what, for them, is the best solution."

REGINA OVESNY-STRAKA,

CEO, Volksbank, Austria in conversation with Arthur D Little

Everyone, it seems, has something to say about the importance of customers. In fact, there are so many quotes on this subject that they could easily fill a book much longer than this one.

Walt Disney said: "Whatever you do, do it well. Do it so well that, when people see you do it, they will want to come back and see you do it again, and they will want to bring others and show them how well you do what you do."

Richard Branson declared: "The key is to set realistic customer expectations, and then not to just meet them, but to exceed them – preferably in unexpected and helpful ways."

Henry Ford chipped in with this: "It is not the employer who pays the wages. Employers only handle the money. It is the customer who pays the wages."

And yet, despite such proclamations – and the fact that most executives will nod their heads in agreement when there's talk about the customer being 'king' or 'queen' – banks have generally done little but pay lip service to this notion.

As a result, they've taken their clients for granted and not given them the care they deserve, even though the customer is key to generating the growth banks need to transform themselves.

If you need evidence of poor customer treatment, look no further than the obsolete IT and processes that are baked banking systems, which slow down and over-complicate every transaction. Faced with the fallout, you're hardly going to turn frustrated customers into raging fans.

Banks haven't yet seen this because they lack the mindset typical of the online retailers, who are continually doing their best to develop new offerings that make things better for their customers. The disruptive recognize this. As Laurence Krieger, COO at the SME bank Tide UK, has said, "Once you strip back a lot of the functionality in retail banking, it's more about the experience than solving issues."[153]

In sticking with the busted old 'universal' model, banks have effectively shown that they're quite content to keep peddling the same unfocused range of products and services – offerings that are wholly unsuited to the needs of their customers.

THE WRONG MEASURE OF SUCCESS

As additional evidence of that, we would point to what Jack Welch, who served as Chairman and CEO of General Electric for 20 years, called "The dumbest idea in the world."[154]

What was it that used to get this doyen of American industry so riled up? That old chestnut: 'maximizing shareholder value.'

Yet, this is the very thing leaders of the world's largest banks have pursued for decades, fixated as they've been on pushing up earnings per share (EPS).

This so bothered Welch because EPS comes with a whole load of baggage and a lot of red flags. For a start, even when EPS rises that doesn't necessarily lead to an increase in stock value. In fact, there's often an inverse correlation – almost 10% of companies with positive EPS growth rates deliver negative rates of return for their stockholders.[155]

On top of that, earnings figures don't accurately reflect inherent risk differences, nor take into account the working capital or fixed investment needed to cover anticipated sales growth. And, because they're based on revenue and cost estimates, they also ignore potential changes to a company's cost of capital or financial risk.

The main downside to chasing EPS is that it makes the leaders of banks think too short-term, because they're fearful of doing anything that might impact this fickle metric. For instance, this drives an abiding reluctance to write off old technology, which legacy institutions have in abundance, even though that's exactly what they need to do. As a result, they stay trapped in the past, constrained by accounting practices that keep them plodding slowly along, plowing the same old furrow, making decisions that never move the bank sufficiently forward. That's not a good look when you're in a disrupted marketplace where white-hot newcomers are doing things differently.

So, if earnings per share aren't the real deal, what should banks be focusing on?

FIND YOUR FLESH AND BLOOD

Instead of chasing earnings, or some other 'cold fish' of a financial metric, bank leaders should turn to their attention fully in one direction: their flesh and blood customers.

After all, as management guru Peter Drucker once said, "There is only one valid purpose of a corporation: to create a customer."[156] If legacy banks ever knew this, it's something many seem to have forgotten.

Drucker's message is clear: if you put everything you've got into meeting and exceeding your customers' needs, they'll be delighted, and they'll pile on the love, and your bank will make money. That means your shareholders' interests will be best served, and they'll be delighted… and that's a big win-win.

Unfortunately, that isn't going to happen if you keep serving up one-size-fits-all products and services, like the ones so many banks are still pushing. Merely trotting out the same old offerings with a bow tied on is hardly going to *delight* when what customers want are innovative solutions that add real value to their lives. This is what the disruptors are giving them, and it's what legacy banks must do if they're to rescue themselves through customer-driven growth.

You can only create this kind of value-added difference when you make the effort to fully and completely understand your customer's requirements, the problems they face, and their ambitions, goals and aspirations. Only then can you give them what they want.

Demographic profiling and purchase history assessment can be used to gain insights into those who bought your products. But these are blunt instruments that can create as much opacity as clarity. Instead, it's better to try and understand what people want to achieve when they use your product or service. Knowing what influences them to buy or not buy from you in the first place is invaluable, as it will inform your efforts to improve the customer experience at every touchpoint.

Group discussions, customer panels, web communities and surveys are all ways to gain this information. Early adopters are great sources of feedback, and if properly encouraged they can become future product advocates. Banks are certainly going to need them as the COVID-19 downturn bites, and really starts to expose the weaker players in the market.

CAPTURE YOUR SHARE OF VOICE, MIND AND HEART

As a means to attract and hang onto customers, banks have historically invested heavily in branding. And because such 'intangibles', which also include buildings, equipment, patents, customer data and software, make up 90% of S&P 500 companies market value,[157] over five times as much as 45 years ago, there was good reason to have done so.

But this 'brand effect' is becoming ever more diluted as customers move away from their traditional banking home. They're quite happy to cherry-pick products and services from multiple providers, even if that means having no more than one traditional account for savings and another for day-to-day checking and cash withdrawls. For many, though, the shift in sentiment goes deeper than this. Middle-class investors, for instance, are now switching away from banks' more lucrative products to stock index and exchange-traded funds, or fixed-income annuities, all of which offer banks lower margins. The more affluent favor alternative assets and equities that are the natural preserve of non-banks.

In part, this altered and still-morphing relationship reflects the loss of the personal connection local branches provided, and their replacement by digital channels that have higher churn rates because they offer a more 'arm's length' experience.

Silicon Valley futurist Paul Saffo suggests that we're in a 'creator economy,' where the real scarcity is consumer engagement.[158] If that's so, banks must do all they can to overcome their customers' 'poverty of attention,' as Saffo puts it, by enriching their experience as much as possible. That means banks need to make sure they aren't just heard by consumers, but find finds ways to capture their hearts and minds. And, of course, they must do so cost-effectively, which really matters when the average acquisition cost of a retail banking customer is $175![159]

THERE IS VALUE IN VALUES

The marketing approach of traditional banks has always been unidirectional, in the sense that they've focused on promoting products and services directly to broadly defined groups of customers. But this doesn't work when the market ecosystem is increasingly complex, and customers can influence one another through review websites like Trustpilot. And it's not just the competence of day-to-day transactional delivery they now want to know about. They're looking far more deeply at what traditional banks stand for, as can be seen in the illustration below.

Percentage of customers who agree with the following statements

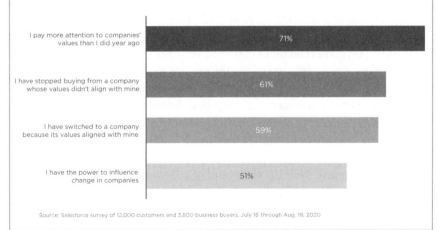

I pay more attention to companies' values than I did year ago	71%
I have stopped buying from a company whose values didn't align with mine	61%
I have switched to a company because its values aligned with mine	59%
I have the power to influence change in companies	51%

Source: Salesforce survey of 12,000 customers and 3,800 business buyers, July 16 through Aug. 18, 2020

The pandemic has shone a spotlight on the wider community-based responsibilities of large organizations like banks. There's growing awareness of and interest in Environmental, Societal and Governance (ESG) evaluation of organizations. Not so long ago, this was little more than a footnote in the annual report, but it's now a corporate game-changer. This is largely due to the pressing need to combat climate change, and very much embodied by younger generations of banking customers. A study by public relations agency 5WPR found that 83% of Millennials want the companies they patronize to be truly aligned with their values.[160]

ARE YOU FOR REAL?

As disruptors become more established, and customers increasingly disloyal, traditional bank brands are becoming ever more diluted. One's brand can even become a toxic asset if it merely reflects vacuous, self-serving 'business' values that customers don't share and probably never did. We saw earlier how one of the world's leading banks, RBS, was fundamentally destroyed by the egos and greed of those who ran it. As investment guru and philanthropist Warren Buffett has said: "It takes 20 years to build a reputation and five minutes to ruin it. If you think about that, you'll do things differently."

If a brand is to mean anything these days, it has to exude the 'authenticity' that customers now want to see in those with whom they choose to do business.

Comedian Steve Martin amusingly summed up the importance of this issue in a sketch: "Say you're going to open a bank. Now say, just, for example, you've got to give it the right name. It's got to be something big and strong like Security First Trust and Federal Reserve. And you have to name a bank that, because nobody is going to put their money in Fred's Bank. 'Hi, I'm Fred. I have a bank. You got $1,500? I'll put it, I'll put it here, in my white suit. White suit, right-hand pocket. Ok, you gotta remember that.'"[161]

If the authenticity isn't there, customers are more than happy to go elsewhere to find it. And if, at any moment, your brand is perceived as 'inauthentic,' there's no quick way to change that, because the values on which it is built will be so deeply baked in. Any attempt to 'overlay' a fresh story on top of the old is likely to be merely seen as a PR stunt, and that could be even more damaging.

If a bank is to give itself the right kind of a 'persona makeover,' it must first understand what values its market is looking for. Next, it must allocate sufficient resources to embed these into its corporate DNA, to the point where they emerge as a natural, appealing and engaging component of the customer journey.

If they don't do this, a bank's likely to be surprised by disruptors who've taken the time to solve their customers' problem better than they can. Indeed, legacy banks should focus not so much on what serves them best, but what it takes to address their customers' needs all along the value chain.

And, of course, creating a great customer journey isn't something traditional banks have been particularly strong at in the past.

TAKE YOUR CUSTOMER
WHERE THEY WANT TO GO

According to a study by Segmint, a marketing data platform, three-quarters of those surveyed feel their bank's performance falls short of their expectations.[162] The quarter of a million plus formal complaints about banking services in the UK alone in 2020/21 says something about what's going on.[163]

What's worse is that this is just the tip of a much bigger iceberg. Research by think tank technologist Esteban Kolsky reveals that only one out of 26 unhappy customers complain.[164] The dissatisfied majority either put up with bad service or, more likely, stay silent and simply take their business elsewhere.

Although legacy banks have used automation behind the scenes for decades to create internal process efficiencies, they've failed to do the same in their front-facing operations, as anyone who's experienced the frustration of being in a call center queue will know.

In contrast, delivering a superior experience is something fintechs are really good at. They're continually exploring how tools like predictive analytics, natural language processing (NLP), machine learning and AI can be used to delight customers across every aspect of their operations.

A table of overall customer satisfaction produced by the UK's Financial Conduct Authority early in 2021 had four challenger banks heading the list. The two frontrunners, Monzo and Starling, had scores of 86% and 84%, respectively.[165] Traditional banks like Barclays, Halifax, Santander and Lloyds lagged some 25 percentage points behind!

If they are to close gaps like this, banks must reinvent who they are, what they do and how they do it. Again, rather than just offering feature-stuffed 'me-too' products, they must strive to build a much more emotional experience.[166] This would be worth doing, as 86% of customers say they'd be willing and ready to pay more for better service.[167]

For instance, by aiming for what's called 'first-time resolution', legacy banks could minimize the need for customers to contact them because their requirements would be met right from the start. That would be good for all concerned and translate into lower costs for the bank. This could be done using automated technology such as RPA to take on repetitive, manual tasks that slow down back-office processes and diminish levels of service.

CONTEXT IS CRITICAL

How this eventually plays out will depend on the behavioral differences between customers and the products or services they want. For instance, the quality and reputation of a financial institution matter much less if it's giving you a loan rather than taking your life savings.

But customer behavior isn't consistent, and it's constantly changing, which means it can vary wildly in different situations and at different times. So, marketing by traditional banks needs to become much contextual – related to the environment customers finds themselves in at that moment. Yet, while more and more of their existing and potential customers are living their lives online, most banks still spend less than 20% of their marketing budgets on digital outreach. Remarkably, some 60% of bankers admit they can't measure the impact of digital marketing on their balance sheet growth.[168]

Of course, effective marketing can only be done when you have the data that enables you to effectively tailor your offering. Once again, we're a world away from the sub-optimal products and services traditional banks have historically sold and cross-sold to their customers.

If there's one thing that has radically changed customer thinking in recent times it has been *the big event*: the pandemic. The coronavirus has left a large and indelible mark on many by depriving them of income and leaving them financially vulnerable. In the UK, a quarter of the population saw their disposable income drop, and one in six homeowners asked for a mortgage payment deferral.

Not surprisingly, this has led many to revise their fundamental financial behaviors.[169] They've either had no choice but to spend more, or were forced to hold on to more of what they had. As the pandemic grinds on, 38% now say they are 'saving a little more,' while 51% vow to save more once the crisis is over. In the UK, for instance, the household saving ratio, which shows the average percentage of disposable income saved, went up from 16.1% in the final three months of 2020 year to 19.9% in the first quarter of 2021.[170]

This now makes savings a growth area for financial services companies, which is good news for most retail financial institutions. That's because savings have long been the foundation of core earning assets, as key sources of coveted 'primary bank' relationship status.

COVID-19 has also reshaped the financial landscape by driving a massive shift from in-person shopping to online commerce. While digital channels have never been a strategic priority for legacy banks, they've suddenly moved front and center. This surge in online customer interactions has put banks' infrastructure to the test. While many have risen to the challenge, for others it has driven home the need to accelerate wholesale technology adoption.

Seven out of ten consumers say that seamless, connected processes that are built on previous interactions are a key factor in deciding who they do business with. Yet, how many banks can say that this is what they're delivering? Indeed, very few.

Consequently, most customers who've gone on a digital journey with their bank will have found it to be a frustrating, disappointment experience. During the pandemic, 56% of banking customers reported being redirected from online interactions to physical locations, while 48% said they'd been asked to print, sign and email paperwork, even though they're supposedly banking online. This meant that nearly half of US customers, for instance, found it difficult or very difficult to complete a loan process digitally.[171]

With societal lockdowns having fundamentally altered how consumers buy goods and services, this definitely isn't what they are after. Forced to change their offline and online behaviors, many came to appreciate online convenience and are now looking for that across every aspect of their lives. That will, of course, include banking. The illustration below shows how much more willing consumers now are to embrace technology in their everyday lives.

Percentage of customers who agree with the following statements

Source: Salesforce survey of 12,000 customers and 3,600 business buyers, July 16 through Aug. 18, 2020

Banks must be mindful of this and respond by accelerating their transformation. The good news is that properly exploiting their vast wealth of transaction data can positioned banks to provide the frictionless experience their customers enjoy from online retailers.

Legacy banks have begun to understand the wide scope of benefits technology can bring – for example, how this can outweigh the scale advantages of the past – and have begun a shift to what they think it means to be a digital operation. As part of this process, they've been attempting to move customers over to internet banking by investing in their online channels and relinquishing their physical presence on the high street. This has resulted in the loss of many branches, which have either been closed completely or reinvented.

Santander, for instance, has turned some into communal Work Cafés, while Virgin has created Money Lounges, where customers can enjoy a more relaxed banking atmosphere. In the US, Chase and Capital One have partnered with upscale urban coffee shop purveyors to open lobby cafés. Time will tell if the pervasive social distancing of the pandemic has doomed those 'public living room' strategies.

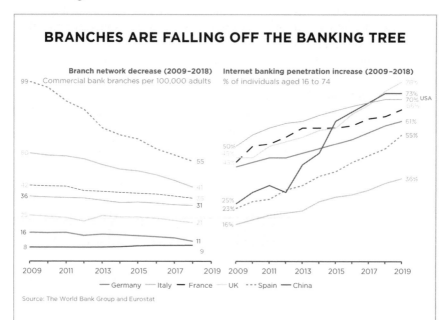

BRANCHES ARE FALLING OFF THE BANKING TREE

Branch network decrease (2009–2018)
Commercial bank branches per 100,000 adults

Internet banking penetration increase (2009–2018)
% of individuals aged 16 to 74

— Germany — Italy — France — UK ··· Spain — China

Source: The World Bank Group and Eurostat

Twenty years ago, Wells Fargo was the first bank to start offering services to its clients over web. Since then, retail banks everywhere have embraced digital channels as an important part of their operations, and a way to migrate customers to lower-cost channels. This became the thin end of the wedge that brought about the decline of the physical branch network, which has withered on the vine worldwide over the past decade. Now, in developed countries, more than 85% of customer transactions are done through digital channels, such as ATMs, computers and mobile devices, with smartphones having become particularly relevant for banking interaction. Physical branches will not disappear completely, at least for the foreseeable future, because a large percentage of the adults don't have bank accounts ('the unbanked') and still need brick and mortar storefronts.

While those that haven't yet embraced online banking find themselves at a disadvantage, it's impossible for traditional banks to resist the pull of the economics. When the average cost of a transaction in a physical branch ringing in at $4, and with PC and mobile banking at just $0.09 and $0.019 in comparison, banks really have no choice in the matter.

Though some may have had plans for making this transition at their own pace, COVID disrupted everything, accelerating the switch to digital overnight. Lockdowns suddenly meant that whole customer segments that historically wouldn't have considered using remote channels as their primary form of banking interaction had no choice but to do so. At the same time, retail banks were unready for full digital engagement, having had no time to ensure that their portfolios and service delivery were prepared for their customers' digital journey. This means they have some work to do.

IT'S ALL A MATTER OF TRUST

Of course, every canny consumer knows that engaging with anyone online requires a large element of trust.

While banks are still seen as largely trustworthy, brand allegiance is on the wane as consumers grow more willing to embrace non-traditional financial providers. Those who are younger and less wedded to traditional banking are more likely to trust their digital suppliers than their bank. Nearly three-quarters of Millennials now say they prefer to receive financial services from digital start-ups instead, while a third believe they won't actually need a bank at all in the future.[169]

This loosening relationship is echoed in a survey by global professional services firm Accenture, which found that one in four customers would consider buying insurance from an online provider like Amazon.[173] This wasn't lost on Amazon, which in 2020 entered the Indian insurance market.[174]

Credit cards and payments are also vulnerable segments, and as non-banks become more confident and gain greater wallet-share, they'll be motivated to move into even more areas. You can see that happening already in the US, where Rocket Mortgage, Chime and Robinhood are competing for mortgages, lending and investment, respectively.

As Jack Ma, co-founder of Alibaba, said the Chinese e-commerce giant's real asset is the trust it has created. "What we have got is not money. What we have got is the trust from the people."[175]

So, financial institutions have to fundamentally review how they can reconnect with their customers in an increasingly competitive landscape, where trust is no longer based on past or exclusive relationships.

If they are to make trust a differentiating issue, banks have to find some way to measure it. Some are beginning to measure customer advocacy metrics like the Net Promoter Score (NPS), which reflects one's likelihood to recommend a company, product or service to a friend or family member. This is a starting point. Another interesting new metric is Return on Consent (ROC), an indicator of what customers believe they're going to get out of giving up their personal data.

As people demand greater transparency and more granular control over how their data is shared and used, intangibles like trust, reputation and affiliation can be leveraged to create market differentiation. This makes them factors a bank must integrate into a values-driven operating model. If a bank can achieve 'trusted advisor' status, it will go a long way to setting itself apart in the market. If it can do that, rather than just entering into some fragmented, transactional process with its customers, it can be absorbed into their lives, remain relevant and be trusted to deliver what is wanted. To do this, a bank will probably have to become part of a wider, trusted ecosystem of partners who are meeting an individual's needs in ways that go beyond banking. We'll look at this a little later.

If you are to differentiate yourself, you need a unique proposition that creates lasting competitive advantage for the bank and added value for its stakeholders. Unfortunately, bankers often convince themselves that their current products and services are key differentiators when they're not, and probably haven't been for a while.

The reality is that today's customers don't necessarily want 'products' at all, but rather a way to help satisfy their lifestyle needs. This is why they're increasingly willing to buy from multiple providers who they think can deliver what consumers want and are aligned with their values.

This puts customers very much in the driving seat. So, banks now have to see the world through their eyes and then let customers' desires and preferences determine the risk, capital and liquidity boundaries of their portfolio. This shouldn't be seen as some kind of marketing ploy, but a new way of thinking that must be encouraged and allowed to permeate every corner of the organization.

That will require banks to connect with their customers with a whole new level of intimacy, which certainly can't be done using the one-size-fits-all models of the past, where they were all treated the same.

If you want to see a real commitment to customer engagement, look no further than Fidor.[176]

CUSTOMER ENGAGEMENT IN ACTION

Founded in Germany, Fidor was the world's first 'fintech bank,' a pioneer in bringing together traditional financial services and technology when it was established in 2009. From the start, its aim was to make banking as fast and frictionless as possible. It began by eliminating all paper and other physical interactions with clients, and greatly simplifying the onboarding process. KYC checks, for instance, are done digitally using video identification, and customers get an e-card delivered to them straightaway. When it comes to loans, credit scoring is performed up front, so funds can be disbursed virtually instantly.

Everything Fidor does is centered round creating exceptional customer engagement through a highly personalized approach. That extends to giving them a voice in how the bank is run. Clients get to say what they think about interest rate levels, or help choose the names of different products Fidor is launching. It's a co-creational approach that may become an enduring part of the future of banking. And, to ensure that anyone who wants to open an account is a 'Fidor kind of person,' new customers are welcomed onboard if they're sponsored by an existing client.

Fidor has exported this kind of innovative thinking to other financial institutions around the world that use its technology platform, like Bank Van Lanschot in the Netherlands and ADIB in the United Arab Emirates. They've been inspired to adopt 'Smart Community,' an initiative that helps tech-savvy members better manage their finances, with a view to becoming customers of the bank. More than 250,000 people have done so since its launch.

The scheme works in large part because it appeals to today's consumers, who want to do research and get feedback from others before making important financial decisions. They're eager to engage with others through forums and comparison sites before making important decisions.

By using this highly innovative marketing approach, Abu Dhabi's ADIB is able to acquire new customers through Smart Community at just 10% of the cost of its more traditional acquisition channels.

BANKS AS 'DATA COMPANIES'

Fidor is an inspiring example of how creating a sense of community could be a real differentiating factor for legacy banks. But, this is only possible because it uses data to act in an insight-driven manner, as its agile fintech rivals are doing.

As Google, with its omnipresence in search, and Facebook, with its dominance of social channels, can attest, the platform that controls the most data possesses the most value. That translates into wielding the most power.

Google's then-CEO Eric Schmidt said in 2010: "One day we had a conversation where we figured we could just [use Google's data about its users] to predict the stock market. And then we decided it was illegal. So we stopped doing that."[177] He probably wasn't joking.[178]

Banks, by contrast, have lagged in their use of data to make products more relevant for customers. That has to change.

Research consultancy Forrester suggests that the bank of tomorrow will be first and foremost a data company that "leverages technology and ecosystem partnerships to deliver value for the customer's financial and non-financial digital ecosystem in a seamless manner."

Some institutions have seen the light and are changing tack. Francisco Gonzalez, former Chairman and CEO of BBVA, declared that the Spanish bank would be "a software company in the future."[179]

And it has to be said that tech firms like the payments processing fintech Stripe are phenomenally good at collecting customer information. In that regard, it would certainly outperform all but a few banks.

So, as Accenture consultants Wayne Busch and Juan Pedro Moreno have written in *Harvard Business Review*: "Instead of simply enabling customers to save money and pay for things, banks have the potential to combine their vast transaction data with new digital tools to help customers make decisions on what to buy, and where and when to buy it – whether it's dinner and a movie or a new home."[180]

The real key here is of course how that data is put to use. Even though banks are sitting on a mountain of potentially valuable customer information, the gems are buried deep, sequestered between departments and imprisoned in lines of business. If data is the new oil, it remains a barrel of 'crude', far from the refined, golden petrol that's needed to fuel the frictionless customer experience.

Legacy banks must reinvent their customer model so products are sufficiently personalized to meet the needs of consumers' lifestyles and how they see themselves. While not based on the use of data, credit card companies have done this to some extent with prestige products – gold cards, black cards, sapphire-colored metal cards! – that suggest exclusivity.

This means that legacy banks must now focus not just on embedding technologies, but using innovative tech-driven solutions to better engage with their customers. And there are exciting ways they can do this. Take the vaunted 'super app', for instance.

CONVENIENCE IN YOUR POCKET

To make sure their experience is as smooth and appealing as possible, some social media networks have developed 'an app for everything'. These super apps give users access to multiple services through a one-stop portal. Beyond messaging, for example, WeChat users can order food, book rail tickets, call a taxi, pay for a hotel room or even look for their next house. They can also transfer money and buy financial services. Users of Alibaba's Alipay can now do much more than simply buy products, including paying their water, electricity, trash pickup and phone bills. Alipay's stated intent is to become a pervasive 'digital life service'.

Watch out, banks. This lays the foundation for the creation of a marketplace, something we'll talk about later.

Currently, the majority of a super app's payment flows will go through traditional financial institutions, because they're the ones originating and underwriting the products. But super apps are beginning to build strong relationships with own their banking arms. So, WeChat uses WePay for payments and WeBank for banking products, while Alibaba has AliPay and Ant Group, which will increasingly sideline traditional payment service providers. This is yet more evidence that the disruptors are taking bold steps into the financial services domains.

If banks don't step up to the plate, they could find themselves relegated to playing a walk-on part. They could end up performing only regulated core activities, while those with the super app actually own the customer relationship and experience.

Much of the super apps' success is made possible by sharing data effectively across different service areas, as this gives them a complete customer picture. Traditional banks, with their silos of data and lumbering mainframe technology, will struggle to achieve anything close. If banks want to be on a par, they must improve both their analytics capabilities and data management, so that information flows freely to where it's needed.

Of course, developing a super app takes significant time, money and resources that a legacy bank might not have. That shouldn't stop it from at least building a reasonable online and mobile presence, the bare minimum expected by modern consumers who are continually increasing their screen time.

At the very least, a bank must find a way to allow simple digital transactions. If not, it will lose existing customers and have done nothing to attract new ones. In a digital world, where there will be an estimated 311 million smartphone users in the US alone by 2025,[181] banks need to acquire a mobile-first mentality.

PLAYING THE BANKING GAME

Peoples' lives are only going to get busier, so convenience is key. Banking tools need to resonate with those accustomed to a digital-first experience, delivered through a desktop computer, laptop, phone or even a gaming station. PlayStation and Xboxes are, after all, interactive computers with an online connection, and if banks took advantage of this they could put themselves in front of a potentially huge, young demographic. Imagine getting credits for playing an online game using your local bank as a portal.

By some estimates, gamers worldwide spend an average of 8.5 hours a week glued to video games. This could make for a great captive audience for banks willing to sponsor a particular game, advertise in the *gameverse* or generate revenue by selling targeted products there, like a first bank account, a car loan or student financing.

The UK challenger bank Atom is already heading in that direction by hiring developers from the gaming sector to learn how to better interact with devotees of Grand Theft Auto, The Legend of Zelda, Halo and Resident Evil.[182] So far, they've created a 3D app for managing finances based on the popular Unity 3D gaming development platform.

With an estimated 3.25 billion regular gamers worldwide in 2021, banks ignore this massive potential audience at their own peril.

RIP, UNIVERSAL BANK –
WHAT NEXT?

To traditional bankers, gaming and super apps may seem like fads and gimmicks, but they're not. They're serious solutions that can help consumers better meet their financial needs, and should be viewed as innovative examples of how banks could begin the process of reinventing themselves.

As we've seen, they need to do something different to counter-punch with the disruptors who've helped kill off the universal banking model. The one-time belief that a single financial institution could profit from a multitude of business lines is now well and truly dead. The old, theoretical benefits are far outweighed by the complexity, cost and difficulty of regulatory compliance, and the sheer attractiveness and utility of new digital approaches.

The argument no longer holds that diversification gives you the ability to invest through the business cycle, or cross-sell a range of products to loyal customers. All you'll end up with is a portfolio of underperforming proprietary products delivered through constricted delivery channels, using antiquated systems kept on life support by an internal team that's consumed with ensuring across-the-board regulatory compliance.

In fact, bringing a laundry list of financial offerings under one umbrella just leads to products and services that are lower in quality and higher in price than what's offered by better-focused, specialized competitors.

For a measure of how this old model no longer works in our age of agile disruptors, consider that in the decade or so since 2010, the top financial services firms have grown by only 30% compared with the six-fold growth of leading fintechs.

While the 20 largest financial services firms are now worth $800 billion more than they were in 2010, the 20 largest technology companies are worth a staggering $3.8 trillion more.[183] That's not a gap, but a yawning chasm.

Given universal banks' seeming inability to transform themselves, investors have looked at this picture of doom and gloom, their potential exposure to risk and fast-rising compliance costs and resoundingly said, 'No thanks!' This has weakened the banks' share performance even further.

And how are banks going to get out of this unholy bind?

It's simple, really.

Make their internal processes as slick as possible to improve the customer journey. Stop trying to be all things to all people. Cut back on their jumble of freeloading products. And then, create innovative alternatives that meet the needs of their market.

When you've done that, you can embark on the digital shift that's needed to turn a legacy bank into the lean, mean fighting machine it desperately needs to be.

CHAPTER 8

MAKING THE DIGITAL SHIFT

"Banks must change their business models so they become more like technology companies. This is a continuous process and something we have been doing for the last 20 years by focusing on areas like superior customer service, digitization, advanced analytics, infrastructure and not just customers, but also staff, because it's by attracting the right talent that we will change our business for the better. Of course, moving a legacy system to a new revenue and business model is not easy, but I think life is easier if you have young minds in your institution, because these forward-looking young brains force the top management to change. The average age in our institutions, for instance, is 37. But this kind of change means moving some people out of their comfort zone. So, good communication is critical, as your team needs to know they are not competing against other banks, but some of the very advanced technology companies. Begin by convincing a few people at first about what you are going to do, build their trust in your team and then make the circle wider and wider."

HAKAN BINBASGIL,

CEO, Akbank, Turkey, in conversation with Arthur D Little

We looked earlier at the Performance Space, a fundamental component of any legacy bank's transition away from its traditional model. Streamlining processes, reducing product complexity and using IT to increase productivity are all elements of this, and a major stepping-stone to acquiring the funds needed to finance a longer-term transformation.

However, if traditional banks really are to compete in a new financial world, they must make a much more profound digital shift and become true technology-led businesses. They must do this because today it's impossible to provide any banking transaction or service without investing heavily in algorithms. It's this digital shift that takes us into the Innovation Space, where the new ideas are created that will drive the bank forward into what for them is new and uncharted territory. So, here, the focus is not so much on doing things better, but on doing things differently.

The majority of banks still do the same things over and over again because they're constrained by old-school thinking that's fixated on capital requirements, or the pursuit of market share, instead of transformation. This is madness. To quote Albert Einstein, "The definition of insanity is doing the same thing over and over again but expecting different results."

There are shining examples of banks that have taken the leap into this digital future, with the likes of BBVA, CBA and DBS drastically changing their business models through innovation.

Then there's the banking giant JPMorgan Chase, which redefined itself as a technology company. It has worked to automate as many of its workflows as possible, and is reaping the rewards. One of its programs, COIN (Contract Intelligence), has cut thousands of hours from commercial-loan agreement processes. Before COIN went live in June 2017, it was taking the bank's lawyers and loan officers a whopping 360,000 hours a year to do that work.[184]

By taking its technology-led approach, JPMorgan Chase has gone from having a worth of $245 billion and 235,000 employees in 2016 to being valued at $365 billion and employing only 165,000 just two years later. Since then, the mega-bank has increased its innovation budget by a further 50% and has rolled out even more digital transformation projects.

At the other end of the size and resources spectrum, you have Capitec.[185] This South African legacy bank has completely transformed itself from an unresponsive traditional institution into a cutting-edge operator that enables its geographically-dispersed customer base to make faster and better transactions, even if they have only an analogue phone. It had to be innovative because there was no infrastructure in place. The only way it could grow was to use mobile telephony to serve a mass market.

One of the reasons many digital banks in Africa are ahead of those elsewhere is that it's impossible to use a traditional branch model to serve sparse populations in remote locations. It would be quite difficult, and disproportionately expensive, to build out an effective physical banking infrastructure, so they've had no choice but to cut deals with telecom operators whose networks then provide the backbone.

The important lesson here for every bank is that you won't get anywhere if you retain your legacy systems. Once again, you need an ambidextrous leader who's dedicated to real transformation. They must intellectually acknowledge the need to do this, and be prepared to redirect resources to where they're required to make things happen. And that's probably going to ruffle some feathers. PwC reports that to derive significant value from their digital investments and make a demonstrable difference, organizations must accept they'll have to spend about a third more than their competitors on technology, processes and operating models.

We talked earlier about a CEO needing the board's buy-in, and it's at moments like this that's their backing is crucial. Carrying out a massive project, which a successful digital transformation will be, can be difficult in the best of times, but all but impossible if everyone isn't willing to play ball.

THE 10 DIMENSIONS OF A DIGITAL SHIFT

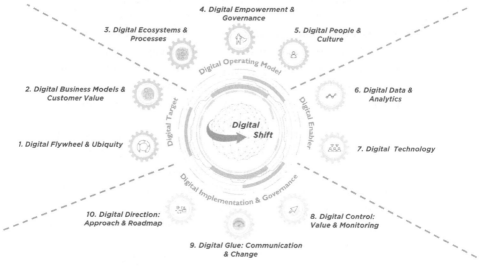

Source: ADL Research

A transformative digital shift will impact the bank's revenue and operating models. The illustration above of a 'digital flywheel' shows that to do this successfully, an organization must pass through a series of mutually reinforcing digital stages that involve its overarching vision, business model, processes, governance, culture, data and technology

MAKING A SUCCESS OF DIGITAL TRANSFORMATION

As the world economy becomes increasingly digitized, investment in digital transformation is expected to reach $6.8 trillion between 2020 and 2023 according to IDC.[186] However, most of these investments will stall or fail for reasons that are largely within the control of the company rather than outside it.

The management consulting firm McKinsey & Company reports that this often happens during scaling (38%) or in the pilot phase (12%). A similar percentage of projects run out of steam at other stages before they achieved what they set out to do.

Resourcing issues were to blame nearly half of the time, although misalignment of culture and ways of working, lack of competencies or having an unclear strategy were also frequent culprits. An MIT-Sloan study points the finger at CEOs who have neither a clear picture of where they want to go nor any real control over the process of getting there.

As a result, you end up with a series of often unrelated, random acts that have little if any strategic thought behind them. Remember, going digital is not a strategy.

Given this kind of poor governance, and a failure to align business processes with internal ownership, perhaps it's not surprising that almost 90% of CIOs admit that one of their digital transformation projects has been delayed, ratcheted down in scope or gone completely off the rails.

Some senior leadership teams won't commit to an explicit set of investments that would get their organizations ready to seize opportunities. They may be tempted instead to hold tight and wait until the winds of change turn into destructive gales. Perhaps they're reminded of Hilaire Belloc's poem about Jim, the boy who strayed and was eaten by a lion at the zoo, the moral of which was to "always keep a-hold of nurse for fear of finding something worse."

Of course, carrying out a digital transformation is always going to be a huge task. For instance, with so many legacy software systems in place, trying to unpick the spider's web of historically cross-subsidized products is virtually impossible, so who'd want to do that if they didn't have to.

But saying 'not me' and passing the buck to the next guy is hardly the definition of leadership. It is also a high-risk strategy decision since you have no idea when things will settle down, and if they don't, by the time change is forced upon you it may already be *game over*. Consumers have become so used to the speed, convenience and low-cost they're getting from online retailers that if a legacy bank gets too far out of step, it will be impossible to catch up.

As it is, legacy banks are already lagging because their current mix of disparate, disconnected online and physical channels just doesn't deliver what people are looking for. When consumers can sign up with a challenger bank with just a few clicks, why would they want your long-winded application process?

MORE THAN A SIDE PROJECT

While more than three-quarters of executives agree that organizations need to do this,[187] it means nothing if they just sit on their hands. And that's to a large extent what's happening. Consider the fact that, although 90% of organizations believe they have a digital strategy in place, just 14% are confident they have the technology or skills needed to deliver it. This gap between belief and reality is a major fault line, and why the vast majority of firms are still struggling to affect a truly technology-enabled business model.

This is yet more evidence that many legacy banks are failing to fully recognize or acknowledge what needs to be done.

In fact, they often fail to treat transformation programs as means to bring about the fundamental change that's essential to their very survival. Instead, they're dismissed as side projects that can be done ad hoc or on a piecemeal basis.

This ensures that they'll run behind schedule, come in over budget and deliver results far worse than expected.

Let us be clear: what we're talking about is a real and proper 'digital shift' that permeates an organization, extending into every nook and cranny of its operating and revenue models, value chain, technology and culture. It must penetrate to the very deepest levels. Digital must revolutionize the way you do everything – how you generate revenue, deliver a service, communicate with your customers and organize and structure your bank.

This means using technology to completely re-engineer your internal systems, to create a much more human-centric experience for your customers. This is no simple process; it involves integrating new and legacy technologies and bringing innovation into areas that aren't normally comfortable with risk.

Even when a bank believes it's taking transformation seriously, under-funding can still be a problem. Penny-pinching is the reason nearly 30% of new ventures fail. The situation is made worse if capital and resources are allocated solely based on 'the stage of business development.' While this might work under normal circumstances, it doesn't for technology-enabled ventures where there are often high investment thresholds from the start. If funding falls below these minimum-requirement levels, you immediately begin to destroy value.

Even ambidextrous CEOs who've fully bought into the need for a fundamental transformation underestimate the difficulty of making the necessary changes to budgets, culture, talent and IT, effectively killing off the digital project before it is born. Research by IT consultant Infosys and Efma, a banking and insurance networking organization, found that just 17% of banks succeed in digitally transforming at scale,[188] while more than half admit that they remain 'too mainstream' or are lagging when it comes to innovative.

What's holding banks back from biting the digital bullet?

Jacob Quorp Matthiesen, founding partner at the digital-sharing platform Prochimp, reports that just 12% of traditional banks consider themselves digital leaders on any level. In fact, most (55%) readily admit that they lack any real degree of digital maturity.

So, although digital transformation is a hot topic of conversation in banking technology circles, it's usually tempered by a dollop of tepid reality.

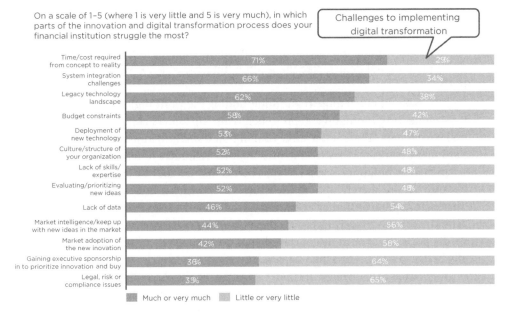

On a scale of 1–5 (where 1 is very little and 5 is very much), in which parts of the innovation and digital transformation process does your financial institution struggle the most?

Challenges to implementing digital transformation

	Much or very much	Little or very little
Time/cost required from concept to reality	71%	29%
System integration challenges	66%	34%
Legacy technology landscape	62%	38%
Budget constraints	58%	42%
Deployment of new technology	53%	47%
Culture/structure of your organization	52%	48%
Lack of skills/expertise	52%	48%
Evaluating/prioritizing new ideas	52%	48%
Lack of data	46%	54%
Market intelligence/keep up with new ideas in the market	44%	56%
Market adoption of the new inovation	42%	58%
Gaining executive sponsorship in to prioritize innovation and buy	36%	64%
Legal, risk or compliance issues	35%	65%

Source: Digital Banking Report Research (September 2020 The Financial Brand)

As the diagram above shows, there are numerous reasons banks fail to complete an effective digital transformation. While the mix of challenges will vary from bank to bank, the main reasons tend to be cost and difficulty of implementation. In many cases, that's another way of saying nobody wants to write off previous IT investments.

This is one of the main historic hangovers, because technology often isn't seen as an overarching solution, but as a cost driver. Bankers just think about the financial cost of going digital, rather than the true cost: trying to support mid- and back-office functions that can't cope with the challenges of obsolete legacy systems and growing regulatory constraints.

That kind of thinking leads to technology being seen as an operational matter rather than something that's of vital strategic importance, which it is. And so, you end up with an ever-growing stack of outdated technology that must continually be patched and repaired, at great expense.

YOUR OLD DIGITAL STRATEGY WON'T WORK

The obstacles to a successful transformation are even greater when a legacy bank continues to believe that past methods will serve it well in the future, or that its halfhearted digital strategy is sufficient.

Financial services firms often think they just need to adopt some kind of off-the-shelf 'technology roadmap,' and underestimate the non-tech organizational challenges involved in transformation. They fail to recognize that a wider cultural change is required.

In taking *some* action, they may become more digitally aware, but it doesn't make them digital-centric like the leading fintechs, which is where they need to be.

This is about much more than simply adding the word 'digital' to your business model or ginning up an app to help your customers check balances and make payments. That's not a successful digital transformation, no matter how hard many banks may try to convince their shareholders otherwise.

In fact, by building an app like this, banks may actually be going backward, because they're merely upping their tech costs without increasing efficiency. That can't happen until they've revamped their internal processes and IT stack. This kind of effort rarely improves the customer experience, as negative social media posts about such ill-conceived apps go to show. You could say it's actually better to be 'app-less than hapless.'

As Francisco González, former Chairman of the Argentine bank BBVA, puts it: "Banks have tried to meet the digital challenge by building their house from the roof down. That is, starting with the channels. But that's a stopgap solution. Without strong foundations, the increased volume and sophistication of online banking will overburden the obsolete platforms and the house will ultimately collapse."[189]

That message is amplified by Charlotte Branfield, Citi's Head of Global Operational Resilience. "There are so many shiny new tech toys and it's easy to think a bank has to have the latest gadgets and be deploying the latest piece of AI, but without actually understanding why," she said. "It's critical to go back to basics and back to your first principles. Ask yourself, 'What benefit is this bringing to either the business or my customers?' It's an exciting time to be involved in resilience and risk management because it means looking carefully at your organizational structure and culture."[190]

Real ambidextrous leaders understand this, which is why they champion in-depth transformation plans, firmly anchored in strategic choices that balance the short-term and long-term imperatives of their organization. They also appreciate the important role technologies have to play in achieving both the Performance Space productivity that's required to support the bank in the short term, as well as the high-level innovation necessary to transform it for the future. Because of that, they're more willing to commit a greater proportion of the budget to exploring their potential.

These leaders also possess a 'technology radar' that's always on the lookout for new applications that might be useful and give them a competitive edge. Most bank executives, however, talk mainly about investing in mobile when asked about digital technology in their organizations. That shows that their focus is too narrow, and they're ignoring the opportunities provided by cloud computing, advanced analytics, machine learning, IoT, RPA, AR and other technologies.

They should concentrate on identifying the right technology, rather than automatically assuming that something 'emerging' is always going to be the best bet. You can often achieve more, sooner, using proven mainstream technologies that are in widespread use than pinning your hopes on tech that's just breaking through. Uber and Airbnb, for example, established themselves in their respective taxi and hotel segments primarily by leveraging the power of mobile phones and simple apps.

ONGOING TECHNOLOGICAL ADJUSTMENT

If they are to bring about a true digital transformation, legacy banks must reshape every customer- and employee-facing system, business process, product and service – even their whole corporate brand – in ways that convincingly differentiate them from competitors.

And since the expectations of customers, employees and partners are continually changing, such a transformation shouldn't be seen as a one-off event, but as an ongoing process of continuous strategic readjustment. In other words, a bank's transformation isn't, as some observers seem to think, a 'Big Bang' that leads to the sudden appearance of a new platform. It's much more of an evolutionary journey.

In other words, to avoid obsolescence banks must continually mutate to keep pace with a constantly changing environment. This is something that even those who've already gone digital can't lose sight of. If they do, they risk finding their transformation slowing and falling out of sync with the marketplace.

Those that don't adapt as necessary will increasingly put themselves at a disadvantage, ever more marginalized and vulnerable to digital disruptors who do have offerings that are fit for purpose.

To achieve what's needed, legacy banks will require a comprehensive, detailed and systematic strategy for 'digitally shifting,' so individual short-term initiatives remain aligned not just with each other but also long-term business objectives. The consequences of not doing so can be great.

As part of such a digital transformation, the ambidextrous CEO needs to ask three questions: Why must I do this? How am I going to do it? What precisely must I do?

The answers will depend largely on whether the plan is to pursue full digitization, where you basically reinvent all your processes to create something new, or pursue a less full-on approach, perhaps by automating only part of the business, so it's improved but not fundamentally changed.

This is analogous to the difference between a piece of chocolate-covered orange and a candied piece. Dipped in melted chocolate, it looks different, and to some extent is different, but when you take a bite it's essentially a piece of fruit with some chocolate on the outside. On the other hand, if you drop a piece of orange into a saucepan of water and dissolved sugar, and leave it to soak, you'll have something completely different – a piece of dense, preserved, candied fruit.

BEGIN WITH A VISION

Of course, a bank can only begin its transformation journey from where it is, and there are many potential destinations. So, it needs to choose a desired end point that encapsulates the unique vision of what it wants to become.

Having a vision isn't just for the enlightened. It's important for any legacy bank wanting to transform. After all, without knowing where you want to go, how can you know where you need to end up?

A case in point is CBA. It began its transformation journey with the stated ambition of becoming the finest financial services organization in Australia, based on the delivery of exceptional customer experience. With this decided, it had a clear objective against which to measure everything it subsequently did. After some ill-conceived forays into uncharted territory, the vision that coalesced for some CBA cooperative banks was to get back to their roots by focusing not purely on profit optimization but also financial stability and their core marketplace.

Digital transformation is a multi-dimensional, multi-year initiative. While the trajectory will be set by the ambidextrous leader, the journey is too complex for any kind of detailed migration plan up front. What's needed is more of a broad-brushstroke roadmap that shows the path a bank must take, from where it is to where it needs to be. Without this, it will be difficult to get a sense of where resources should be allocated.

And while there is a need for banks to make quick strategic decisions about which technologies to adopt, this should be followed by a far more measured implementation that takes into account organizational constraints and complexities. If the need for speed overwhelms everything else, you end up with service delivery problems and the like, as RBS did in the UK when major tech outages left many of its customers fuming.

This means a bank must define its own ambitions and think deeply about what it wants to become, and what it then must do to best align its business activities with customer needs.

Since there are very few banks with the mix or depth of resources needed to anticipate and meet the needs of a diverse and demanding client base, across a wide range of service areas, the strategy is going to involve making big choices.

UNDERSTANDING WHERE YOU ARE

Where do you start in making a wholesale digital shift?

A good starting point is running an initial diagnostic across all parts of the organization to check how well equipped it is for the journey. This includes evaluating the marketplace, your organization's current capabilities and its future objectives. Some banks have developed their own proprietary tools for doing this. Citi, for instance, has a 'Digital Diagnostic Framework' with detailed checklists and client use cases to examine such things as overall strategy, organizational culture, innovation processes and customer journeys.

From this deep dive, a bank can get a better overview of all points of strategic exposure and competitive weaknesses across its portfolio, lines of business and geographies.

Such an assessment has to be as realistic as possible. Banks must be careful that the rewards and benefits from previously picked low-hanging fruit don't create a false and overly optimistic view of what may actually be a dying market segment. If that reality is recognized, divestment and quick forging of new partnerships should be the order of the day, rather than self-congratulation.

Some degree of benchmarking against competitors and the wider industry is always useful as a means to assess your current position and get an idea of progress, but we don't believe that's something to be relied on. And, others' benchmarking results certainly shouldn't be taken as an imperative to do what they do. Every bank is different, and blindly following someone else with copycat policies is likely to take you down the wrong rabbit hole. This may be one of the reasons that three-quarters of companies that go digital find they aren't hitting their revenue expectations.[191]

VISION, GOALS AND TARGETS

While being mindful of how it is doing relative to its peers, each bank should be prepared to plow its own furrow. It's best to focus on the effort and resources required to successfully implement your own particular digital shift.

Remember, the point of digital transformation isn't to replace legacy systems, as such, but to drive change by creating a more efficient technology-based business model. The goal is a differentiated value proposition that enables creation of new revenue streams. Amazon, for instance, achieved its preeminent position not only by being cheaper than traditional stores, but also by offering consumers so much more variety and convenience.

While each bank's uniqueness means there is no one recipe for success, there are some guiding principles they can follow.

One: assess where you are and where you need to go. In other words, be well aware of the industry's perceived point of arrival. We'll talk more about that in the next chapter. Force yourself to really reconsider your existing business model. Forget the status quo; be bold and ambitious in your ideas by embracing non-traditional thinking.

Two: create an overarching strategy for bridging the gap between the two. This will require you to understand what must be done differently to achieve your new target state. That involves identifying gaps in your offerings and developing innovative products and services to fill them.

In a later chapter, we'll look at how organizations can develop their internal capabilities and structures using powerful tools like the breakthrough incubator to constantly develop, pilot and scale new product and service ideas.

Three: set aggressive stretch goals for achieving what must be done. As discussed earlier, merely going after marginal improvements isn't good enough in the current environment because the timelines are condensing too quickly. Set interim milestones that are linked to concrete implementation actions. Ideally, some 'quick, early wins' should be baked in to help build momentum. This is something many banks have done by capitalizing on the potential of customer interfaces. It's much harder to do with more complex, end-to-end processes.

Four: with a concise plan in mind, communicate clearly to various stakeholders. If the CEO, board, markets and external third parties aren't in alignment with what's being proposed, it will be difficult to make sufficiently fast progress. In fact, it's likely that any transformation will fail.

Five: invest in the technologies and capabilities needed to digitally solve the bank's problems. These technologies will include AI to help make interactions frictionless; live streaming that gives customers the information they need in a way they want; AR to add a new dimension to the customer experience; Big Data that enables deeper personalization based on real insights; and a range of payment nodes and chatbots that smooth transactions.

This will mean migrating away from current complex architectures and 'replatforming,' by moving legacy software to the cloud, which will be far more cost-effective and free up resources. Once this is done, processes can be reengineered to make them much more customer-oriented. This may involve building new code to replace the legacy software, but banks shouldn't shy away from using commercial software, as this could offer significant savings.

Six: implement with speed and determination. If you've chosen the right customer segment, you may even be able to benefit from first-mover advantage, which will enable you to not only capture the lion's share of that specific market but also create a real barrier for those coming afterwards. They'll need to discount prices and increase marketing spend to attract customers, which will push up their break-even point and lower returns.

Seven: measure your progress frequently. The acid test for whether any digital transformation exercise has succeeded or failed is the 'digital ratio' – the percentage of the digitization achieved in a process, compared to the original objectives. If this ratio is good, the impact will be positively reflected in real ongoing metrics, such as revenue, profit, cost, customer engagement, retention, repeat buying and, perhaps most importantly, customer value. Your bank will only be successful when customers appreciate your products or services enough for them to buy. Period.

Since banks can no longer be all things to all people, that begs the question of where to focus your digital shift. Where do you now really need to be playing? In payments? Lending? The mass market, or zeroed in on niche spaces? Only by answering such questions will you know where to pick your battles... which we'll delve into in the next chapter.

CHAPTER 9

PICK YOUR BATTLES

"What makes a good bank is how fast they reach the customer to solve their problems and provide financial services conveniently, efficiently and responsibly. Therefore, it's the concept of evolving from the traditional bricks and mortar bank to an embedded finance model, driven by the concept that by the demand for high quality, seamless customer experience and fintech partnerships, banks will become hubs where products can be plugged in and out. When you think about changing business models, that's pretty revolutionary. The whole system is changing."

CHARLOTTE BRANFIELD,
Head of Global Operational Resilience, Citi[192]

When marketplaces are stable and steady, a solid value proposition combined with the right capabilities can be enough to secure your position and help build strategic assets long-term.

Mass disruption changes that. It breaks the 'comfortable' patterns of business and leaves CEOs with only one thing they can rely on: the presence of uncertainty. When that's the case, you can't just extrapolate your strategy from what's gone before. That will just keep you where you are. Why would you want to stay put if, as a legacy bank, you're seeing your revenues dry up because disruptive newcomers are cherry-picking the product battlegrounds where you can't compete on price or customer experience?

Of course, even during disruption, some very large players may be able to maintain *business as usual* because they have the financial wherewithal to survive the new norm. For most, remaining some kind of 'detuned' universal bank just isn't an option, because they don't have the ability to scale to a size that will keep them competitive against tech-enabled new entrants made efficient by AI, machine learning and the cloud. They have no choice but to reinvent themselves. Blindly hanging on to the past, in the belief that what once worked will do so again, when it patently won't, is fatally misguided.

If you open up the traditional banking cookbook, all you'll find are recipes for disaster based on balancing risk, capital and liquidity, improving productivity by cutting costs, and cross-selling tired old products to a dwindling customer base.

You may choose to argue that traditional banking frameworks and strategies can still be adapted and made to fit our new financial environment. We respectfully disagree, based on the preponderance of evidence we've laid out here. You can't argue with the facts.

When the game changes, you have to change. Instead of following old paths, legacy banks must now have the courage to take their current business model and pull it apart, before their competitors do. Bolt by bolt. Rivet by rivet. And then, step by step, rebuild it.

This involves doing far more than just adding extra features to existing products, or making a few organizational changes here and there, or launching an app that doesn't quite do the job, or calling yourself 'digital'. These are exercises in futility; they'll give you absolutely no traction.

Since there's no longer any commercial benefit in being a universal bank that serves everyone, this will require a retreat from historic segments, sectors and geographies, where cost and risk are now too high. It calls for the reallocation of capital and resources to where some degree of competitive advantage remains. Swiss banks, for example, are increasingly specializing in their core competence of wealth management and sliding away from everything else.

Such strategic repositioning doesn't mean letting go of every old, core capability, of course. Where would a corporate bank be without hedging? They'd suffer the pains of higher costs, increased risk exposure and dramatically reduced profitability.

What's needed is a core business model that isn't merely reactive to what's happening, but actually drives change. This is the only way traditional banks will be able to cope with significant shifts in their revenue and profit pools.

MORE STRATEGIC OPTIONS

Many financial organizations waste time, energy and resources on doing the wrong things because they don't have a sense of what the future of banking is going to be like. They haven't grasped the industry's *point of arrival* that we've been talking about.

If this vision is lacking – because leadership doesn't know what they need to do, or wrongly believes that what they're doing is right – they won't ever be able to build a new and improved bank that's fit for purpose. This will just lead to further poor, unprioritized resource allocation, which is the opposite of what's called for when you need to improve short-term performance.

A legacy bank requires the kind of ambidextrous CEO we've described, who can intuit a left-right brain approach to charting the right course.

In defining this unique vision, it should quickly become apparent which historic but unprofitable business lines, sectors or geographies should be relinquished. This will be the logical response to the *do-it-all* universal banking model's obsolescence. Those segments where the fintechs are now dominant would also be sensible areas to cull.

THERE'S NO USE IN STANDING STILL

Legacy banks can't delay too long before making these kinds of choices, given the seismic disruptions altering the industry's fundamentals. The fallout from the COVID pandemic has added to this sense of urgency. Societal lockdowns have given people the space to look more closely at their spending and rethink how they can make their money work harder by managing it online. Such behavioral change is leading more and more to the doors of the fintechs, lured by the slicker, more user-friendly, digital-first experience they offer.

If banks dawdle over this transition, they may find that they have neither the financial resources nor the ability to raise more to do what needs to be done.

As we've noted, legacy banks are notoriously slow to adapt, which is an unhelpful characteristic in a fast-moving digital world. This poses a significant test for those more used to the measured rigidity of banking's traditional business model. While it may well be easier for senior leadership to sit on their hands over this, they'd be ignoring what is perhaps the most pressing business imperative of the age: creating growth around innovative new products, services and business models.

We can see what a challenge this will be if we look at the top 20 business transformations of the last decade. We've seen game-changing companies suddenly burst into our consciousness, like Netflix (top of the list), tech giants (Amazon and Microsoft), and fintechs and marketplaces (Tencent, Alibaba). Only one mainstream financial institution seems to have done enough to make the list: DBS Bank in Singapore.

By adopting the cultural vision of a '27,000-person start-up,' DBS was able to successfully reposition its core business model, develop new products and services and deliver the growth and financial performance sufficient to position it among those heavy-hitters.[193]

So effective were the changes DBS made that it was able to go from a traditional regional player to being crowned *Global Finance* magazine's 'Best Bank in the World' in 2018. It did this by turning its business model on its head, embracing innovative ways of thinking and creating a fresh, new 'digital culture.' We'll take a closer look at that later.

While adopting this kind of free-flowing mindset is a prerequisite for change, the natural instinct of many banking CEOs is to batten down the hatches in turbulent times and ride out the storm. If they do anything at all, these timid folk will look to optimize what exists rather than trying to invent what's needed. And though their reticence may give them a certain sense of being control, this is little more than a comfort blanket. That's particularly the case when every business sector, not just banking, is being hit by that most convulsive disruption: convergence.

THE EMERGENCE OF CONVERGENCE

Convergence is the coming together of once disparate sectors over time, and this is happening more widely and rapidly than ever. So strong is the wave that global research and advisory firm Gartner describes it as "the most fundamental growth opportunity for organizations."[194] Gartner attributes this to way convergence enables 'value innovation' through the creation of new products, features or services, with simultaneous destruction of less valuable ones.

Nicolas Negroponte, Director of the MIT Media Lab,[191] first drew the world's attention to convergence in the early 1980s, with his diagram depicting how computing, communications, and the publishing and broadcasting sectors would converge over time.

THE FIRST INDUSTRIAL CONVERGENCE

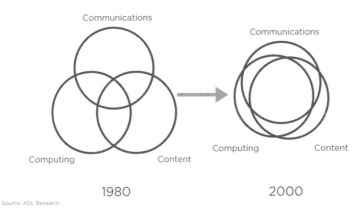

Source: ADL Research

Initially, there was little overlap between the three, but Negroponte predicted that they'd begin to converge because of their common reliance on digital systems. Forty years on, it's pretty obvious that he was right. By some estimates, convergence has had an impact on more than half of the companies in the S&P 500 Index.

Convergence occurs as similarities between different industries draws them together, blurring and dissolving the boundaries that once separated them. The speed and extent of this maps to the degree of attraction between sectors and the extent of any barriers that might keep them apart.

You can see this happening in many areas, with the convergence of e-commerce and IT being one of the most obvious examples. Amazon, the ultimate e-commerce company, has entered into the software-as-a-service (SaaS) market with its Amazon Web Services (AWS) offering. That's made it just as much an IT provider as a seller of consumer goods. Microsoft has moved in the opposite direction by developing its own e-commerce platform, Azure, to offer personalized marketing solutions and scalable e-commerce apps.[195]

Of course, we've already mentioned Amazon's full-on foray into financial services without ever having been a conventional bank. Amazon Pay has evolved into a digital wallet for both online and brick-and-mortar merchants. By leveraging its scale, Amazon can reduce card transaction costs for retailers, encouraging their participation in its ever-expanding ecosystem.

Another example is Amazon Lending, which between 2011 and mid-2017 issued $3 billion in loans to 20,000 SMEs in Japan, the US and the UK.[196] More than half of those who received a first loan through the service took out another. These Amazon loans have enabled small- to medium-sized enterprises to grow their sales by an estimated $4 billion. Inevitably, the pandemic has dented these numbers, but that's unlikely to hold the tech giant long-term.

In a sense, Amazon is building its own financial institution by taking the core components of the modern banking experience and tweaking them to suit its merchant and consumer audience. This is a much more interesting development for the company than just launching a deposit-holding bank.

BANKS AND TELCOS

While creating opportunities, convergence – like all disruptive forces – can also be a threat to those who don't spot or react to what's happening.

Take the natural convergence between telecom operators and financial institutions, and the potential to monetize phone users' data through cross-selling partnerships that target a particular price or risk profile. We've seen how this works for France's Orange Bank, given the close relationship with its sister phone company. For insights into how the relationship works read our interview with Paul de Leusse, CEO of Orange Bank on page 153.

Telcos are well equipped to converge with banking because it's relatively easy for them to embed financial services, like money transfer and payment processing, into their offering. They generally also have larger customer bases than retail banks and are better at marketing to them.

This means that a telecom could be a formidable rival for a legacy bank if it chose to start providing financial products to its customers, with whom it already has a strong connection.

In emerging economies, where the internet and mobile telephony have much greater penetration than banks, telcos have even more of an edge. The only major drawback for them would be the cost of regulatory compliance. For many, the expense of deposit insurance alone could pose too high a barrier to entry.

WHERE ARE THE CONVERGENCE OPPORTUNITIES?

Convergence can take various forms, depending on the nature of the attraction between sectors or segments. When a traditional financial service joins with a more sophisticated one, for instance, the lure might be penetration convergence. This happened when new technology enabled the creation of ATM services, which provided convenience and reach, saving customers time and helping bankers extend basic services to remote areas without opening branches.

Cross-convergence supplements what's already there. An example is the creation of the mobile banking services that were made possible by new internet and telecoms services.

When you have industries that are symbiotically close to each other, like business and banking, or insurance and securities, reorganizing convergence can happen. This improves competitiveness, for instance, by allowing banks to bring a wider range of different, better products to the market.

Industrial convergence is the integration of new and traditional industries. Although banking, NBFCs (Non-Banking Financial Companies), insurance organizations and securities firms all offer different financial products and services, they share some functional commonalities and features based on the technology, policies and customer groups. If businesses in these different sectors came together, it could spell trouble for a traditional bank's business model.

Then we have technology convergence. This is perhaps the most transformative confluence of all.

Blockchain, for example, will be the foundation of many new products and services, including cryptocurrencies, because of the way it creates a 'single point of truth' transaction ledger. This allows producers and buyers to directly exchange goods and services without oversight from an administering organization. It could transform banking by enabling fintechs to offer faster, lower-cost payment transactions than banks can. This could lead to real-time clearance and settlement systems; introduce non-traditional routes for raising capital; improve the efficiency of capital markets; and establish a lower interest rate market for borrowing and lending.

Such are the possibilities offered by blockchain technology that nine out of ten members of the European Payments Council believe that it will have fundamentally changed their industry by 2025.

WHO'S ALREADY TAKING ADVANTAGE OF CONVERGENCE?

Convergence is a way for legacy banks to do something radically different, and there are plenty of opportunities waiting to be exploited by those willing to explore the connections between the seemingly unconnected.

Take agriculture and fintech, for instance. You might not think there was a lot of synergy between the two until you consider that in some markets, only 30% of farmers have access to finance from formal sources, according to a study by ThinkAg, a platform for agriculture and food innovation, and MSC Consulting.[197] And, about half of the small and marginal farmers in many countries are unable to borrow any money at all because standard banks consider their income flows too unpredictable.

Fintechs have seen these sorts of opportunities and are starting to move into the space. In Australia, there is Agrihive, which collects data and generates live reports on commodity and stock prices that local farmers can use in their dealings with accountants, law firms and lenders.[198] In Kenya, you have FarmDrive, a company that calculates a personalized credit score for the many smallholders without adequate financial records, who can use this to apply for a bank loan.[199]

There are also specialist insurance providers and payment platforms specifically set up to connect farmers and distributors through a digital trading platform.[200] These are using the blockchain technology we just talked about to enable direct, transparent and verifiable trading between farmers, cooperatives and agri-buyers.

There's also a convergence between fintechs and health technology providers. FitSense, for example, is an online analytics platform that gathers data about an individual's stress levels and sleeping patterns from wearable devices and smartphones, and uses it to obtain the best possible insurance premiums.[201] The healthier you are, the lower your premium.

Since financial expertise isn't a core competency among healthcare providers, perhaps the greatest opportunity lies in 'medical banking', with the coming together of finance, insurance, hospitals and healthcare providers. The potential here is enormous because of the current poor integration between different parts of the supply chains, opaque procurement processes and manually driven systems that create inefficiencies in delivering, distributing and processing medical services.

Banks would do well to create platforms that can better connect all participants in ways that would reduce risk, improve the quality of decision-making and speed up transaction processing. This would be of immense and immediate benefit to the many healthcare providers already at a financial breaking point because of patient bad debt, market shrinkage and demand for increasing quality. With healthcare costs already spiraling because of the aging populations in many countries, there's real potential here for legacy banks ready and willing to step out of their traditional comfort zone.

Exante Financial Services, a division of UnitedHealth Group, is one organization that's recognized the opportunities in this area and is already handling credit card payments and member IDs for more than 20 million medical plans.[202]

Sberbank is another that's involved in healthcare administration. Russia's largest banking group signaled its intent to move into the potentially lucrative medical sector when in 2017 it bought DocDoc.ru, a leader in the online medical appointment market.[203] Sberbank put it at the center of an e-health platform that brings telemedicine, medical records, consultations and treatment delivery together by linking doctors, hospitals, insurance companies, drugstores and patients. This should create opportunities to cut costs and improve services. It will also allow Sberbank to capture a mountain of patient data, from which it can reap valuable insights.

Of course, as regulations tighten around the digitization of health data, medical banking is likely to remain specialized, because few want to wrestle with the complexities of compliance.

MOVING INTO NEW PASTURES

Any time you see convergence occurring, it's a sure sign that the old certainties are dissolving… or being roughly torn apart. In banking we're seeing that previous ways of dividing the industries along vertical business lines, such as retail, corporate and wealth management, are no longer appropriate.

The traditional boundaries are already shifting. LendingClub has redefined the making and marketing of mortgages, while outside of financial services you can see how Starbucks has reinvented the coffee drinking culture.

For legacy banks, this might mean that there's now a much greater need to focus on 'origination and sales' activities, where the bulk of global banking profits lie, and think about strengthening areas like customer relationships, financial advice, product development, speed of transaction processing, HR and recruitment. And, of course, IT. There might also be sector-specific vulnerabilities to consider around risk management, regulatory compliance and financial analysis.

To those with the vision and courage, there are countless opportunities to look at the world in new ways.

You could, for instance, target those 'over-served' with products that are too complicated, expensive or low-quality, as Honda did in the 1970s by focusing on 'basic and no frills,' and as Walmart and Dell have done since.

In China, WeBank exploited an opportunity when it began selling mass-market products into segments not serviced by large banks, like the SME space. Or, you could go in the opposite direction, as private banks do by targeting 'underserved' customers who are willing to pay more for extra features or service.

Alternatively, what about finding a new use for an existing product, or subdividing bigger markets into new micro-segments based on a common customer characteristic? Or, aim at those not currently using your product, or those who don't in another geography?

One key segment that's ripe for such an approach is the B2B (business-to-business) e-commerce market, which is currently under-served by legacy banks. Valued at $12.2 trillion in 2019[204] – six times more than the consumer market – B2B e-commerce has been described as the next 'El Dorado.'[205] With an anticipated compound annual growth rate of 18.7.% between 2021 and 2028,[206] this sector will offer plenty of opportunities for financial services firms with something to offer.

Once again, this is an area where newcomers are already taking the initiative. Payability is a leading funding platform that provides cash flow and payment solutions tailored exclusively for e-commerce.[207] To date, it has provided more than $3 billion in funding to thousands of sellers attracted by immediate loans to cover cash shortfalls, as they wait for online purchaser payments to be processed. The application process is fast and simple, and quick decision-making means Payability customers get their hands on the capital they need in less than 24 hours. So, no more having to wait for Amazon to pay you following an e-sale.

On the broader SME front, there are significant opportunities waiting for legacy banks ready to tackle this sector, which to date they have largely neglected. And since this market has been treated with little affection, it's been poorly served by a small portfolio of ill-conceived offerings that are essentially underperforming hybrids of personal and corporate banking products.

In the EU, for instance, it's difficult for SMEs to get financing in an efficient and timely way, with traditional wait times for loan decisions of 3–5 weeks.

With the average 'time to cash' extending up to three months, targeted products related to different business stages and lifestyle needs could prove immensely popular.

This is a potentially huge market, given that SMEs are responsible for about two-thirds of jobs in the private sector and wield a combined $46 trillion in annual spending power.[208] Each year, SMEs generate $850 billion in global income for banks – about 20% of their current worldwide revenue.[209] The OECD predicts that this enormous revenue pool will grow by about 7% annually over the next seven years, as central banks come to view it as a powerful engine for economic growth.

Opportunities for creating a richer digital banking service for small business will only expand as the world of open banking evolves. An Accenture survey found that some 60% of small businesses would use their bank more heavily if it offered more business-focused services. This suggests that in the UK alone banks could have generated £8.5 billion in new revenue streams in 2020 if they'd better engaged with SMEs.[210]

Legacy banks' lack of interest in this segment has opened the door to smaller new operators, alternate lending institutions, authorized fintechs, retail organizations and technology firms. Thanks to the Europe's PSD2 regulations, they can now easily gain access to small businesses to offer them a far wider portfolio of lower-cost financial products. If they switched away from their traditional bank, many SMEs could drastically lower their financial transition costs.

Challenger banks and alternative financing providers will be eyeing this area with ever greater interest, especially as regulatory changes have made it easier for them to provide loans to what is in many ways an ideal banking segment, and to then cross-sell other products.

That's important because, unlike most retail consumers, SMEs need a range of services on both a daily basis and as they go through lifecycle phases, from launch and growth through to maturity, and even recovery and renewal should things get tough. Added to this are the requirements of entrepreneurs and directors who own and manage the business.

If banks want to start servicing this sector better, they'll face growing competition from peer-to-peer and specialty lenders, such as Prosper and Funding Circle, balance sheet lenders like Kabbage, and lending platforms, of which Fundero and Lendio are just two examples.

Some banks have already recognized the opportunity. France's Banque Populaire is a specialist in this area, employing a team of 1,000 focused on servicing a customer base of about 128,000 SMEs through 150 dedicated business centers.[211] The bank aims to add value by creating a truly differentiated experience for each customer, based on their turnover. It provides different offerings for their micro, small and corporate clients, who are further segmented based on their profile and specific needs.

Scandinavia's leading bank, Nordea, does something similar by defining five groups of business customers, based not on their size but their behavioral patterns.[212] For instance, those just starting out, who would generally find it hard to get a line of credit from a bank, are offered payment services to get the company off the ground. Another level of segmentation is by industry type, in recognition of their particular needs. Plumbers and carpenters, for instance, may have significant cash flow challenges.

The bank also works with professionals and knowledge workers who are typically early adopters of new products like payment wallets, as well as larger employers with more complex needs. For instance, because they often issue business credit cards to many peope, they need a more sophisticated expense management to ensure cards are relevant to a user's needs and will be used responsibly."

Established players, like Mastercard, are also looking at what is a huge market segment that's deserving of more bespoke set of products and services. Dick Paul, head of SME products Europe at Mastercard, is the one has overall responsibility for identifying both the needs of SME customers and keeping a watch on regulatory trends and changes in retail banking that might provide opportunities. "Banks have been very happy to help SMEs with their cashflow by offering an overdraft or a small business loan, which is going to cost those businesses more money," says Paul. But as he points out: "A more positive way is to offer a set of tools and services that enable small businesses to receive money from their customers quicker and give them more payment flexibility with suppliers."[213]

CRACKING THE SME MARKET

If banks are to really benefit from this SME opportunity, they must first create differentiated products and services tailored to the small-business market in areas like invoicing, payment collection, payroll tools and trade finance. And, if they're really serious, legacy banks will look to create a powerful, simple-to-use platform that helps SMEs better navigate the complexity of their day-to-day administrative and financial activities. In particular, they'll need to help these clients better manage cash flow, because this, rather than P&L, is the key metric for small businesses.

On top of this, it would be helpful if they didn't treat closely connected SME business accounts and their owners' private accounts as separate entities. Another plus would be to offer fast, flexible decision-making about potential funding, and pertinent advice about credit control, legal matters and supplier management. Add in virtual relationship assistants, as some more advanced banks are beginning to do, and that would be a pretty strong set of offerings for resource-strapped SMEs.

One reasons legacy banks may be reluctant to go after this market is the lack of transparency and reliability of financial statements when dealing with SME clients. Unlike publicly traded companies, privately held companies don't have the same disclosure requirements, and this opacity can make banks less willing to engage.

Fortunately, this is another area where technology can help. Big Data solutions enable banks to analyze structured and unstructured lending alternatives to assess and monitor the ongoing risk posed by SMEs.

BUILDING ON WHAT YOU HAVE

Where then should you focus? Moving forward based on the strength of current competencies is obviously a sound policy, but only up to a point. Just because you've been historically successful in a particular area doesn't mean you should double down there if it's a low-margin segment.

This is where you need to break out of the old universal banking mindset if you are to create a fresh package of products and services. But this isn't about being different just for the sake of it. A large corporate bank that mixed investment and retail services, for instance, would end up with a complex mess that didn't bring any tangible benefits.

Instead, this is about creating an optimal and differentiated mix of products and services that builds on a bank's competencies, plugs gaps where these are lacking, exploits opportunities and helps defend against threats.

And it's important to do this in a controlled manner. Even if competitors are flashing attractive value propositions in all directions, this isn't about responding by adding new features to old products. That won't work, and may actually make things worse by adding yet more complexity to an already obsolete model. That will only make product management and a risk measurement all the more difficult.

The last things a bank needs are exotic offerings that add additional levels of unquantifiable risk, which could lead to problems when it comes to restructuring a balance sheet. It would be much better to use predictive analytics to identify your highest-risk customers and manage them accordingly. If, for instance, you can capture 70% of your overall risk in just 20% of your loan portfolio, you can feel much more confident about where the risk lies.

When financial markets are unstable, as they've been over the past decade, liquidity management is more complex than ever. Sudden market movements, shifts in depositor behaviors, or disruptive events – like the deluge of bad loans in the wake of the pandemic – need to be allowed for and considered in any transformation strategy.

DON'T FORGET LIQUIDITY

Whatever the strategic position, there's going to be a consequent impact on a bank's liquidity, which is perhaps the most important consideration of all. The last thing you want is to walk down a road that will see you run out of money.

The financial crisis of 2008 showed how quickly this could happen. The EU's new accounting standards have forced banks since 2018 to take a more forward-looking assessment of borrowers' financial health, and will make the impact of future write-offs and debt restructuring on current earnings and capital position much more apparent.

As it is, with the instability of the financial markets and corporate debt overhang that grew substantially during the global financial crisis, banks have been much more cautious about extending new credit, despite the availability of cheap and ample liquidity.

There's benefit in this because liquidity will become much more of a focus over the next few years, as legacy banks will need to restructure their balance sheets to address two black holes.

The first of these is the increasing amounts of regulatory capital required to maintain business lines and product portfolios, which can be addressed by backing out of some markets and culling obsolete product lines.

The second is the need to set aside extra capital to cover bad loans, post-pandemic. Dealing with the looming NPL situation is going to be more of a challenge, and one that will have to be managed very carefully. While banks have been gradually writing off non-performing loans, they haven't yet factored this into lending margins, which will weigh heavily on their profitability when they do.

So, banks must be sure that when converting short-term deposits like checking and savings accounts and other assets into long-term loans, this doesn't have a negative impact on their liquidity and increase their exposure risk.

With liquidity management becoming increasingly complex, banks must prepare for future market shifts and changes in depositor behavior through a robust strategy for evaluating future cash flows

---

based on assets, liabilities and items not on their balance sheet. And, to anticipate potential liquidity shortfalls, they'll need regular financial stress tests to assess the bank's tolerance to liquidity risk under various scenarios. If the results don't align well with particular 'liquidity events,' products may need to be redesigned to meet client needs and optimized for capital and liquidity.

If banks do need to generate liquidity, they can get some relief by selling non-liquid assets; buying more liquid assets; shortening maturities of assets; lengthening short-term wholesale funding maturities; reducing lines of credit already committed; increasing retail deposits to reduce cash outflows; or issuing long-term wholesale debt to buy liquid assets.

Because competition among banks tends to drive equity levels below their efficiency point, it becomes increasingly important to use capital more effectively and achieve an optimal mix of debt and equity financing that maximizes a company's market value while minimizing the cost of capital. Although debt financing may have the lowest theoretical capital cost because of its tax deductibility, too much debt increases financial risk for shareholders, who will demand a higher ROE in response. This makes another case for trying to reach an ambidextrous balance.

Ensuring capital efficiency will involve continually monitoring asset quality to identify any deterioration. The Reserve Bank of India's (RBI)' Financial Stability Report (FSR) has highlighted the fact that the profitability of banks when measured by ROA and ROE has significantly declined.[214] And, we all saw what went wrong with the subprime mortgage market.

Regulations like Basel III have compelled banks to ensure that they have sufficient capital provision. However, with margins on much conventional business falling, banks have begun developing off-balance sheet products as a way to boost fee income – things like loan commitments, letters of credit and derivative securities.

PICKING THE RIGHT BATTLE

It would be impossible to prescribe in these pages what any individual bank should do, as this is something that would require an in-depth analysis of its structure and profile, market and customer demographics, legacy technology, compliance obligations and competitive pressures. Not only that, but each would differ in how it saw itself fitting into the future financial landscape, based on its unique perspective of the industry's point of arrival.

With that said, it is possible to identify the core positioning opportunities for legacy banks, though not all would prove suitable for every particular institution. But one thing that all banks should be, irrespective of their long-term ambitions should be to make themselves as efficient as possible. There should be no debate about this. Regardless of where you see banking's point of arrival, pursuing greater efficiency is not so much a matter of choice but a necessary condition for success.

As we've previously discussed, this is going to involve such things as trimming product portfolios, reducing process complexity and eliminating the silos created by vertical business lines. You will also need to start using AI, RPA, data analytics and machine learning. Once you've started this process, there will be no stopping the technological cascade, since every manual process that remains will put unendurable pressure on every other process around it. Until every one of these weak links is removed, you won't be able to provide the seamless, hyper-personalized experience consumers are looking for.

And if you lack the resources to scale effectively, then don't even think about trying to reinvent the business, just concentrate on driving productivity to make your bank as efficient as possible. Without real innovation, of course, it won't be possible to remain competitive with the disruptors, but you will be maximizing the bank's value for a later sale.

But, as we've said repeatedly, it's crucial that technology isn't just brought in for the sake of doing so, as that can lead to expensive IT mistakes. Learn the lesson from the 1980s, when organizations introduced expensive Customer Resource Management (CRM) systems that were meant to give a complete customer view but weren't able to capture the quality or quantity of data needed to effectively feed them. That left expensive IT like Oracle's CRM solution lying idle. When introducing new systems, banks must already have the capabilities to manage integration with their other business systems, or acquire them, before going there.

If you are in it for the long-haul, then you will need to do more than just become efficient, perhaps you could 'pick a spot' and become a category killer in a specific product area or segment by creating an exceptional value proposition, which no one else could match. Excellence then becomes a barrier to entry.

If banks are sufficiently confident they could attempt to do this on their own as Orange Bank has done, which launched in France in 2017 and now has more than 1 million customers with 20,000 more signing up every month. In 2018, the bank moved into Spain, where six months later they had created a 100% mobile business offering payment services through Apple Pay, Samsung Pay and Google. They've since also signed a partnership with real estate services platform Nexity to offer home loans. Three-quarters of the bank's new customers now come through bank accounts and make at least one transaction a week; the rest are acquired through loans.

Orange Bank has now moved into Africa, where it focuses on providing highly accessible solutions, like micro-credit services, that enable people to borrow small sums of money instantly using their phones. This is all part of the bank's ambition to become a leader in financial inclusion in West Africa.

But before legacy institutions think about going down this path, they need to accept an uncomfortable market reality. So, though many banks may instinctively believe they can do this, their optimism will be misplaced because for the most part, they won't be able to emulate Orange's success.

The nature of the marketplace is now such that most banks simply do not have the firepower to compete against a powerful fintech that's occupying the same space. But if you can't win a head to head fight, what's the solution?

The answer is obvious. If can't beat them, then the only sensible course of action for most banks is to join them. And here our message to banks' leaders is very clear – do not see this as some kind of defeat, because it is not. Rather is a smart, and strategic move, in response to market reality. Do not resist it. In fact, it's the only play possible since by working with a fintech, rather than diminishing your bank you will actually be adding value to it since it enables you to focus on what matters most to your customers rather than worrying about your technology infrastructure.

What banks must understand is that technology is no longer a differentiator in the marketplace. It is now the essential enabler that ensures you are capturing the information you need from your customers, and then use powerful analytics to give them the rich and relevant experience they're looking for. Remember that today a bank's performance is being compared not so much with other banks, but with the exceptional service and experience consumers enjoy from major retail platforms like Amazon. Rightly or wrongly, they will increasingly expect the same from anyone they deal with.

Australia's CBA got that message when it integrated information from real estate companies with GPS technology to simplify and enhance the house-buying process for its customers. That created real value because it allowed a person to stand in front of a property that was on the market, find out all about it, and get a pre-approved mortgage to buy it.

In effect, by working with a fintech, you will be throwing off the straitjacket that your IT department has been keeping you in for all these years. And released from it, suddenly, you have much more flexibility and a newfound ability to focus on what truly creates value.

By capitalising on their expertise, you can go on to create an e-commerce platform. Or, better still, use that partnership to forge a marketplace that uses embedded finance to leverage the bank's core products, unique infrastructure or license. If well done, this back-end model could create significant revenue and value for a legacy bank. Of course, taking this route will make a bank part of a much wider ecosystem, which will require a different corporate mindset. We'll take a look at that later.

But this is how banks that seize on new opportunities in areas such as cryptocurrencies (like Bitcoin, Ethereum, Ripple, Omni, Nxt, Waves and Counterparty) could steal the march. Though these altcoins are still a relatively small component of the financial landscape, appetite for them is growing fast. Their 2019 market value of $240 billion is nearly double that of the year before ($128 billion). With central banks now contemplating launching their own coins, this presents an opportunity that some big players have already recognized. In May 2021, it was revealed that Goldman Sachs had set up a cryptocurrency desk as part of its global currencies and emerging markets trading division. While the firm's initial focus seems to be bitcoin-linked derivatives, the aim is to start working with selected crypto trading institutions to expand its offerings.

When you realize how such collaborations expand your horizons, then the whole world opens up because immediately you can start seeing fintechs not as threats but as stepping-stones that can lead you to a new point of arrival. Imagine not being held hostage by what your 'techies' can or cannot do, as in the past. Instead, you can move from fintech to fintech as the need arises, plugging into what each offers as your requirements change. There is a light at the end of the tunnel, which is why growing numbers of banks are choosing this option.

Toronto-based RBC is a good example. It's partnered with digital payment infrastructure provider Extend Enterprises to create a virtual credit card offering that's delivered through a mobile app without compromising security or control over spending.

There are many other fintech-bank partnerships like these, such as BBVA (which is working with Simple, Digit, Catch, Azlo, Wise) and Radius Bank (with Brex, Treasury Prime) in consumer and business banking; or Cross River (with Affirm, Upstart, Seedfi, Stripe, Upgrade, Best Egg, Coinbase, Finix, Rocket Loans) and WebBank (with LendingClub, Prosper, Avant, Petal, Upgrade, Klarna, PayPal Working Capital) in consumer lending.

Rather than finding a third-party fintech, some banks are joining together to create their own like a consortium of Nordic banks, which includes giants such as Danske Bank, Nordea and SEB. All have pooled resources to launch their own fintech, Invidem, which aims to improve the partners' KYC and AML operations by acting as a central clearinghouse for sharing, validating and reporting transactions and customer data.

And having used fintech power to establish your preeminence in one area, by piggybacking with a fintech, you could then widen your offering into other parts of the market and perhaps cross-sell new products to your existing customer base. In some ways, we can see how this happened with Orange Bank. It followed a strategy specifically designed to adapt to local market opportunities and competitive intensity.

Of course, all such initiatives require an ambidextrous CEO who's comfortable looking beyond what is normal or 'what we've always done.' If you are to stand out, you must be able to look at the current business with new eyes and not just command others to 'find me more mortgage products,' because they are just a commodity.

While working with a fintech will be the best route for many smaller banks, for larger institutions, another possibility is to become a wholesaler of its own portfolio of white-label products which it develops and then sells to or through third parties. Again, this is a venture that's probably better down with the help of a fintech.

There are also opportunities for providing infrastructure-as-a-service (IaaS),[215] or even 'renting' out your balance sheet to small or non-financial players. Banks are already doing this when they provide credit card processing to retailers. And for over 20 years, Bancorp, has been providing non-bank companies with the people, the processes and the banking technology they need to as they put it "move our partners' businesses into the future."

Many more opportunities will emerge as digital banking evolves, though most of these are likely to remain open to large financial institutions.

Finally, there is 'play to win' where an institution completely reinvents itself to take advantage of a perceived opportunity or to better equip itself to compete in several segments against the insurgent digital natives. Ally Bank, for example, began as a GM car leasing company before moving into full banking, and then digital-only. It then zeroed in on online brokerage services, before finally majoring in digital wealth management.

This is the most challenging option and one that's really only feasible for the biggest banks with the deepest pockets. And even then, not everyone gets it right. No matter how good your strategy is, the timing of execution is everything. Knowing how to pace implementation can spell the difference between success and failure because you have to balance urgency with the need for processes to embed into and start working within a wider ecosystem. If you're too hasty, you will create an internal environment that's constantly in flux, eventually leading to the corporate equivalent of a nervous breakdown.

Take what Deutsche Bank did in the 1990s and 2000s when it pursued what perhaps could be described as 'a policy of over-excitement' and ended up running around like a headless rooster. This was just asking for trouble, which is exactly what Deutsche got.

The 150-yer-old bank had expanded rapidly overseas, so much so that at one point it was the world's largest lender and a top trading firm. But in the wake of the 2008 credit crisis, it incurred fines of $1.93 billion from US regulators,[216] heralding an era of lossmaking. Its troubles resulted from a combination of strategic mistakes and operational inefficiencies that others would do well to take note of.

A relentless pursuit of fast growth had left Deutsche vulnerable, requiring a period of rapid retrenchment that created a sense that it was out of control. The bank had to shrink its fixed income team and axe its entire equities trading arm because of a lack of capital. This was followed by a costly 'shrink to grow' strategy predicated on moving closer to its domestic roots after years of investment elsewhere. A failed merger attempt with Commerzbank added to the chaos, prompting COO Kim Hammonds to call Deutsche "the most dysfunctional bank" she'd ever worked for.

This all transpired under chairman Paul Achleitner, who presided over every one of the bank's failed turnaround efforts since 2012. Need there be further evidence of how important the right leader is for any bank looking to transform itself?

WILL IT MAKE THE BANK GO FASTER?

This chapter has been about where legacy banks should pick their future battles, not finding ways to fight those of the past.

Creating a strategy that enables you to do this will require considerable crystal ball gazing about the industry's point of arrival, as well as much introspection about what the bank should do and what it can do. This means asking many hard questions at a granular level.

To paraphrase the question facing Great Britain's gold medal-winning 'men's eight' rowing team at the 2000 Sydney Olympic Games, regarding any and all decisions: "Will it make the bank go faster in future?" The ambidextrous CEO must ask this about every action the bank takes, every management process that's created and every piece of technology that's installed.

This is about throwing off the shackles of accountancy practices and the fear of writing off past investments in IT. It's all about what needs to be done.

And if what's being done doesn't better 'servitize' your customers (a terrible word, we know, and one we use through gritted teeth) by adding value through an offering that's truly tailored to their needs, you'd better think again.

A bank's leadership must set themselves stretch goals and 'impossible' timelines that force them into a bold rethinking of their business model, and quickly.

Having done that once, they must be prepared to keep on doing it. Even if you've created a clear and settled picture of the banking industry's point of arrival, this is not a one-off exercise. The world is changing too fast, particularly in a post-COVID environment. This means decidedly *not* following the lead of half of all CEOs, who never review their own strategies. Once written, most of these overblown manifestos are filed away and forgotten.[217]

That's a mistake the leader of a legacy bank cannot afford to make. They must continually revisit their thinking if they are to keep open water between themselves and their competitors, and plug the gaps and weaknesses that make their organization vulnerable to attack.

If they don't, their business will become irrelevant, like the 52% of Fortune 500 companies that have merged, been acquired or gone bankrupt since 2000. This fate isn't inevitable, of course. It doesn't have to be a legacy bank's destiny if it starts seeing 'enemies' as friends and finds ways to work with those disruptive fintechs. We'll look at that in the next chapter.

CHAPTER 10

DISRUPTORS' THINKING

Since this book is about the future of banking, we looked to those who are actively reshaping the industry. In a series of wide-ranging question and answer sessions, we asked the CEOs of two industry-disruptor organizations for their perspective.

The first of these is Ricky Knox, one-time CEO of Tandem, a British challenger bank that's focused on providing banking through mobile applications. Co-founded by Knox in 2013, the bank is based in London and has grown significantly since its launch. In 2018, for instance, in a deal that brought in a near-£200 million loan book, more than £300 million of deposits and nearly £80 million of capital, Tandem acquired Harrods Bank. By the end of 2020, it had approximately 800,000 customers who'd been attracted by features such as 'Autosavings', a service that allows users to automatically redirect money in their account to specific savings pots.

We had the following conversation with Knox.

WHAT DO YOU SEE AS THE INDUSTRY END POINT FOR BANKING?

RK: I think the UK will be dominated by a new breed of bank that owns the consumer interface and provides a very differentiated, much-improved level of service. Existing banks, like RBS, will have to retrench and become wholesale operations, the kind of 'plumbing bank' you go to if you don't want to run a high-grade Treasury operation and are happy to ride on someone else's rails.

So, we'll end up with some of today's big players alongside a set of consumer banks and industry specialists who understand a particular segment and can build a bank to serve it.

In the US, things are developing slightly differently, with non-banks being front-end companies that own consumer segments. Though, I believe you will see banking institutions developing the front end in the UK and large parts of Europe.

So, I think the universal banking model will go and be replaced with a more fragmented space.

And I can see that it will have a much larger fee element. In the US, you already have a charging model for current accounts and other banking services. In the UK, instituting this will be tougher, because it fundamentally challenges consumer thinking. But I think you will see increasingly subscription-based services in part driven by Millennials and Generation Z consumers who are used to paying for things on a subscription basis. But I do think there's a significant opportunity to shift some of the revenue model overall in the industry as consumers grow up.

HOW IS TECHNOLOGY HAVING AN IMPACT ON THE MARKETPLACE?

RK: Historically, technology gave you, say, 20% of your competitive advantage. Now, that's 80%, because the customer acquisition cycle that's so critical is being done online. From a disruptive point of view, this happened extremely quickly for us. So, we went from zero to ten million banking customers, new banking customers in the UK, in about a couple of years.

With a newer bank, for instance, you can now download an app and open a credit card in three minutes. Our app is so easy to use that people play with it and end up with extra products they didn't think they needed. It also creates a customer interface that gives us a lower acquisition cost and higher stickiness, which are both useful, but more than anything else it also generates customer love. On Trustpilot, for instance, we have 80% positive reviews, and these largely come from one awesome feature – Autosavings – which people love. And those who use Autosavings have double the customer lifetime of those that don't.

You don't get this so much with an old bank. For example, until a few years ago, Barclays didn't have a digital loan process on their website.

And the pandemic has definitely accelerated digital penetration. Now, in the UK, there isn't an 80-year-old who doesn't have an iPhone so they can FaceTime with their grandchildren. They may not be brilliant at using it, but it means that you now have children who are teaching granny about how to open an online account.

This means traditional models based around branches with nice, smiley staff will be permanently excluded, and that will hit the competitiveness of small building societies and credit unions, which could see them dying out. This doesn't mean you can't continue to serve people who don't want an online interaction, but it's going to be harder.

So, over the next ten years, the old players who can't compete when it comes to new customer acquisition will eventually have to consolidate or fade away. By the time legacy banks wake up to this, potentially they won't have the scale to respond because the money flows will have already been captured by the new disruptors, who will by then be established brands themselves.

CAN LEGACY BANKS PROTECT THEMSELVES STRATEGICALLY?

RK: If I were a big bank CEO right now, I'd be doubling down on my big corporate clients, because there the relationship model works quite well. And if a large corporation is getting great, personalized service, they've no reason to move. But I'd cede SME and retail to a new breed of specialist front-end banks.

Then, I'd be investing in systems really hard and looking at the next segments across, and build out something amazing. I would choose a segment of medium-sized enterprises that's big enough for me to specialize in and own.

And so, I could compete against those with a clever IT system that are getting banking licenses and coming toward me down that vertical. I would actually increase my offer. So, I might start giving systems away for free – for instance, in the front-end for medium-sized point-of-sale systems – or even buy a point-of-sale vendor themselves, and have a little factory making stuff so I could be absolutely king of online and offline high street.

HOW DO DISRUPTIVE BANKS LIKE TANDEM MANAGE TO CAPTURE AND MONETIZE DATA BETTER THAN A LEGACY BANK?

RK: Well, you have to be on the cloud, because it's not possible to run any more on physical servers, and here's an example.

Our CTO built a Big Data array for an Israeli bank that cost $580 million and took five years. Then he came to Tandem and basically replicated the process using mostly cloud tools, and it took two years and probably cost about £2.5 million.

Now, with Google's latest cloud release, you could almost build your own Big Data array in 12 months with just ten people, rather than take three years using 200.

But it's still hard and requires a lot of very technical expertise that banks find hard to hang on to, because really good tech people and really good data scientists don't love banks.

Data gives you a massive advantage. So, insurance and banking are both super exciting sectors because they both have huge data sets. Since the core of their business model ultimately is risk assessment, if they have more data, they can better assess risk.

But you can only do that when you have the tools to leverage it. So, the challenge is to get the right Big Data array set up to leverage the quantity of data you have. And in theory, once you have this working properly, your decision-making should be much better than other banks long-term. So, at Tandem, we have a master model against which we can test all variables to make sure the ones we go with drive better decisions.

HOW LONG WILL IT TAKE FOR THE BIG BANKS TO CATCH UP WITH THE LIKES OF TANDEM?

RK: The tools are moving so fast, and eventually the big banks will start to put this stuff in and begin to use. Will Tandem still be at an advantage in ten years? I don't know.

HOW DO YOU EVALUATE THE OPPORTUNITY OF EMBEDDED FINANCE AND POWERING E-COMMERCE FOR A NATIVE DIGITAL BANK?

RK: I don't know whether embedded finance will be driven as payment was, which was all around who could build the simplest, most beautiful API (application programming interface). Or, whether we will end up with a disintermediation layer that essentially allows really easy embedding with very flexible software in between.

It's clear that banks struggle with building interfaces, and so may never be able to properly build their own APIs, and may be better doing a deal with someone who basically builds them a very beautiful API in the front end. So, a new breed of orchestrating company could develop that sits between the banks and the slightly clunkier wholesale, embedded finance banks.

Firms that aren't super good at tech could partner with a couple of different API providers to create embedded finance, which is where I see the market structure going. The winners in embedded finance will either be technology intermediaries who work with specific institutions, or an API bank, much like Griffin.

WHERE ARE THE OPPORTUNITIES GOING FORWARD?

RK: I think there's a really interesting opportunity in the API banking space that will start with very technology-driven companies at the front end providing API banking services and embedded finance to other tech companies.

There are two other big opportunities in digital banking, which is to either create a digital bank that owns a system and therefore is able to differentiate itself, or to build and become the new platform of choice.

DO YOU SEE BANKING-AS-A-SERVICE AS A NATURAL EXTENSION FOR A CHALLENGER BANK, OR IS IT A COMPLETELY DIFFERENT BUSINESS MODEL?

RK: I think it's a different business model, and one that offers almost more opportunity for banks than it does for tech companies.

ANY ADVICE FOR ANYONE LOOKING AT TRANSFORMATION RIGHT NOW?

RK: First, definitely do it. Big banks need to replace their systems wholesale. Until banks replumb completely, they won't be able to compete, because they won't be able to offer the same level of service as someone like Tandem.

And don't think your transformation is ever done, because there will always be things you need not just to reconfigure, but actually rebuild. For instance, we started

Tandem thinking that if we built a clever data stack and front-end layers, we could differentiate over time and utilize the back end, but it didn't happen like that.

So, in our old stack, we built what I call a universal origination chain, which meant you registered for Tandem and not a specific product. It's only when you start entering your data that we save it to a specific application. But because of the way the back end worked, we couldn't ever create a one-click journey, because we were using two systems that were architected differently, each generating a different sequence of data requests. So, we never did get to universal origination. But we did ensure there was zero friction to that additional journey.

Two, think of it as changing up all of your systems, which you could do incrementally. And perhaps, if I were a fine old-fashioned bank, I might also wait a year or two until guys like Mambu and Thought Machine had stopped experimenting and were on top of the back-end systems they offer.

Three, absolutely choose a vendor that's between five and eight years old – no more or less than this – so you are dealing with someone that has the right kind of maturity. I would also want to see that they are using AWS or one of the other more tech-driven platforms. I wouldn't want to work with the company that uses Azure, for instance, as that pretty much tells me that they don't respect technology.

And four, don't think about putting millions of people onto a transformation project, as that won't actually de-risk it and will just waste more money. Instead, work with a team of 50–100 people.

And that was our conversation with Tandem's Ricky Knox.

Like many leaders of fintechs, Knox believes that the old traditional banking model is dead, and what will take its place are a new set of players, like Tandem, which are segment-focused and heavily driven by technology. However, he still sees some hope for legacy banks if they can reinvent themselves in an appropriate manner.

But what about our other Q&A participant, Paul de Leusse, who heads up Orange Bank? His company has been on a journey much like Tandem's. Did he have a similar view of the marketplace?

Since its launch as a completely mobile banking service in 2017, following the acquisition of the Groupama bank the year before, Orange Bank has certainly brought a new energy to the marketplace. It has grown to the point where it now has about 1.6 million customers in Europe and 0.6 million in Africa. At the start of 2021, Orange expanded its banking services portfolio and customer base with the acquisition of Anytime, a French neobank that's focused on small businesses and professionals.

Though largely focused on France at present, it has expanded into Spain and the Ivory Coast, and is looking to grow internationally with further launches planned across Europe. It aims to acquire five million customers by 2023, though this figure will almost certainly be adjusted in the light of the COVID-19 pandemic.

AN ORANGE PERSPECTIVE

We had the following conversation with de Leusse.

WHAT ARE THE BENEFITS OF BEING A TELCO BANK?

PdL: Churn is always one of the biggest concerns for telcos, because at 15–20% it's much higher than for banks. So, anything we can do to reduce that is welcome. Because of (the bank's relationship with the telecom provider) Orange, for instance, we have a much more intimate relationship with the customer than a traditional bank. So, in Spain, for instance, that enables us to divide that churn by two.

That not only helps protect us from the GAFAs (Google, Apple, Facebook and Amazon), or a Chinese counterpart that could disintermediate the relationship with our clients, but it also gives Orange Bank access to (the telecom) Orange's customer base. As with most telcos, this is much bigger than a bank's – in France it's about 25 million, with at least 500 customers a day going through our network of 600 shops.

We're also able to capitalize on customer data in ways that legacy banks can't. So, by looking at how someone uses their mobile phone, we can see if they might be ready to change banks, and then we can target them with our banking offering.

Or, we can use phone data to anticipate credit risk. In fact, we have found that telco data is much better than banking data for doing this. In Africa, for instance, we can lend money to those that banks would never lend to because we know their cost of risk based on how they use their phone and mobile wallet.

Another example is Romania. Even if a bank has access to tax data and the credit bureau, it appears that the telco data is a better proxy of the client"s credit risk than these public data.

Banking data only gives you an idea of what was happening three months ago. But this kind of information, along with tech data, tells you who someone is today, and that makes it much more accurate. So, if you become unemployed, I know the day this happened, because the pattern of your phone calls changes – when you call, and how many times, will alter dramatically.

Of course, data privacy is a key topic for us, and we leverage these telco data only if the customer allows us to do so.

Having accurate data like this means we are helping democratize banking. In Africa, for instance, half our current customers come from the informal part of the economy, so our digital banking model gives them something they never believed possible. Even in Europe, we have many customers who had never previously considered using a new digital bank because they thought it was something only for the rich. But in France, we have more mass-market customers than affluent. Orange Bank customers earn around €1,900 a month, which is around the French national average.

DO TELCOS HAVE TO PARTNER WITH A BANK?

PdL: I see no benefit in telcos partnering with banks in emerging countries. There are many established African banks interested in accessing our 100 million-plus customers, but I don't see any value in sharing our customer base, our data or our network with them. We created Orange Bank Africa on our own, without the support of any bank.

The situation's more complex, of course, in more mature markets. But even in France and Spain, we chose to create our own bank because we wanted an intimate link with customers, since this is something that's very important to us. Of course, while we believe we can do without banking partners now, that might change.

DOES YOUR TECHNOLOGY GIVE YOU AN ADVANTAGE OVER LEGACY BANKS?

PdL: Being on the public cloud – in our case, Amazon – does give us a competitive advantage, but this is more to with the greater agility we gain than in lowering costs. As an example, it means if I decide to launch a new product, it's done in six months rather than the two years it would take a bank.

We're always looking to optimize our app by adding or changing features, and as cloud natives, we launch new functionalities at the rate of three a week. A traditional bank I think could do no more than seven or eight, perhaps ten, releases a year. This makes us much more efficient.

WHAT ABOUT BANKING-AS-A-SERVICE? IS THAT OF INTEREST TO YOU?

PdL: Yes. Our IT is really excellent. We score 4.95 out of 5 on app stores. In terms of app quality, that makes us by far the number one bank in Spain. So, we've been approached about BaaS and have initiated discussions with some non-European telcos – so there's no risk of competition – who might be interested in receiving BaaS from us.

WHAT'S YOUR OUTLOOK ON THE FUTURE OF BANKING AS A WHOLE?

PdL: I think we are at the end of the universal bank model, because it is not needed. But I'm not that pessimistic about legacy banks because they've proven their ability to change. Yes, their legacy IT is a problem, but they do have a huge customer base and I think the COVID crisis has made them more aware of what they need to do.

If I were a legacy bank, my biggest concern would not be from dying, but having my profit pool significantly reduced by new banks with offerings at a lower price point I couldn't match. That means they need to reinvent themselves to be much more cost-efficient if they want to compete.

IF UNIVERSAL BANKING IS DEAD, WHAT WILL THE TELCO BANKING MODEL LOOK LIKE IN TEN YEARS, NOT JUST IN EUROPE BUT ALSO IN AFRICA, FOR INSTANCE?

PdL: I'm quite confident that in a decade the four big retail banks in Africa will all be telco players, and that we will be one of them. The telecom players here already offer loans and mobile money, and now are considering setting up banks to meet the needs of the 80% of the population that's unbanked, who aren't being served by traditional institutions. Orange, for instance, has gone into the Cote d'Ivoire, and then there's Vodafone in Kenya.

But, of course, telco players are much more prudent about launching banks in what can be called mature markets, because there's the question of achieving critical mass and having a sufficiently rich offering. So, while the payment business is good for attracting customers, it's not a very profitable one, which means you need to add in consumer loans and other products.

And that was our conversation with Orange Bank's Paul de Leusse.

He was largely in agreement with Knox on most of this, with neither thinking it's all doom and gloom for the legacy banks. But if they are to start competing effectively against companies like Tandem and Orange Bank, the traditional institutions might have to start looking at fintechs not as rivals, but potential partners in a much wider financial ecosystem.

CHAPTER 11

PLAYING TOGETHER NICELY

"We are witnessing the slow destruction of financial services, rearranging itself around the customer. Who does this in the most relevant, exciting way using data and digital, wins."

ARVIND SANKARAN,

Director, Product Development and NPI, Google Cloud

Once upon a time, banks were large, cozy clubs. They invested in a brand that made them appear respectable, to capture customers who remained loyal for years, never turning elsewhere for someone to look after their money. This was the case because all banks were pretty much the same and moving from one to the other was a complex and time-consuming hassle. So, in the 'good old days,' banks owned the customer and were able to cross-sell them products and services even if they didn't quite fit.

But then the banking landscape started to change. Back in the 1980s and '90s, as we've seen, the first intruders arrived in the form of ING and the Egg card. Over the next decade, technology began to reshape the financial marketplace. But the real catalyst for change was a shift in banking regulations, particularly initiatives like PSD2. This brought about the era of 'open banking,' which since 2018 has required financial institutions to allow third-party access to a customer's transactional data if the customer requests it. This is now a common public resource that banks can no longer claim as their own.

Previously, such a depth of customer information could only be acquired by creating something like your own payments platform, such as Apple Pay. But now, non-banks, with their cutting edge technology, create better products based on customers' actual spending patterns.

Rafa Plantier, the Tink open banking platform's country manager for the UK and Ireland, put it this way: "The combination of technology and open banking provides a fantastic opportunity for the industry to innovate and create sophisticated digital products that would previously not have been available to customers walking into a branch."

Open banking has uprooted all the old certainties and fragmented the marketplace by helping to create a whole new financial ecosystem that goes well beyond the realms of 'normal banking.' This means that all manner of players can now pursue a bank's plum customers, offering them the best deals on a whole range of financial products and services. Such cherry picking by the new disruptors has increasingly left legacy banks with only low-margin products and the cost of trying to serve more and more unprofitable accounts.

OPEN BANKING OPENS DOORS

What really made open banking work was the advent of new collaborative technologies like API middleware, which we touched on earlier. This allowed different computer systems and databases to connect and share information. It's this that's now enabling the creation of whole new financial ecosystems that go beyond the standard one-to-one bank-customer relationships of the past.

And as Jason Maude, Chief Technology Advocate at Starling Bank, says: "If you as a bank cannot offer that connectivity … you will be like a town the railroad missed, and you will weaken and die. Customers, including small and medium-sized enterprises, are not going to do business with a bank that relies on paper processes. In the next decade, affording customers immediate and secure access to the data in the same way they have access to their money will become a requirement rather than a *nice to have*."[218]

Of course, given how open banking reshaped financial services, it was massively disruptive to legacy banks' everyday business, not least because it led to an explosion of potential competitors. In 2020, the number of third-party providers (TPPs) in the UK banking industry rose from 204 in February to 289 in November.[219]

Not surprisingly, it's easy for banks to see open banking and all that it brings as a threat. In reality, it's actually far more of an opportunity because of the way it allows them to diversify their income streams, which is especially important during times of market turbulence.

Some banks have already begun embracing the opportunity. Back in 2018, for instance, BBVA launched Open Platform in the US, a BaaS offering that allows third parties to deliver financial products to BBVA's customers. HSBC has its Connected Money app, which customers can use to view information about all their bank accounts, loans, mortgages and credit cards. Barclays has done something similar by allowing account aggregation through its own mobile app.

Although such banking apps were once a differentiator in the marketplace, they've now almost reached the point of commoditization. However, that shouldn't detract from the value they bring to consumers. Some 82% of those who use an open banking-enabled app say it has helped them improve how they manage their money.[220]

THE NEED TO COLLABORATE

All told, the really distinctive feature of open banking is the way it enables collaboration between different players in the markets, and ultimately the creation of connected new financial ecosystems. This is where the market heading.

Standard Chartered Bank is one example. Mark Lever, its European COO, calls partnerships with technology specialists "critical to our strategy, because we know clunky, pap platforms and traditional banking methods are not sustainable."[221]

If they are to stay relevant and remain in a position where they can duke it out with the newcomers, banks need to be part of this bigger picture. For all but the largest, being a lone wolf in this world just isn't a viable survival strategy.

Those with the vision and collaborative reach can strengthen their own capabilities in ways they otherwise couldn't, develop innovative products and get them to market faster. Only through joining forces with others will they be able to start offering the higher-quality experience their consumers are looking for.

Chirag Patel, Executive Vice President and Global Head of Digital Payments at Santander, puts it well when he says: "Partnership is about complementing the skills and capabilities you have when you've found that customer pain point. It is not necessarily the latest technology that solves it. Often, banks can get a much faster path to market by partnering rather than building in-house. This approach allows you to do something with more incredible speed, with lower costs, potentially, and enables you to test and see if these are the right solutions quicker. It's essential to get it in front of the customers and see if it works or not."

All this means that banks do not need a 'fintech strategy' as such, because working with others should now be an accepted part of an integrated business, revenue and operating model. More and more banks are acknowledging this new reality and looking for help from fintechs.

However, some banks remain so confident in their own abilities, or are so skeptical about partnering with fintechs, that they'd never indulge the idea of full-on collaboration. They'll continue to think of any teaming up as an incremental step or a mere side project. This is wrong. While such a tangential connection may better equip a bank in the short term, to perhaps handle higher transaction volumes, it won't be enough to sufficiently differentiate them in the marketplace. Eventually, they'll see their customers slip away and be left with nothing but generic, low-value services associated with checking account balances and payment processing.

If a traditional bank doesn't want to find itself there, it must see working with fintechs as an opportunity to fundamentally restructure its business model, so it can start to offer much more specific products and services. These must be better tailored to a particular customer segment or consumers' changing needs. This is something a traditional bank could never do on its own.

Banks could steal the march by capitalizing on new opportunities in areas such as cryptocurrencies – Bitcoin, Ethereum, Ripple, Omni, Nxt, Waves, Counterparty and the like. Though these altcoins remain a relatively small component in the financial landscape, appetite for them is growing fast. Their 2019 market value of $240 billion nearly doubled that of the year before ($128 billion). And with central banks now contemplating launching their own coins, some big players have already recognized the potential. We talked earlier about Goldman Sachs having set up a new cryptocurrency desk.

Beyond the creation of original products, there are further benefits to a bank in collaborating with a fintech. Research by Manuel Sosa, INSEAD Associate Professor of Technology and Operations Management, suggests that 'innovation dust' from companies like fintechs seems to rub off on those they work with. When he and his team looked at US design patents over a 35-year period, they found that those who collaborated with 'stars' in a particular field were more likely to turn into stars themselves.[222] It seems that those who possess special skills – such as the creative ability to combine unrelated elements into novel ideas – can unwittingly pass these on to those they work with.

This means that the mere fact of working with a fintech can change a bank's DNA over time, as new behaviors and mindsets are transferred and then evolve to create a more dynamic cultural environment. We'll look at that in more detail later.

THE EVOLUTION OF THE BANKING ENVIRONMENT

Business Model Archetype			
	Servitization	**Marketplace**	**Ecosystem**
Focus	• Customized, asset-heavy solution • Close, long-lasting relationship • Vertically-integrated offering	• Broad product/service offerings • Ability of matchmaking of products and customer needs	• E2E customer experience • Broad, complementary product/service offerings
Why ?	Increase customer lifetime value	Increase existing customer base	Reach out to new, adjacent customer segments
How □→O	Transform products into digital services: sale of access/rights instead of ownership of product	Offer product portfolio on established marketplace or setup new digital marketplace	Participate on platform as producer, business partner or ecosystem orchestrator

Source: ADL Research

We can see something of the evolution of the banking environment, and how it's moved to become a far more interconnected space, in the diagram above. We begin with what's known as 'servitization,' an ungainly term coined in the late 1980s for peddling an outcome as a service. It isn't about one-off sales, but rather selling products that provide an additional service. Consider Netflix and Spotify, whose service that delivers individual pieces of film or music (a product) is very different from just selling someone a CD and that being the end of it.

In essence, this is the traditional banking model: asset-heavy, divided into vertical business lines, and dependent on building long-lasting relationships with customers to maximize their lifetime value. If banks are to escape from this way of doing business – which they must, because it no longer works – they have to digitally reinvent their products and services, and how people access them.

Marketplaces are a big step in that direction because they allow customers to satisfy their needs with a wider range of products, not just from their bank, but through networks of third parties. Being able to deliver others' products creates a more attractive offering that banks can then use to increase their customer base.

Ecosystems take us even further down this path by extending the marketplace into non-financial and lifestyle products, creating interconnections with many more providers. Ultimately, this creates a one-stop shop for consumers, as their needs are increasingly met in one place. For ecosystems to be really successful they must be able to extract deep insights from data, so, they can deliver the rich, satisfying experience that customers increasingly demand.

These are the most evolved of all banking spaces, and legacy banks need to make sure their products are being integrated into this wider environment as it ripples out into adjacent segments of the market.

Yet, becoming part of such an ecosystem isn't going to be easy for many legacy banks. This is due in part to the complexity and inefficiency of their outdated IT infrastructure, which can't even cope with existing demands, let alone a multitude of other players trying to plug in.

Of course, ecosystems inevitably mean that old supply chains and marketing channels become redundant, since a bank's customers now have direct access to a vast array of new and different products and services. This will require a readjustment of the corporate ego.

WHO'S WHO IN THE ECOSYSTEM?

If legacy banks are to become part of a broader dynamic ecosystem, they need to get a better idea of who's out there, and their respective ambitions.

Among these inhabitants are the orchestrators or aggregators, like N26. Typically, they're more interested in the customer relationship than creating products themselves. Their aim is to fulfill as many of their customers' needs as possible by providing access to a wide range of financial products from multiple providers. This allows them to create high levels of customer satisfaction without investing in the development of their own products. If a traditional financial institution provided an orchestrator with access to its customers, it would risk losing the relationship with them because they could buy directly from the actual product provider.

Next, we have the producers who use technology to develop and deliver best-in-class financial products. Oaktree offers laser-precise risk management services; Nutmeg emphasizes its investing acumen; Coinbase focuses on delivering advanced crypto capabilities; and PayPal offers an easy-to-use payments system. While producers do engage with customers directly, they tend to do so through an orchestrator or marketplace.

Then there are the integrators. They own a banking license that they use to deliver private-label products and technology solutions, like banking as-a-platform (BaaP), to non-banking companies. Bancorp, for example, provides back-end banking services in conjunction with its partner, the banking start-up Simple.

BANKING-AS-A-PLATFORM CREATES AN ECOSYSTEM BANKS CAN USE TO RETAIN CUSTOMERS

Source: ADL Research

BaaP is a way to integrate the offerings from multiple fintechs into a single ecosystem that can be accessed through a central app. This allows a bank to connect its customers with things like robo-advisors, marketplaces, investment services and fintech lenders. It's the opposite of BaaS because the bank still owns the customers and adds value by bringing them others' products. Being able to run such a model is dependent on having APIs that can connect core banking processes with outside TPPs. The 'API layer' that's created sits on top of the bank's own systems, enabling the flow of data between them. This platform banking approach is flexible, relatively easy to scale quickly and enables a bank to stay in control, so it can be confident that it is remaining regulatory-compliant. This is a defensive strategy that can be put in place to prevent customers from being lured away by flashy offerings from fintechs.

An integrator's strength comes from sophisticated IT architecture and how they use this to better manage processes. By working with integrators, banks could brand as their own a whole range of high quality, strategically important products. These might include current accounts or payment services, or leverage areas where they have a greater competitive advantage, such as in lending.

Banks could even choose to become wholesalers of white-label offerings by developing close relationships with many producers and selling their products to other banks in the retail and corporate segments. This would be a readily scalable model that banks could use to deliver innovative products faster and with less friction.

Finally, we have the processors. They're great at improving the efficiency of middle- and back-office services. They are the ones who take on things like transaction and payment processing for incumbent banks constrained by old-fashioned processes and monolithic architectures, like mainframes. First Data was one of the first with this kind of model.

Many of these players will work through marketplaces, which are often set up by fintechs that excel at data management, to leverage their capabilities. This is something we'll talk about in more detail later.

THE PENNY BEGINS TO DROP

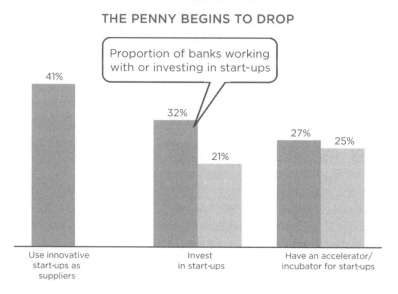

Source: Efma-Infosys (November 2016 the Financial Brand)

One of the ways banks can deal with the new reality is to seek greater integration with fintechs, which have the necessary technological expertise and innovative mindset. More and more banks seem to be creating this kind of relationship. Arthur D Little's research has found that more than 40% of banks are now using start-ups as suppliers, and 32% have actually invested in them. That's a significant increase over the 21% that had done this in 2015. What's more, a quarter of them are running accelerators or incubators to help with innovation. BBVA is a good example. It began by buying the start-up digital bank Simple[223] (Spain) in 2014, subsequently acquired a 30% stake in Atom Bank[224] (UK), and then purchased Holvi (Finland) outright.[225] Similarly, BPCE in France got hold of Fidor Bank (Germany) in July 2016.[226]

In a sign of the consolidation that is going to take place in the digital banking space, BBVA has announced that it will be shutting down Simple and moving customer accounts over to its US operations.

THE REALITY OF WORKING WITH OTHERS

Working with others gives banks a much-needed push out of their comfort zone and helps them confront their own 'that's just the way we do it here' cultural mentality. However, capitalizing on this opportunity requires a degree of structural and cultural adaptation, as well as the creation of new decision-making pathways. This is needed to ensure that there's clear accountability between bank and fintech about who decides and who provides.

Since this kind of collaborative working is still a relatively new phenomenon, everyone is on a learning curve. And so, best practices have not yet been fully developed or firmly embedded. There often remains a certain proprietary thinking about who owns what data. This makes it essential that everyone understands the need for effective knowledge distribution and process innovation. If that's not properly managed, you can end up with information silos and ill-structured databases – exactly what's *not* needed in an ultra-competitive landscape where speed of response is paramount.

Unfortunately, while banks are beginning to see the benefits of working with fintechs, the fintechs themselves often feel that collaborating with big banks is too slow. They view it as a painful 'teeth-pulling' process that creates an innovation-stifling environment, which is the antithesis of what's actually required.

If they are to get over this hurdle, the legacy banks must accept that they're now part of a much broader, far more complex financial ecosystem in which no single bank can be all things to all people. Again, this requires a spirit of openness and willingness to adopt new technology, as the distinction between banks and fintechs becomes increasingly blurred.

The need for this new mindset is not exclusive to banking, of course. We see a similar philosophical rebooting in many other industries where new ecosystems of players are being created in ways that dissociate asset ownership from revenue. Airbnb, for instance, owns no rooms but generate fees from those who do. Similarly, Uber has no taxi fleet itself but earns money from drivers who are the vehicle owners.

Microsoft has used the term 'symbiotic' to describe the increasingly interdependent ecosystems that are now crisscrossing business borders, all cemented together by APIs.

In this new era of openness, the success of financial services organizations will be measured by how well they're able to move away from *business as usual* and embrace more dynamic business models, such as platform-as-a-service (PaaS)[227] or infrastructure-as-a-service (IaaS). These are much more the norm across the industry's segments, spanning retail and wholesale banking through to capital markets and wealth management. Sharing data will be at the heart of everything.

Even if they were to build the kind of digital app through which customers could receive a tailored service, banks as they now operate wouldn't be able to deliver it. That's largely because they aren't able to reap any real insights from the disparate, disjointed mountain of current account and credit card transaction data they're sitting on.

We have the vertically divided traditional banks, still reliant on in-house solutions; those that have become fully digital, or are in the process of doing so, and have eliminated any physical distribution layer; others that are developing marketplaces where they double down on the relationship layer by providing products from third parties; and the players who've relinquished the customer layer entirely, as the integrators and processors have, to concentrate instead on products and underwriting by becoming BaaS providers.

In this increasingly fragmented environment, where the very definition of what it means to be a bank has changed, the only way traditional financial institutions can find their place is to hitch a ride on the back of the fintechs. That's because they'll only be able to reinvent themselves through innovation, which as we will see in the next chapter is the engine of future growth.

CHAPTER 12

WHAT GOT YOU HERE WON'T GET YOU THERE

"Innovation does not mean launching a product that only helps the bank. It means doing something that genuinely helps the customer."

MATTHIAS KRONER,

CEO, Fidor Bank, Germany

In 1972, journalist Tom Wolfe wrote of the abstract nature of bank logos when he said they "create a feeling of vagueness and confusion." This "somehow makes it possible for the head of the corporation to tell himself: 'I'm modern, up-to-date, a man of the future. I've streamlined this old baby,' [and] if the [design] fee doesn't run into five figures, he doesn't feel streamlined."[228]

That same theme was taken up in a 1983 review of bank logos in *ID* magazine, which complained about the unfortunate tendency "to look over one's shoulder and see what the other guy is doing, and to base one's design accordingly. As in the banking industry itself, risk-taking is frowned upon."[229]

So, what were they saying? That banks are boring? Yes. That they all look the same? Yes.

While a corporate identity or branding project may set out to give an organization its distinctiveness, the reality is that many banks have been more interested in looking good than being different. In fact, in the past banks have actively wanted to look like everyone else because it presumably made them appear more respectable and 'legitimate.' If you're too *off the wall*, how can you be trusted with someone's life savings?

So, 'boring and safe' came to be seen as good, and in fact the only way to operate. This is why banks actively sought out the homogeneity of the pack, adopting names and identities that were all but indistinguishable from their rivals. This phenomenon was dubbed 'symbolic isomorphism' by Boston College Professor Mary Ann Glynn.[230] Bank of America, CBA, Deutsche Bank, UBS and HSBC... they're all *much of a muchness.*

With little choice in the marketplace, a bank's customers were left with no option but to tolerate the slow, poor. Perhaps that tradeoff was acceptable if you were fearful that your life savings were at risk. But times have changed.

Outside of banking, consumers have become used to getting what they want – and getting it quickly and effectively – from the large online retailers. They want more of the same from their banks, and with all the new alternatives available, they're unwilling to accept the blandness of vanilla.

LOUD AND PROUD

The once-shackled banking customers are turning to a new breed of financial institutions who want to stand to out, loudly and proudly flaunting their difference.

Starling's namesake is a bird that's fast, adaptable, sociable and friendly. N26's 'N' stands for number and 26 the total of smaller cubes that make up a Rubik's Cube. Then there are Chime and Revolut and Tide, all names you wouldn't naturally associate with financial institutions.

They've uniquely christened themselves because they understand that, in today's digital landscape, there's no benefit in being a shrinking violet in a financial services sector that's becoming ever more commoditized.

For the same reason, they're continually investing and testing to generate new ideas, learning from those that work and killing off those that don't.

This is the kind of approach that's been successfully used by private equity firms and venture capitalists, with the aim of achieving rapid performance improvement followed by transformation. It's precisely the ambidextrous approach we've set out in these pages.

THE ENGINE OF GROWTH

As such, innovation is the true engine of competitive advantage, and therefore the generator of growth. As Professor Amit Seru of Stanford Business School says: "When firms innovate profits go up, and labor and financing flow to them and away from their competitors, who suffer from this creative destruction."

So, if you aren't innovating you aren't even standing still. You are going backward.

From our own research at Arthur D Little Global innovation excellence, we can see that the most radical innovators enjoy greater success than those who take a more incremental approach.[231] For instance, those in the top innovation quartile enjoy 19% more sales and 13% greater profit than those who aren't.

Innovation has always been around, of course. The big difference today is that we now have 'digital.' This completely transforms the way we interconnect, allowing previously autonomous, independent IT systems to communicate and work together.

Much as electricity did this, digital connectivity has a profound impact on business and revenue models. It breaks down barriers, driving the convergence we've talked about by blurring the lines between sectors and business lines, and completely disrupting the existing value chain. Embedded finance is a good example.

Digital shift is at the very core of innovation, and it is an inexorable force. Those who make the change-over successfully will redefine their business model, value proposition, distribution channels, customer interface and much else. They'll do all this in ways that give their customers something that's simply better, cheaper or faster than what they'd received before.

Innovation creates discontinuities, and the more disruptive these are, the greater the opportunities to reach out to new audiences through fresh distribution channels and cut the cost of customer acquisition.

In other words, innovation is the trigger that releases an organization's energy. When linked to an inspiring point of arrival, innovation has the potential to mobilize the entire organization and turn existing and emerging threats into future opportunities.

But to capitalize on these, banks must be prepared to retool their whole business.

This means the question a CEO should now ask when looking at radical proposed action is not 'why?' but 'why not?' One could argue that the more disruptive you can be, the greater the potential for winning the big prize.

Of course, innovating is never easy in any industry. Even those who are good at this have a hard time sustaining their performance. This can be particularly problematic in a complex organization, like a traditional bank that's constrained by regulatory realities. Here, innovation is much more of a challenge than it would be for a gung-ho fintech. Just consider that as recently as 2017, 76% of senior bankers didn't believe that digitization would affect their business model. That's a shocking statistic, and a sad indictment of where banking is at the moment in terms of its thinking.

Even when so-called innovations emerge in traditional banking, they're often just slightly different ways for customers to interface with the institution and not about core banking transactions, like deposits, loans, mortgages and payments. That wasn't always so – back in the '70s, bankers seemed much more cutting edge in their thinking. They were the ones who introduced ATMs, debit cards and the like. Since then, this crown has slipped and been taken away from them by the fintechs.

Getting their innovation mojo back isn't so easy for traditional banks, given that they tend to follow rigid product development paths that don't encourage new thinking. Bankers will say this is due to the checks and balances required for regulatory compliance. There's a kernel of truth to that – developing a radically different product could have huge, unintended financial and compliance costs that might be hard to swallow. But is this truly a valid impediment, or are there other reasons at play?

Perhaps it is more a case that banks tend to lack experienced innovators who are able to initiate and push through changes. This can certainly happen. When a bank's culture is all about risk minimization, it becomes the norm to do nothing rather than something that can get you fired. And if there is any possibility that some maverick idea may actually be implemented, there are always excuses to hide behind.

As a result, leaders are reluctant to step up and sponsor or take ownership of change. This can be particularly true with expensive technology that bankers don't fully understand. So, innovation is pushed to the margins, where it's compartmentalized and made a separate 'thing' that doesn't become infused into the core thinking of the business.

The comfort zone for most legacy banks remains the efficient implementation of their current business model, rather than considering how they can innovate.

That's the case even though this is the very thing that will enable them to grow and compete long-term.

That leaves them to plod on, relying on the same stale products, even as they deliver few sales and cost a king's ransom to maintain.

Even their best products will eventually reach the end of the line. After the usual life cycle of attracting the 'easy pickings' customers, and then being countered by competitors' offerings that are lower-priced, faster, more efficient or provide greater convenience, they see a drop-off in sales, and the bank provides less and less support. Finally, when too many customers are lost, the old product is finally laid to rest. With an offering like a mortgage, this process can take 30 years.

EATING YOURSELF FOR BREAKFAST

This process was described by the economist and business consultant Clayton Christensen, in his 1993 book, *The Innovator's Dilemma*.[232] The pattern he observed in various industries was that the dominant incumbent had the resources and opportunity to innovate, but failed to do so because of the challenges associated with disrupting themselves when they were still in a leadership position.

While this sequence of events is entirely predictable, it still seems to catch many business leaders unaware. Blindsided by what's happening, they miss their 'innovation moment,' which came and went when the product was beginning to lose traction in the market.

In fairness, it should be said that even the best companies can't tell exactly when this moment will be. That's why they make innovation a continuous process, with many following the principle of 'creative destruction' by launching new feature-rich products while there's still life left in the old ones. Such creative 'cannibalization' enables them to disrupt the market in a controlled way, and keep barriers to entry high. As Tim Cook, CEO of Apple, of one the most self-disrupting companies around, has said: "Our core philosophy is to never fear cannibalization. If we don't do it, someone else will."[233]

In other words, if you aren't the one initiating change, you'll find yourself continually reacting to the changes created by others… and that's not the best place to be.

But taking preemptive action like this just isn't the DNA of a traditional bank. Perhaps understandably, product managers who've spent years nurturing and protecting their 'babies' will be loath to see them replaced. They will ferociously resist any attempts to do so. This is one of the reasons they end up with those large, ungainly, underperforming portfolios we've been talking about.

However, in a highly dynamic market – and financial services is certainly one – you will quickly lose market share if you aren't eating your own products.

IF YOU AREN'T INNOVATING, OTHERS ARE

Unfortunately, too few banks develop effective, coherent innovation strategies in response to market shifts even as they recognize that they should. A study by Efma and Infosys Finaclef of 140 retail banks in more than 70 countries revealed that while 84% had increased their innovation budgets, just five European banks had actually made innovation an executive responsibility and allocated funding for it.[234] In other words, innovation seems to be viewed more as a whimsical notion than a serious commercial objective.

That's why banks can get caught off-guard, as they were by the concept of open banking. This hardly came out of nowhere, but few banks seemed to realize that it would mean they could no longer rely just on rates to bring in new customers. Nor did they bother to review how this might affect how they segmented, distributed, priced and marketed their products. This encouraged their customers to move to those with radically different value propositions and differentiated products that better suited their needs.

That's why companies like Ant Financial have radically reshaped the financial services industry through their innovative approaches.

With innovation happening on many fronts, if banks aren't careful they can be caught unawares. As we saw in the previous chapter, telecom operators around the world are creating new risk factors by developing mobile-first payment systems that could disrupt the whole world payment network.

A good example of this is KlickEx.[235] This service-infrastructure provider is based in the Pacific Islands and has a staff of just 14, but it offers global money transfer, foreign exchange and inter-bank settlement services. If other companies around the world start working with non-bank service providers, most probably telecom carriers, they could be a significant source of competition to legacy banks. This is a genuine case of 'reverse innovation,' where new ideas flow from less economically evolved regions to stimulate better and cheaper financial services in more advanced regions.

Of course, changing direction necessitates breaking away from conventional thinking. It calls for a departure from the same old exclusive focus on short-term annual financial management, and the same tired program of cost-cutting, branch closures and basic performance improvement. Instead, it demands a sharp new focus on well-tailored service delivery.

As a result, most banks are following no more than a 'me too' strategy rather than one that will give them a sustainable competitive or commercial advantage. Research by Global Innovation 1000 shows that there is a demonstrable difference in both revenue terms a clear difference in both revenue (11%) and growth in Earnings Before Interest, Taxes, Depreciation, and Amortization (EBITDA) in the favor of those organizations that are more innovative.[236] Not only that, but they are also normally much better at 'deploying at scale' since they are investing less in maintaining obsolescent technology and spend more on digital transformation.

INNOVATE EVERYWHERE

Until just a few years ago, it made sense to not stray far from what you knew. Best to only to expand outwards through adjacencies. But that's all changing. Because of convergence, the notion of *core and adjacent* is effectively dead. You can no longer stay anywhere close to where you are.

You now have no choice but to come up with a radically new business model, and it's only through innovation that you can do this.

Fortunately, because the marketplace has become so nebulous and fragmented, it's possible with the right idea to set up your stall practically anywhere. As a business, you are the one setting the boundaries within which you're going to operate.

Once again, it will be up to the ambidextrous leader to spot what the rest of the world *hasn't* seen by taking a contrarian view.

If a bank wants to be truly innovative, it can't confine itself to one area. Instead, it should look across all aspects of the organization and its value chain. Everything should be scrutinized with a fresh eye, from the ground up and the top down. This includes product differentiation; service delivery; the development of complementary services to enrich the customer experience; greater vertical integration that gives more control of the value chain; focusing on a particular core activity; introducing new technologies to automate back-office processes; creating efficiencies by outsourcing time-consuming, unprofitable tasks; and new recruitment procedures that bring on board the talent that's needed.

While there has to be widespread innovation, that doesn't imply a need for it to be pursued at the same level across the entire bank. That would probably be unsustainable. Instead, there must be a 'continuum of innovation' that recognizes some operational areas requiring less innovative attention than others. For instance, systems involving records, back-office core operations and customer transaction data probably need to be looked at only periodically, while middle-office systems involved in decision-making, pricing, analytics and risk-management should be revisited more often, to accommodate changing business practices.

Customer-facing apps must be updated most often, so they remain not only fit for purpose and continue to engage, but also because these interfaces are ways to capture information about how your customers act and behave. If you change the interface, that can have a massive impact on the way people unconsciously interact with your technology, leading to new insights from which you can then create competitive advantage.

INNOVATION – YOU CAN'T GO FAR ENOUGH

Economist Joseph Schumpeter said that "the function of entrepreneurs is to reform or revolutionize the pattern of production," and that's exactly what those who set up a fintech are doing. As far back as 2015, JPMorgan Chase CEO Jamie Dimon was warning shareholders about the "hundreds of start-ups with a lot of brains and money working on various alternatives to traditional banking."[237]

Given the size of this external threat, it begs the question of whether legacy banks can ever be *too* innovative if they are to successfully transform themselves. The answer is probably no, although there are of course those who've reinvented themselves by not straying too far from their core.

The Singapore bank DBS, which we talked about earlier, is often cited as having one of the most extensive transformation programs in the financial services sector. It was certainly the first bank in the world to develop a methodology for measuring digital value creation. Its unique differentiator is that it focused on creating an 'innovation culture' that feeds a very successful digital banking model. In India, its digital retail customers now generate twice the income, at a 20% lower cost-to-income ratio. This segment also generates a 9% greater ROE than DBS's traditional banking segment. Digital customers now make up more than 40% of the bank's customer base and generate about 70% of its profit.[238]

While this wouldn't have happened without a commitment to innovation, in reality, DBS is not a true innovator since it has stayed relatively close to its historic core business.

For most banks, this won't be good enough. In fact, it's actually going to be riskier than moving into uncharted territory. Instead, they'd be better advised to strongly innovate in spaces that fintechs are likely to disrupt, as a preemptive innovation strike. If you can remove the potential for customer dissatisfaction by providing great products and services, you cut the ground from beneath the disruptors, who then don't have anything to differentiate themselves.

PLANNING TO INNOVATE

Innovation doesn't happen by chance. It needs to be planned, encouraged and fed with the latest market insights and data. The rapid growth of Berlin-based N26 and Tandem in the UK is underpinned by product innovation, process simplification and a transformative 'fast to market' business model. This has enabled the founders to steer their organizations forward without losing the creative, innovative team members they've recruited.

They have only been able to accomplish this because of their specific mix of competencies, capabilities and resources. Other banks that try to do the same with different DNA might not be so successful. So, while it may be tempting to copy someone else's system, don't. Such a system must be tailored to the specific needs of the innovating unit.

If you don't currently have an innovation program in place, you need to create one. If you do have one, you need to review the entire process to ensure that it's fit for purpose.

And you must decide whether you want to focus on internally driving innovation or using external partners, which is likely the way to go if the internal structure and nature of the organization is too rigid to allow for other than traditional thinking.

If they have the right mindset, banks can innovate from within, and can often do so by tapping into the knowledge of their own frontline employees, service development teams, executives and back-room staff. This is what Standard Bank, one of South Africa's largest financial services groups, aims to do by running an annual event, where employees talk about how they've implemented innovation.

Bank of America doesn't have an innovation lab as such, or even a dedicated budget set aside for development, because its philosophy is that innovation is part of everyone's job. Or, at least, it stems from the efforts of 5,600 'employee inventors' in 42 states and 12 countries, who are tasked with generating a steady stream of ideas. This culture of internal innovation seems to be delivering, since the bank now has a portfolio of more than 4,250 offerings, nearly half of which relate to AI, machine learning and information security in the banking sector.[239] This wouldn't have happened without a commitment to radical thinking, both constructive and destructive.

When it comes to innovation, Brazil's second-largest retail bank, Banco Bradesco – a 75-year-old financial services giant with more than 71 million customers – acts more like a fintech start-up. As part of a technology-led strategy, it set up the inovaBra platform, which gives micro-entrepreneurs access to a range of financial and non-financial tools,[240] and put employees through a major skills-improvement program to support it.

In China, you have ICBC, the world's largest bank in terms of assets. Almost from the moment it launched, ICBC began establishing an organization-wide innovation culture by setting up a fintech research institute to help deliver a smart banking strategy that leveraged blockchain technology, Big Data, AI, cloud computing, 5G and IoT.[241] In partnership with Ant Financial, it has now developed a means for merchants to collect payments through Alipay or ICBC's own app without making any time-consuming changes to their existing payment collection systems.

Of course, in a complex organization like a bank, internally-developed innovation is more of a challenge because of the different entities, geographies and business lines involved. Such an undertaking has to be endorsed and driven by senior leaders, given how extensively it will cut across many departments. Innovation certainly isn't something that can be vaguely delegated to 'someone' in 'some' department.

Once an innovation strategy has been determined, it should be managed by a dedicated team that can focus on turning an idea into a commercial revenue-generating reality.

When redesigning any process, it's important to get feedback early, or the team could end up going down the wrong track. Feedback loops should be integrated into project workflows, and the responses rapidly communicated to others through informal networks.[242] If things go wrong, don't cover them up; that's counter-productive and will just slow down adoption.

You can simulate the effectiveness of new processes by running virtual 'what-if' scenarios with real data, to test the effect and feasibly of any changes. Once evaluated, processes can be rolled out in phases and the results assessed. This reduces uncertainty and protects the organization from a major and expensive failure. The managers of such pilot projects can then act as the 'change agent' who sells it into the rest of the organization. Once the details of the pilot are codified, the process can be replicated elsewhere.

An MIT-Sloan study found that this pilot phase will typically take twice as long as the rollout itself and may consume 2–3 times the staff and management time.[243] So, local managers must allow for that degree of commitment.

LOOKING OUTSIDE FOR HELP

The focus of innovation must be on value creation, which can be something of a culture shock for both management and employees – for whom this has never been prioritized – because of concerns about cash, short-term performance and internal politics.

As innovation isn't something that banks have done well in the past, it makes sense to not only develop internal capabilities and structures but also seek outside help from those more experienced and better equipped to develop, pilot and scale new product and service ideas across business lines.

This might be particularly beneficial when it comes to the commercialization handoff of a novel concept or product to the wider organization for execution and implementation, which is often one of the biggest challenges.

Through a group effort with others, legacy banks will not only move forward faster, but they'll overcome the 'innovator's dilemma' of whether to cater to their customers' current needs or go for disruptive innovations that anticipate their future needs.

There are several ways to do this. They could, for instance, create a separate environment outside the company where innovation can take place and be nurtured. This is something we'll look at in the next chapter.

Or, they could use external consultants and technologists to help reconfigure the business model and develop disruptive cannibalizing solutions, which might be a route to pursue if you want to counterbalance your existing product portfolio. Through a process of osmosis, key innovation competencies of the 'outsiders' will also be absorbed into the bank by default.

Another option is to invest in fintech start-ups and incubate them. This is the corporate venturing route that more and more major banks are taking, as shown in the illustration below.

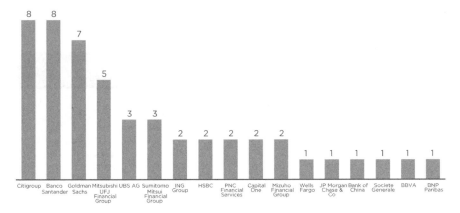

**MAJOR BANKS ARE INCREASINGLY
LOOKING TO INVEST IN FINTECH START-UPS**

Major Bank Investments to VC- backed Fintech Companies (Q3'15–Q3'16)

Source: The Pulse of Fintech, Q3 2016, Global Analysis of Fintech venture Funding, KPMG International and CB Insight November 16th, 2016
Note: Chart includes largest banks in US, Europe and Asia by AUM with disclosed fintech investments

THE FOUR DIMENSIONS OF INNOVATION

If you want to create more than a little bit of noise in the marketplace, you need to think of innovation in four dimensions.

The first of these is to ensure that what you are doing is human-design innovation. New technology only has value when it's useful and usable, so you need to put the human experience at the core of what you do.

This means focusing on the problems that underpin your customers unmet needs. Fail to do this, you just create a gadget – a mechanical lemon squeezer that provides little benefit because it has to be taken out of the cupboard each time and takes so long to clean.

You can only effectively address your customers' problems if you truly understand them. So, the second dimension is to use advanced data analytics and AI to provide a continuous stream of real-life information about customers that will help you make their lives better. The insights you'll get from this are much greater than anything coming from traditional customer research initiatives, which are infrequently done to begin with. As Paypal's co-founder Peter Thiel has said: "What people *aren't* telling you can very often give you great insight as to where you should be directing your attention."[244] You will get this from analytics.

Third, you should innovate not just for your customers but also for your internal teams. If you employ smart automation, for instance, you will release them from doing and mundane work to make them more creative and productive. In effect, automation combined with analytics will put your bank's cognitive powers on steroids and augment decision-making in ways not otherwise possible.

In doing so, you will be creating the digital workspace that connects people and makes them more effective.

Finally, you should innovate using open technology that enables you to better collaborate with others in what is becoming an ever-developing financial ecosystem.

ALIGNING IN FOUR DIMENSIONS

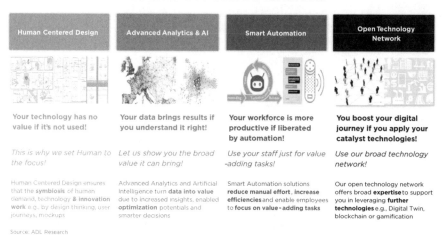

Human Centered Design	Advanced Analytics & AI	Smart Automation	Open Technology Network
Your technology has no value if it's not used!	Your data brings results if you understand it right!	Your workforce is more productive if liberated by automation!	You boost your digital journey if you apply your catalyst technologies!
This is why we set Human to the focus!	*Let us show you the broad value it can bring!*	*Use your staff just for value -adding tasks!*	*Use our broad technology network!*
Human Centered Design ensures that the **symbiosis** of human demand, technology **& innovation work** e.g., by design thinking, user journeys, mockups	Advanced Analytics and Artificial Intelligence turn **data into value** due to increased insights, enabled **optimization** potentials and smarter decisions	Smart Automation solutions **reduce manual effort**, **increase efficiencies** and enable employees to **focus on value-adding tasks**	Our open technology network offers broad **expertise** to support you in leveraging **further technologies** e.g., Digital Twin, blockchain or gamification

Source: ADL Research

A bank is about both people and technology. The way it encompasses the two in its operating model will largely determine the success or failure of any transformation. To achieve this, the four critical elements of any digital shift must be aligned.

WAITING FOR BANKING'S UBER

Innovation disrupts by displacing the old and replacing it with the new in a way that's rarely, if ever, smooth sailing. This is the case not just in financial services, but in pretty much every other sector as well. We talked earlier about how print media revenues fell off a cliff when they reached the trigger point where digital advertising suddenly became dominant.

There are many more examples. For instance, countless retailers didn't embrace home delivery soon enough and discovered they didn't have sufficient internal systems in place when they tried to catch up.

"There hasn't truly been an Uber for banking," Pascal Bouvier, Venture Partner at Santander Innoventures, says.[245] But that doesn't mean there won't be. Even as you read this, there might well be such a fintech waiting in the wings that in a year or two will knock the whole industry off its axis.

To a large degree, the purpose of innovation is actually to prepare for such trigger points. And there are going to be more and more of them coming down the line, ever closer together, as we enter a new era of innovation driven by technological developments. The 40% annual improvement in central processing unit (CPU) performance that underpins Moore's Law – which states that computing power tends to double every two years – may be starting to slow, but that's more than offset by alternative processors that are improving at a rate of more than 100% a year. So, rather than technology slowing, we're on the verge of cheaper-than-ever processing that will lead to an explosion in AI and machine learning applications that financial institutions will be able to use to great advantage.

This is going to completely alter how we think about applying technology to businesses. If you're in banking and you aren't excited about the possibilities this presents, you will be – it's going to be game-changing.

Any bank that doesn't see this doesn't truly understand the ambidextrous approach we've set out in this book. Of course, there are no certainties, but the scenario we've been describing is pretty likely at this point.

Constant innovation is the only way to reach a relatively safe haven, which makes it a business imperative in a world that's constantly evolving. And although technology is at the very center of any digital shift, this isn't something that can be left to the IT department. Good as it may be, your tech team is simply too disconnected from the business to have any real understanding of the customer. The bank's leadership must be the ones to inject a new spirit of innovation, where trial and error, experiment and techniques like rapid prototyping become the norm.

Again, we can't emphasize enough that the CEO and board must be aligned in this endeavor. Otherwise, what would be a multi-year process of transformation is going to fall apart before it has begun. And since a focus on short-term profit is often the enemy of innovation, because of the way it makes institutions try to preserve what they have, a set of new, less inward-looking transformation metrics will need to be adopted, some of which we discussed earlier.

In the next chapter, we'll look in more detail at how a legacy bank can begin to turn itself into an innovative powerhouse by using 'sandboxes' and breakthrough incubators to play around with new ideas without seriously injuring itself.

CHAPTER 13

HOW TO SHORTEN THE JOURNEY

"The way market share is being transferred from banks to players is already a clear sign that banks need to find the right alliance with those players. I don't see, for instance, universal banks in five years from now really competing in the traditional retail business. If some are still able to it's because they can leverage completely different product propositions. That's why I believe the point of arrival in traditional banking is very close, and will consist of a very lean proposition. When I say lean, I don't just mean the physical footprint, but also the set of products and services provided, which definitely won't be as rich as it was in the last decade, but will be driven by new-generation needs. I expect the Amazons of this world and even Microsoft will very soon replace banks, thanks to the trust that they have gained from clients, and their capacity to spend money on technology and innovation. I have kids of 11 and 13, and I think they will never go to a bank branch and will exchange money with friends only by using apps that probably won't belong to a financial institution brand. That again could be Apple or Amazon. This part of history has already been written, it's just about how long does it take to get there."

ROBERTO PARAZZINI,
CEO, Deutsche Bank Italia, in conversation with Arthur D Little

The multitude of digital-only banks emerging in Europe and elsewhere, like Monzo, N26, Revolut and Starling, embody the kind of venture that banks need to create.

This new sort of light-on-its-feet business is a world away from the stodgy complexity of a legacy bank's business model. So, how is it possible to bridge the gap between the two?

This certainly isn't going to be a side project for the IT department or an 'overnight operation,' where a bank can simply reverse itself out, bit by bit, from an old model. At least, it shouldn't be. This is something much bigger. For some who have crossed the divide, it's been a decade-long exercise in transformation. These banks have still had to abide by all their regulatory restrictions and continue to deliver services to their customers, while shaking free from outdated technologies, inefficient work processes and staid corporate cultures.

While sweeping digital transformation is necessary and essential for legacy banks, it doesn't come without risk, which means that things don't always end well. One of the most striking examples of how things can go wrong is the digital bank Bó, a sorry tale of an improperly handled transformation.[246]

THE STORY OF BÓ –
A DIGITAL DEBACLE

Bó was set up by high street lender RBS to combat the likes of Starling and Monzo. As a quick 'digital fix,' RBS had at one time tried to buy Monzo. When that didn't pan out, it embarked on building a new venture that would offer the security of being linked to a respectable, traditional bank while having many of Monzo's features. The key differentiator was to be that Bó would focus on money saving.

RBS sunk more than £100 million to the project, and in June 2019 brought onboard team members from Loot, a digital banking app that had recently gone insolvent and was in legal administration. Loot's chief executive, Ollie Purdue, joined as Bó's Chief Product Officer in September of that year, and with everyone in place things were gearing up.

Six months later, Bó was dead. Closed down. Kaput. It became yet another example of how even big banks, with the resources to create a business that could go head-to-head with their digital-only competitors, can seem incapable of doing what's required.

Why did Bó fail so miserably?

RBS's chief executive, Alison Rose, hinted that COVID-19 was a primary factor, with falling profits and heavy credit losses related to the pandemic influencing the shutdown decision. However, while Bó had experienced a downturn in customer engagement during the crisis, so had established digital banks like Monzo and Starling, which also saw a drop in sign-ups during March 2020.

But there was something more. Besides the coronavirus and the need to cut costs, there were deeper issues at play. In fact, the decision to liquidate the venture did not come as much of a surprise to many.

Bó's technology stack had been plagued by problems from the start, and remained troublesome through the rush to go live, in a scramble to head off the possibility of the project being cancelled. The tech team spent the first three months post-launch consumed with fixing bugs. Then there was the compliance glitch that forced Bó to replace thousands of users' cards. And then, soon after its launch in December 2019, Bó was hit by a string of critical reviews on the App Store. Users rated it 3.2 out 5 on the iOS mobile operating system, for example, while Mettle, RBS's other digital bank, enjoyed a much healthier 4.7.

This all worried RBS investors, especially since this poor performance was in vivid contrast to the relative success of Mettle. Focused on business customers, Mettle was achieving much greater customer engagement than Bó, as evidenced by far higher numbers of transactions, deposits, spending and app usage.

Since engagement is such a crucial data point for digital banks, this wasn't a good sign for Bó. Mettle was also better protected commercially because business clients generate more revenue per capita, since they generally hold larger deposits and credit applications. Mettle's way of working was also much more like that of a tech company than a bank.

Even though it was a so-called 'flanker brand' that sat outside RBS's core infrastructure, Bó was bound by the inherently cautious mindset of its parent company. Starling Bank Founder and Chief Executive Anne Boden, who once held a senior position at RBS, conceded: "It's very difficult to replicate the energy and technology of a start-up."

It was also apparent that all was not sweetness and light among those running the show. From the beginning, there were rumblings about what was going on. There was talk of a clash among leadership from early on about the new bank's future. When CEO Mark Bailie stepped down in January 2019, there was no one around to defend Bó or champion its ambitions.

The seeds of failure had been sown early, since RBS executives saw Bó as something of a side project rather than a pivotal part of their banking transformation. This meant they were never fully engaged or emotionally invested in its success. And because they had set it up as a separate brand, they could close it without lasting embarrassment.

Nonetheless, the demise of Bó was a serious blow to the bank's digital transformation and yet another example of the dismal failure of corporate innovation projects.

PLAYING WITH SAND

So, how can a legacy bank begin building a new digital operation in a risk-averse environment like financial services, where the consequences of getting things wrong are extraordinarily expensive?

The answer is *isolation*. When developing any new digital venture or introducing untried technology, make sure there's no possibility that some rogue element of the project can 'escape' and contaminate the parent business.

You can do this by creating a 'mirror' environment that reflects real-life conditions, where you can experiment with new ideas in absolute safety because the space is separated from day-to-day business operations. This closed environment is often called a sandbox, like the play space where children can creatively scoop, sift and mold, learning how things work as they go. In a technology innovation sandbox, financial institutions can mimic a production environment, test out ideas and simulate responses to any changes without regulatory risk, which could have a disastrous impact on their business, revenue and operating models.

In this way, it's possible to work out how much 'compliance pain' may be involved when launching a new product or entering an unfamiliar market. Some regulatory authorities, like those in Singapore, Australia, the UAE and the UK, have actually created regulatory sandboxes. These fenced-off test environments allow fintechs to experiment with different business models and get behind-the-scenes feedback, with no chance of making costly real-life errors.

This enables a bank to learn from its mistakes, which inform and shape future actions rather than becoming the source of a major public embarrassment.

Sandboxes can be valuable for testing out new technologies, products and services, improving internal processes and efficiencies, or strengthening security capabilities to see what works and what doesn't. However, for bigger projects, such as setting up a new digital bank, something meatier is required. This calls for a laboratory that enables the rapid development of ideas that fall outside a bank's comfort zone and couldn't otherwise be done.

Debbie Brackeen, Head of Incubation at Citi Ventures, talks about wanting Citi's banking innovation centers to make "a significant impact to the overall business, not just incremental changes."[247] She said their purpose was "to pioneer and test new disruptive solutions for our customers" and "new business models and technologies that advance our position in the market."

Such centers tend to be called accelerators, incubators and labs, and while terms are often used interchangeably, there are some differences between them.

As its name suggests, an accelerator aims to speed up the development of a start-up concept. This usually is done by giving the project intensive support and guidance over a period of time, typically three months or so. During this time, the start-up's founders – who could be from inside or outside the bank – receive advice from mentors on how to develop their baby. They then have a 'demo day' opportunity to pitch their well-formulated product or prototype idea to potential investors, the press and other interested parties.

Separately, incubators are designed to help those with a germ of an idea develop their thinking over an extended period, using resources and capital support provided by a bank potentially interested in an ownership percentage.

An incubator allows a bank to pursue innovation while the legacy part of its business manages ongoing, traditional activities. Once created and proven, the resulting 'inside-out' ventures can be scaled up and grown into successful new companies that could offer potential equity opportunities to those who set them up. In some cases, they will become separate entities, and other times they'll be plugged back into the parent bank to become a functioning part of it.

While many organizations have created in-house incubators, most simply don't live up to expectations. Research by Arthur D Little shows that 85% of companies that set one up are dissatisfied with its performance. This generally isn't because the ideas, concepts and prototypes were bad, but due to subsequent problems with an incubated venture's commercialization and scale-up.

The primary reason most incubators fail is that they were set up with a sole purpose: to create a new business and then grow its value. While this may seem to be an obvious objective, it typically results in a series of disappointing, unfocused 'trial and error' experiments in peripheral business areas, in the vague that hope one of them might come to some kind of fruition. The simplistic thinking seems to be: 'If something good comes of it, fantastic... let's scale it up and away we go.' If things don't pan out, it's back to the drawing board, to try and try again.

While the ability to manage existing bank business while simultaneously developing new ventures to capitalize on convergence opportunities is a real sign of ambidextrous management, embarking on fishing expeditions is decidedly not. You're unlikely to stumble upon your next big idea, but will certainly create frustration and impatience among senior leadership.

If they have unrealistic expectations about timelines or a new venture's potential commercial returns, a project is already in deep trouble. This is a common reason many initiatives are killed off too soon. While banks need to change, and do so quickly, it can easily take 2–3 years for a new business to become profitable. Even then, it often takes 7–10 years to become truly successful. And so, everyone involved – and particularly those in the executive suite – needs a healthy dose of patience.

MAKING A BREAKTHROUGH

In view of the failure of traditional incubators and accelerators to deliver because of their ad hoc, experimentation nature, we think a much better plan is to concentrate on what an incubator's true purpose should be, and that is to identify gaps in the value chain and find ways to fill them.

This is best done through a breakthrough incubator. Instead of simply doing something and seeing what might happen, this kind of development space is designed to build a prototype of a new venture from initial idea through to launch and scale-up. With this 'build-operate-transfer' approach, there's a much greater chance of creating a commercially viable venture that can then be successfully integrated back into the parent bank.

And, because they're designed to make things happen in a more controlled and focused fashion, breakthrough incubators can typically move a new venture to launch in just a year or two, rather than three or four normally required for a start-up. They can do this because of the way they really integrate technical, commercial, operational and strategic elements, and move them forward simultaneously. In that way, multiple solutions can often be developed in parallel.

To explore more marketable ideas as quickly as possible, financial institutions could build a portfolio of multiple fintech start-ups as digital 'bets.' In 2018, Alabama-based BBVA did this by starting its own internal venture group, with offices in the tech hubs of London and San Francisco. The aim was to fund and foster big ideas that would disturb the banking establishment.

The whole aim of this New Digital Business (NDB) concept is to partner with, invest in and acquire disruptive technology companies of any size or stage of development.

BNP Paribas sought to do this when it set up BNP Paribas Capital Partners, with a view to taking direct minority stakes in innovative start-ups that are reinventing financial services and insurance.

The bank is now supporting a wide range of entrepreneurs who are focused on AI, data, blockchain and cybersecurity. To date it has made strategic investments in Serena Data Venture, Viola Fintech and Ventech China.

THE GAME-CHANGING BREAKTHROUGH INCUBATOR

If you aspire to stand out in your marketplace, a breakthrough incubator can be a game-changer by enabling you to create new revenue streams and develop new services, business units and ventures, as shown in the illustration below.

Breakthrough Incubator for growth in the core business, diversification, convergence...

Creating a new product/service	Creating a new capability/Business Unit	Creating a NewCo/JV
▪ End-to-End approach: opportunity assessment, product development, commercialization, product launch and scale-up ▪ Example: Sycamore	▪ Outside the customer's comfort one ▪ Strategic for the company ▪ Typically adopting new technologies, skills, etc. ▪ Example: X by Orange; VW Elli	▪ Fully funded by customer or with financial/industrial partners/investors ▪ Example: Snaps, EOS-X, Orange Seguros

Source: ADL Research

A breakthrough incubator can be used for rapid prototyping, a concept usually associated with manufacturing. It can be used to develop financial products, through a process of 'ideation,' to determine proof of concept; 'evidence gathering,' to see if the proposed solution addresses the challenge and provides proof of solution; and 'transformation,' the make-it-happen phase, where the project goes mainstream. By using rapid prototyping, banks can invest more time and resources in creating a minimum viable product (MVP) that can then be integrated into the business and rolled out into the marketplace.

ESTABLISHING AN INCUBATOR

The first step in the breakthrough process is setting up the incubator itself. This must be based on a detailed and inspiring vision of what you want to achieve: a precise understanding of future customer needs and how these might be practically met. If you don't know this up front, you'll just be flying in the dark.

What's needed is much more than merely espousing some broad goal, like 'finding new ways to include AI in the supply chain.' Such bland, directionless statements are of little help when it comes to prioritizing investment or choosing the best external innovation partners.

Of course, there's also the opposite danger: being overly prescriptive. If you second-guess what the best technological solution will be when establishing the scope of the incubator, or decide in advance the number of experiments you're going to run, you will close down potential avenues for innovation. There has to be wiggle room for ideas to develop, sometimes unexpectedly.

The set of parameters used to measure the success of an incubator project should also be determined at the outset. Possible metrics could include how well a new start-up scales; the degree of collaboration with other parts of the bank; the level of internal buy-in that's been achieved during the process; the quality of talent attracted to the project; the number of challenges overcome; or the effectiveness of a particular incubator element. These 'soft' output measures are much better indicators of success than speculative revenue or profit numbers that *might* be achieved at some unknown point in the future.

Once such parameters are agreed upon, the project needs to be championed by the senior leadership team, and particularly the CEO. Without a top-down approach, the project won't be taken seriously. The greater the visibility it has in the organization, the less likely it is to be pigeon-holed as just a bit of 'R&D.' That would of course be the kiss of death.

WHO'S IN CHARGE?

The next step is to create a governance team made up of stakeholders representing all business lines. This way, the incubator won't feel isolated or disconnected from the rest of the organization, something that again would lead to people seeing it as a side project.

When choosing the stakeholders to bring onboard, be careful that none has an agenda that could compete with the aims and purpose of the incubator and – intentionally or not – be counter to its success.

After this, there's the question of whether the incubator is going to be an internal or external vehicle. An internal model, where the incubator is managed by an in-house team, would certainly provide more potential for control. However, without third-party involvement, it could also lead to much slower progress. And, there's always the potential for contamination from distorting corporate influences, because there isn't complete isolation from the rest of the bank.

This is why we suggest that a breakthrough incubator be managed by an independent outsider. This helps keep operations at arm's-length from existing brands that might otherwise smother a new venture before it's born.

Whichever option is decided on, the incubator must be run by a cross-functional 'dream team' with diverse capabilities and experience. Members should be motivated, vested in making the incubator work and entrepreneurially minded. They should also have a strong understanding of the way large banking environments work, and know-how to get the most commercial pull from the latest technologies. Ideally, they should also have fintech experience or a track record in building a start-up.

They must also possess the right attitude, as these are the people who are going to shape the incubator's culture, ensure that it leverages solid technical skills, and steer how it engages with the bank and others. HR must make sure that they're not recruiting square pegs for round holes, because that will prove problematic in what's going to be a relatively small team.

And while new technologies, processes and ventures are the most obvious candidates for 'incubation,' there's no reason why they could not be used in exactly the same way by banks to accelerate changes in their broader corporate culture.

We will look in more detail at the notion of creating a digital corporate culture in the next chapter.

WHEN INCUBATION'S DONE

Once you have proof of concept (POC), we move on to the penultimate step, which is the point at which the new business must either be integrated into mainstream operations or killed off.

This is the most difficult phase of all because it's where all the bear traps are hidden. It's now that the bank must answer some hard questions about who's going to be responsible for any transition. If you leave this to an existing business unit, they might try to shoehorn it into existing operations or brands. This could lead to the dilution, or even undoing, of all the good work done in the incubator and prove detrimental to the potential value of a new venture.

There is also the question of timing. If integration is attempted too soon, the new venture could be crushed by the sheer weight of legacy processes that it's trying to reshape. On the other hand, err too much on the side of caution, and delay for too long, and it could lose momentum and end up increasingly sidelined. This would have implications for how quickly a bank can scale up.

A better approach is for the new business to go through a transitioning process during which it is given its own standalone governance and structure.

This would involve putting in place key functions – supply, operations, marketing, commercial and finance – to support it. After this, there would be a 'get to know you' period during which the new venture and the existing business would learn about each other and make adjustments accordingly. The knowledge gleaned during this handover phase should be documented, for use in setting up future breakthrough incubators.

The speed with which all this happens depends on how well the bank's C-suite and innovation leaders agree on what integration will actually look like. For instance, will the new venture be run as a completely separate business unit, or as a wholly owned subsidiary? How is it going to be financed and controlled? And then, how and when will it be brought to market? There will also need to be consensus on revenue expectations for the new business.

If all goes well, such issues will be resolved without bloodshed. With luck and a fair wind, the new venture will seamlessly transfer from its surrogate mother into the parent bank, where it will flourish as a subsidiary or perhaps even become the new model for the entire bank.

WHO'S INCUBATING WHOM?

Incubators and accelerators offer great opportunities for testing disruptive new solutions, business models and technologies. Unfortunately, 80–90% of innovation centers are a massive waste of resources because they don't deliver on their innovative promise. But, there are financial institutions that are using them to great effect.

The Barclays Accelerator, which is run with the bank's Colorado-based technology partner, Techstars, offers 13-week introductory programs in London, New York and Tel Aviv.[248] They give participating financial start-ups access to mentors, marketing wherewithal and investment opportunities. Barclay's and Techstars take a joint 6% share in each company thereby 'accelerated.'

Then there are Deutsche Bank's Innovation Labs.[249] These support the bank's digital strategy by developing solutions through a global network of start-ups. The labs make it easy for start-ups to find their way into Deutsche, helping their ideas become reality faster.

In 2019, the Spanish bank BBVA launched its Open Innovation Acceleration Program, a nine-month course for start-up entrepreneurs. Participants receive expert guidance and support from senior leaders in the bank on topics such as sales, marketing and implementing technology.

Societe Générale in France has its internal intrapreneurship program, which supports the development of some 30 start-ups at any one time.[250]

Once the bank has confirmed a venture's potential, it is either developed as a project that will become a business unit or passed to the group's investment fund, Societe Générale Ventures, which is dedicated to growing internal and external start-ups.

Also in France, BNP Paribas has a lab 100% dedicated to developing intrapreneurial ideas.[251] In 2019, it deemed 12 projects out of 150 applications worthy of putting through a four-month acceleration program, with the aim of finding business sponsors and further financing.

Goldman Sachs's in-house incubator, GS Accelerate, enables its employees to develop "ideas that can deliver best-in-class solutions" for the bank's clients.[252] The lab has helped Goldman move into new business areas, manage risk better and tackle inefficiencies in its operations. So far, it has invested in all kinds of fintech ideas, in areas like blockchain, data analytics, insurance, personal finance, wealth management, financial services software, lending, real estate, regulatory technology, payments and settlements. Through this mechanism, the bank is currently invested in some 25 start-ups.

When Citi Treasury grew tired of its expensive, labor-intensive accounts-receivable processes, the bank's VC arm invested in High-Radius Corporation, a firm specializing in 'receivables technology.' The result was Citi Smart Match, a software program that can use AI and machine learning to create more efficient automated systems for comparing payments expected and payments received.[253]

Citi Group now has innovation labs in Dublin, London, New York, Singapore, Tel Aviv and other cities, where the work is often focused on internal innovation and research. It also offers a four-month accelerator program for outside start-ups, 100 of which have been accelerated since the program's inception.

In 2016, JP Morgan launched In-Residence, an incubation program that gives emerging fintechs access to the institution's facilities, systems and expertise for six months.[254] But it's not just outsiders that can benefit. If any of the bank's 50,000 tech employees want to come forward with an idea for a fintech venture, they can. If they get green-lighted for development, founders can become chief executives of their brainchild. That's quite an incentive to innovate.

Of course, large banks have the resources to take more chances with their information. They can afford to take more 'punts' that fail, but this doesn't preclude smaller banks from also exploring new ideas and generally being more innovative.

Akbank in Turkey is a good example, because they see themselves going through a process of continuous change rather than aiming to meet particular milestones. "As a bank we are a very pro-change," explains the CEO, Hakan Binbasgil, "and have been actually changing our institution for the last 20 years."

This means that every day, the bank's focus is on creating superior customer service, introducing digitization, capitalizing on advanced analytics, building new infrastructure and, above all, people. That encompasses both customers and staff. "It's by attracting the right talent that we will change our business," says Binbasgil.

TECH MATES

Of course, it's unlikely that a legacy bank will want, or be able, to do all the work involved in setting up sandboxes or any kind of breakthrough incubator on its own. Most will need to find a tech partner to help them, either right from the start or once the incubator structure is established. There is the added benefit that the fintech approach to life will potentially rub off on a bank's employees.

Finding a suitable collaborator isn't necessarily easy. It can be particularly vexing if you're a smaller institution, without the resources to identify and vet potential partners and then develop a meaningful relationship with them. Another potential stumbling block for banks looking for a 'tech mate' is their culture. The staid, slow, conservative corporate aroma they exude isn't all that attractive to a tech firm that's built on speed and innovation.

If that can be overcome, there will still be a need for both sides to possess complementary visions, values and goals. Perhaps most importantly, it's critical that each side feels the other is sharing some degree of risk. Having skin in the game helps ensure that everyone is committed to a project's success, and it makes them less willing to walk away should things get difficult.

Any kind of partnership is likely to require the bank to make considerable adjustments to the way it works, if the sheer weight of its internal processes isn't enough to defeat the whole point of the partnership and kill an initiative before it's begun.

This hopefully is much easier to achieve if a bank understands the need for a new openness and collaborative approach, where data flows seamlessly between departments and isn't locked away in silos.

In large part, this will hinge on instilling an appropriate corporate culture. There's more on that in the next chapter.

CHAPTER 14

HOW WE DO THINGS AROUND HERE

"In 2020, COVID-19 forced organizations around the world to enact radically new ways of working and operating amid the pandemic's human and economic impacts. Organizations had to respond to a sudden, unforeseen crisis whose rapidly changing nature confounded efforts to predict and plan for events. The pandemic brought into sharp relief the pitfalls of strategies that envision moving from point A to point B on a static path, and that assumes one has years, not months or weeks, in which to rethink outdated views and establish a new set of truths. As we all learned the hard way, in an environment that can shift from moment to moment, the paths and timeframes to achieving one's goals must shift as well."

2021 DELOITTE GLOBAL HUMAN CAPITAL TRENDS REPORT[255]

Technology is great, but in the end, transformation is all about people. For success, making a digital shift requires a fifth dimension, which is culture. This is something banks hate to talk about because it feels soft and fluffy and so 'unbanklike.' But that's a big mistake, because culture is absolutely key. As Peter Drucker put it: "The culture eats strategy for breakfast."

Unfortunately, for legacy banks, one of the biggest barriers to change is that their leaders don't know anything other than the universal model they've grown up with. And, with no experience in how fintechs and technology companies operate, they have no sense of how their reinvented bank should look, feel or be run.

So, they guess.

That's why organizations often make token nods to change that result in things like dress-down Fridays, or redesigning a workplace to create a cool warehouse look. These things have been tried, and they don't work.

This is rather like 'putting lipstick on a pig,' to use that quaint American expression frequently trotted out at election time to deride one candidate's idea or another. These cosmetic gestures do nothing to make a bank's legacy culture fit for purpose, nor do they appeal to the hype-sensitive younger employees they presumably aim to please.

Millennials prioritize 'people and culture fit' above everything else. They're more interested in work environment and growth than being patronized by tone-deaf senior management.[256] How management chooses to treat them has an impact, for better or worse.

Every organization has a culture, even traditional legacy banks, even if it's just there by default. The amalgamation of attitudes, beliefs, habits and behaviors reflects a mix of adherence to organizational norms and how far employees stray from them.

Bringing about cultural transformation isn't a nicety that can be dealt with superficially. It is a prerequisite for any legacy bank interested in implementing a wider transformation. Lacking this, it wouldn't be able to achieve the speed and lightness of touch necessary to compete with the fintechs.

This is important stuff, given that 90% of unsuccessful digital transformation attempts failed because the underlying culture did not change. That's often because business leaders believe they know what a 'good' organizational culture looks like, while in reality they have a vague notion, at best. They don't fully understand or appreciate the skills that will be needed by banks in the future.

All too often, old-line CEOs see anything related to 'training' or 'people' as wholly the preserve of the HR team. As a result, the workforce is not strategically reshaped, employees lack the requisite skills and competencies, and they're ill equipped for the journey ahead.

That is no longer acceptable for any bank looking to move forward.

THE COMPLEXITY
OF CHANGE

Achieving any kind of cultural change is difficult because it's not like a technology stack you could just buy tomorrow on the open market. It involves uprooting people's routines, which can be an altogether wrenching experience. But that, of course, is the whole point of transformation: to break away from the norm.

This will in all likelihood create a psychological strain, and people will resist, because stretching them away from their comfort zone is bound to involve discomfort.

"Every organization has an immune system and defense mechanisms against change that is often linked to individual agendas, conflicting key performance indicators or unclear instructions," says Martin Lindstrom, a consultant to Standard Chartered's Ministry of Common Sense, an initiative aimed at cutting the bank's tangle of red tape. "This creates a second invisible layer within the business."[257]

So, what we're dealing with is a complex organism that is being made ever more complex by technology that significantly multiplies the number of interactions between employees, departments, suppliers and customers. That's even the case in a 'non-digital' workplace. All of this makes organizations increasingly disparate and fragmented, which inevitably shapes their culture.

If you want to make a difference to a bank's zeitgeist, any successful change management requires unwavering commitment from those at the top. Leadership must effectively rebel against the organization, as it exists, and its entire infrastructure. This is why the old grandees, with their 'wisdom' from the past, are seldom the risk-takers needed to take a bank forward.

CHANGING THE STRUCTURE

Creating such a new culture within any organization is going to involve disruption and contrarian thinking if previous ways of doing things are to be expunged. And expunged they must be, because if they remain embedded, old employee habits just won't die. Ingrained behaviors rooted in 'the way we do things here' will once again bubble to the surface and take up residence by default.

If you are to become a more agile business, you need to focus not on organizational hierarchies, which are all about control, but on roles. The focus must be who's going to do what, and how, and why.

This is a big thing for a bank, because you're asking people to move on from the typical, staid hierarchical structure, where the scope for free thinking is limited. Instead, you're pushing them into an utterly new environment, where people are allowed to think and make decisions for themselves. Where information is shared rather than kept protectively hidden away by departments. Where the onus is on making things happen quickly – getting things done – instead of 'waiting to see' or cautiously tiptoeing around and second-guessing everything.

An ambidextrous CEO will be willing to create that internal revolution, but not everyone will. Some will shrink from becoming leader of the pack and pulling the organization along on the ambidextrous journey it needs to pursue. They'll be happy to lay low and simply go through the motions.

The ambidextrous CEO must pivot toward outward orientation versus navel-gazing, delegation over control, boldness rather than caution, and action over endless planning. In a risk-averse business like a legacy bank, such wholesale rewiring will not come naturally or easily.

As a result, there will always be internal resistance, especially in the face of fundamental changes to the bank's existing business and operating models. This doesn't mean the senior leadership team needs to embark on an orgy of reckless organizational change, or expect their employees to behave like a bunch of thrill-seeking adrenalin junkies. Far from it. We've seen what can happen when the foot comes off the brake too dramatically; that didn't end well for RBS.

Such rethinking forces a bank to become far more tolerant of risk and potential failure. This sort of personality shift will not sit well with a tentative, micro-managing CEO who will almost certainly fail if they take on such a task. Again, we need a truly ambidextrous leader who can roll with the punches and commit to making it happen.

Assuming that senior leadership is up for the challenge, what needs to be done?

CULTURE – THE CEO OWNS IT
BUT EMPLOYEES MAKE IT

For any transformation-focused CEO, one of the first jobs must be to decide what the bank's culture is going to be. As we've said, this might sound a bit warm and fluffy in the buttoned-down world of legacy banking, but it's incredibly important. More than three-quarters of us would consider a company's culture before we'd apply for a job there, and over half consider culture more important than salary when it comes to job satisfaction.[258]

Internal culture is in large part determined by an organization's business ambitions and how it wants to position itself in the marketplace. If it wants to be perceived as modern and cutting-edge, that had better be reflected in its employees and the overall 'sense' of a business.

Inevitably, the culture somewhere like WeBank – where 80% of employees are engineers – is going to be very different from somewhere like HSBC. In any event, one's culture just wouldn't work for the other.

Simply put, the culture must be fit for purpose. To ensure that it is, the CEO must recognize that cultural change is an essential component of being a strong, ambidextrous organization. You have to look at what you're trying to achieve, and what sort of workplace, employees, attitudes, skills and values will take you there. One thing is certain: a culture must be completely aligned with the bank's evolving business model.

The importance of technology in the modern banking organization almost certainly guarantees that a legacy institution will err on the side of 'nerdiness,' given the need for a high percentage of engineers and software technicians.

On the other side of the fence, many tech-focused companies may have to question whether their original start-up culture remains applicable as the company matures. Google has a reputation for putting its engineers and computer scientists first, but could that do it future harm longer-term, because of the way it limits diversity?

This is another issue where the CEO must take an ambidextrous approach – one culture for now, but with an eye on what's needed heading into the future.

But while a company's culture is essentially 'owned' by the CEO who will decide its nature, their ambitions will always be hijacked by those who actually make an organizational culture: the people who work there. They shape the culture in the first place, and reinforce it daily through their behaviors and actions, some of which will be consistent with the culture that's required and others of which won't.

This means that any CEO wanting to create a specific cultural state must first change existing employee mindsets to fit, and then recruit only those who align with the new environment. More than 90% of leaders acknowledge that some kind of talent change will be required if they're to succeed with their digital transformation, with 44% believing this will need to be extensive.

That's up 7 percentage points up from 2020 to 2021, which suggests managers are starting to grasp the scale of the task ahead.[259]

This puts the leadership team at the very center of things. They have to constantly reinforce the new norms, not so much by telling people what to do, but by inspiring, nurturing and persuading them to act in another way. If the vision is painted compelling enough, people will naturally come under its gravitational pull.

Savvy leaders may want to identify and train 'change champions,' to serve as local advocates in their departments. They can sell in change and become a channel for both negative and positive feedback about proposed initiatives and actual pilot schemes.

This obviously makes strong, transparent internal communication immensely important, since this is the only way to build the trust and engagement that encourages compliance with what at first will be an 'alien' set of rules.

Not least of these will be how performance is measured. Building trust with customers requires a review of promotional mechanisms, since rewarding individual employees for high-volume sales could be at odds with trying to provide the best possible client service.

Leaders can never communicate too much or too often during a legacy bank's transformation, if the benefits of major change are to be fully understood by their teams.

And, such communication needs to go far beyond the usual, superficial 'feel good' speeches indulged in by CEOs. Instead, they must include hard facts, detailed information and real-world case studies showing change in action. If employee feedback is asked for and given, it should always be acknowledged and never dismissed as trivial.

While using every channel available and engaging clearly with employees is important, so is strong external communication that will influence customers, attract new talent and gain the support of all other outside stakeholders. Once a board is fully signed up to support a transformation plan, the bank must communicate its intentions effectively to the capital markets, so analysts are in the loop and can track the right performance measurements.

NURTURING CULTUR

While many struggled during the recent recession, USAA, a financial services firm serving American military families, experienced some of the most robust growth in its 88-year history. Bloomberg, *Businessweek* and others gave it top marks for financial strength and customer service.

This is largely a reflection of the inspirational leadership of Joe Robles, a former US Army general who took over as president and

---

CEO in 2007 with the ambition of taking the company to even higher levels of excellence. That required shifting the strategy away from siloed lines of business that served members individually to an entire enterprise that did the right thing because it was the right thing to do.

Robles took on this role with enthusiasm. Calling himself the Chief Culture Officer, he created six cultural principles he dubbed 'My Commitment to Service.'[260] Robles, who retired in 2015, attributes much of USAA's success to these.

"People ask me all the time, what is USAA's secret sauce?" he once said. "I keep telling them that a big piece of it is the culture of this company, and it has given us a huge business advantage. You can see the improvement in customer satisfaction. You can see the business results and how we outperformed a lot of our competitors over the past three to four years."

He said that improving and strengthening the company's culture was an ongoing objective. "Culture is not a gimmick, a promotion, or a one-time event. People think you can take a strong culture and build it up, and then just move on to something else, and then it's going to sustain itself. Unfortunately, that's not the way the world works."

And what's Robles' advice to other leaders and CEOs who are leading culture change?

"People ask me all the time if I think it's important for the CEO to own the culture or whether I should have a Chief Culture Officer on my staff. I am the person most accountable to the board of directors for the results of this company and the culture of this company, so I am, by definition, the Chief Culture Officer.

"One of the things that I will pass on to my successor will be a strong and vibrant culture that is focused on our customers, that is focused on our employees, and that continues our history of service and strong financial results. If I can do that," he said, "then I will have done my job as a CEO."

Under Robles' leadership, USAA membership grew by 53%, revenues by 45%, and assets owned and managed by 59%. This was all in the midst of one of the worst economic downturns in recent history, during which the company still returned $7.3 billion to members and customers through dividends, distributions, bank rebates and rewards. It also remained among just a handful of companies to earn the highest ratings for financial strength from Moody's, AM Best and Standard & Poor's.[261]

NO SQUARE PEGS
IN ROUND HOLES

One thing is clear: whatever its trajectory, a bank will require a workforce with higher cognitive skills, particularly those with creativity, critical thinking abilities, decision-making chops and an understanding of complex information processing. As Georgetown University professor Cal Newport, author of *Deep Work*, points out: "Two core abilities for thriving in the new economy are the ability to quickly master hard things and the ability to produce at an elite level, in terms of both quality and speed."

For HR, recruiting like this has never easy in the best of times, and will only get harder when an organization is in the throes of a cultural change. As it is, 80% of financial services firms say they have trouble hiring and retaining the talent they need.

And it's not just a case of hiring the best people; it's very much about hiring the *right* people. If employees are out of synch with you as their employer, that will hurt your business, particularly in a small team.

Historically, banking management has tended to blame their lack of dynamism on an inability to attract the right people. Perhaps there is a grain of truth in this, as not having the right people on board will certainly have an impact. But why can't legacy banks get the people they need?

Part of that stems from the perceived image of legacy banks. Who wants to work in what you think is going to be a rigid, unexciting place when you believe you'd have a much better time in the weird and wacky world of a cool, young fintech?

If banks are to adopt the mentality of a start-up, they'll need a far wider range of talent from outside their comfort zone, and the more diverse the mix of candidates, the better. A 2013 study by a team of European researchers found that this better-blended workforce will be less constrained by existing solutions and more likely to bring novel ideas to the table.[262]

In part, legacy banks are being forced to cast recruitment nets ever wider because they're fishing for specialist skills in what are often small talent pools. And the demand for those with the right skills is only going to become greater as technology suffuses the workplace. After all, you can only make the most of innovative new systems when your people know how to make, run and use them.

And right now there's extraordinary demand for those with the right skills, since even in Europe's most technology-focused banks, only 20–25% of jobs are currently tech-oriented. In many institutions, it could be as few as 10%. Imagine what will happen as more and more traditional financial institutions finally recognize the need to recruit cutting-edge skills to run their new systems?

As it is, banks are turning to recruitment methods they haven't previously used to find potential hires. This is another area where banking has been slower than other sectors, which have been more creative in their new-hire processes. The digitization of HR has helped other industries bring much greater speed, focus and effectiveness to the war for talent.

Unilever, the consumer goods giant, has augmented its more conventional recruitment and hiring tools with AI, social media, and even online games. The technology firm Cisco is now running recruitment 'hackathons' and has set up digital HR initiatives, like its YouBelong@Cisco app to help new hires and their managers during onboarding.[263] Even an old-school corporation like IBM is now using innovative HR solutions, like the digital learning platform that's customized for each of its 350,000 employees.[264]

CREATING A DIGITAL WORKPLACE

Along the way, it's increasingly important that new staff are comfortable with evolving technology, because AI, machine learning, automation and other systems will increasingly transform the workplace and require everyone to interact with ever-smarter automation.

Fortunately, this is exactly the kind of workplace where many want to spend their days. A Deloitte survey found that nearly two-thirds of employees would prefer to work in a digital workplace where they could tap into strong online social networks. Rather than distracting workers, there's evidence that digital networking can actually make them 7% more productive and lead to a 20% increase in employee satisfaction.

By leveraging instant messaging, using virtual meeting tools and automating workflows, banks can create more transparent working environments where all team members can track the status of every task or project they're involved in. Of course, while these tools can be a force for the good in a bank's transformation, it all boils down to their benign application by senior and middle management. If used as a means of control rather than a route to creative efficiency, they'll instead create an intrusive culture that will ultimately affect the bank's performance and reputation.

Such things all feed through to improved employee retention, which can increase by as much as 87% under the right conditions. That's a good sign because it means employees are happy, and customers like businesses that are 'being nice.' Happy staff are good for business. According to research by Glassdoor, the anonymous employee-company review site, every percentage point increase in customer satisfaction can be linked to a 4.6% increase in a company's market value.[265]

GETTING READY FOR
A CHANGING WORLD OF WORK

One difficulty facing both legacy banks and fintechs – as well as every other kind of tech-based firm – is that in all major economies' populations are aging, and that's shrinking the workforce.

So, there will be an increasing need to cater to a younger generation of 'digital natives' whose attitudes toward work and the workplace can be very different from older generations'.

Younger people want to be part of an organizational environment where diversity, social consciousness and environmental issues matter. They're also looking for better work-life balance, convinced that work should be fun and not take over your life. This means that many younger employees don't want the long hours or the onerous commute their parents endured. If they don't see their employers adopting progressive policies, such as flexible work hours, they'll find a job elsewhere.

If further evidence were needed that banks must become more culturally flexible, look no further than the pandemic lockdowns that have required employees to work from home. Financial institutions have had to react quickly to that dramatic change, which few could have imagined just two years earlier. But while they posed immense challenges, lockdowns forced organizations to creatively reinvent their systems and how they perform under pressure. Those that have been able to maintain client focus and overall user experience through the turmoil will surely emerge better equipped and stronger.

This global experiment in remote working has proven that it's possible to adopt a new model that has minimal impact on productivity. In many cases, in fact, it may even have enhanced it.

Having seen the promised land, many people don't want to return to the tedium of their time-consuming, energy-sapping daily commute. There are indications that half would look for another job if they couldn't work in their preferred location. In the UK, that would mean 7.42 million people switch jobs rather than go back to a traditional, full-time office setting.

Legacy banks need to be ready to accommodate that kind of change in sentiment, because you can be sure that many fintechs will. If they try to impose old ways of working there will be an inevitable pushback.

There are signs that some large organizations are starting to see the way the wind is blowing. Around a quarter of big corporations now say they're open to employing those who don't live close to their offices, and that figure is likely to rise with the seeming success of large-scale remote working.

Goldman Sachs, where Millennials and Gen Zers already make up 75% of the workforce, has done the unimaginable and relaxed its corporate dress code to create a more informal environment, in hopes of being more attractive to younger employees.

Many of the technical, HR and management challenges that come with working from home have already been dealt with, so this shift will not be nearly as seismically disruptive as it might have been.

If legacy banks allow a greater degree of homeworking, this may also enable them to throw out some of the old ways that have hindered innovation and siloed information along business lines. That requires a shift from the static team paradigm to an open operating model, where more can be done by free-lancers and contractors. Many challenger banks already do this, with variable spending associated with third-party fintech and regtech vendors accounting for some 75% of total operating costs.

For legacy banks, of course, changing models like this raises a whole host of governance issues. That will need to be worked through, to achieve the right balance in monitoring employees and preventing risk. Doing it wrong could damage an organization's reputation, productivity and brand. One example of this: robust policies must be put in place to ensure that employees understand the importance of securing confidential information if they're allowed to work in a location of their choice.

ENCOURAGING CREATIVITY

Having said all that, it's not just about technology.

Arthur Yeung, Senior Management Advisor at Tencent, put it this way: "When we think about the digital economy, we sometimes think that everything has to be new or revolutionary. But in the digital world, things like trust and integrity become even more important. Technology has become such a powerful force and can improve our world so much, but without trust and integrity it can also do lots of damage to society, so we must be responsible with this power."

To that end, in 2019 the Chinese conglomerate adopted the mission state-ment, 'Value for Users, Tech for Good.'

Because innovation is so crucial to the future of the legacy banks, one of the most important 'soft' competencies that must be instilled in any new culture has to be creativity. This is not optional for a bank looking to have a sustainable future. Creative entrepreneurial mindsets will be needed to improve relation-ships, simplify processes, cut costs, speed up communications and generally evolve beyond the boundaries that have so limited banks in the past.

Since stagnation and repetition are the enemies of creativity, employees should be encouraged to become 'lifelong learners' who seek new knowledge and regularly explore alternative ways of doing things. This is why some for-ward-looking banks use job rotation to challenge the leadership team.

Creativity must also be sought in recruits and nurtured once they're in posi-tion. Banks can encourage creativity within the organization through problem-solving exercises that stimulate employees to think beyond the obvious.

One challenging exercise is to require people to stretch beyond their well-worn lane, which can be quite energizing. And if they work in creative teams, the more diverse these are, the better. As we touched on earlier, cognitive styles that are too similar lead to groupthink, and that doesn't get you anywhere. An optimal mix of thinkers will help scrutinize and address problems from different angles.

Of course, in any commercial environment, creativity must have a point and purpose. It goes well beyond blue-sky daydreaming. Creativity must be captured and directed through a managed process, aimed at delivering tangible results that are in line with clear business goals. This requires employees to work in a creatively focused way on achieving those objectives.

Giving team members some degree of latitude will help foster creativity, and play to their strengths, which inspire and motivate. Nevertheless, a close eye must still be kept on progress, so adjustments can be made as necessary.

While improving creativity will take time and effort – especially in legacy banks, where there's little tradition of doing things differently – this is one area that isn't notoriously budget-heavy. Even a simple creativity tool like an old-school suggestion box can be an effective way to get the anonymous feedback, sidestepping cultural or corporate 'correctness.' At a more sophisticated level, a Slack or WhatsApp group could be set up for informally sharing ideas.

Regular lunchtime brainstorming sessions are another way for groups to break bread together, share creative ideas and help build a sense of cohesiveness. They can also provide a forum for challenging old assumptions that might prevent a bank from moving forward.

Whether you have an online forum or a physical meet-up, it's critical that participants aren't judgmental about any new ideas, as fear of criticism will discourage participation. A sure-fire killer of creativity is an 'unsafe' environment where people don't feel they can say something different or challenge assumptions, which is precisely what's needed. It is of no help at all to have everyone just agreeing with the status quo when they should be questioning the way things are done.

Managers must give credit for original thinking, even if senior leaders may not always like what they're hearing. This sends a clear signal that creativity is important and valued by the bank.

That's not to say that new ideas shouldn't be put under the microscope. While there should be a focus on creative thinking, *critical thinking* should not be forgotten.[266] In fact, the two go hand-in-hand. Steely-eyed scrutiny is necessary to evaluate potential solutions that spring from creative thinking. Still, new ideas should be given room to breathe before they're subjected to rigorous dissection.

Even the most creative ideas will come to nothing if no one thinks about how they can be commercialized and implemented. Ideally, this should be done by a separate team but, in the hand-off, leaders must ensure that quality ideas don't become hopelessly diluted in the interest of implementation.

While getting the right data to the right people at the right time can create a significant competitive advantage, that isn't going to happen if senior management doesn't support such initiatives by making them part of a data strategy that's aligned with the overall business model.

Delivering such support, particularly during tough times, is at the heart of creating the cultural change that keeps a financial institution alive and relevant in a rapidly reshaping world.

'Survivor organizations' will evolve and adapt to this changing world. The question is, will yours be one of them? In the next chapter, we'll reflect on whether you have what it takes.

CHAPTER 15

CAN BANKS STRIKE BACK?

"It is not the most intellectual of the species that survives; it is not the strongest that survives; but the species that survives is the one that is able best to adapt and adjust to the changing environment in which it finds itself."

CHARLES DARWIN,
On the Origin of Species

So, let's round things up.

We're approaching the end of our look at how the world of banking is changing, driven by a technological disruption that's taking us into uncharted waters, where some will thrive and others will perish.

While this may feel all very new to some, it's actually anything but. If we go back a couple of hundred years, to 18 June 1815, we can see how financial services were being disrupted by technology even then.

On this wet and muddy Sunday, the fateful Battle of Waterloo was fought. Although many knew it was coming, only one among the financial elite — the German financier Nathan Rothschild — had the foresight to station people close to the battlefield, equipped with the best communication technology of the time: the humble carrier pigeon.

The moment it was known that the Duke of Wellington's alliance army had defeated Napoleon, the birds were released to carry that valuable information back to London. This enabled Rothschild to steal the march by using that knowledge to place huge bets in his favor.[267] The killing he subsequently made in UK Commonwealth treasury securities called *gilts* became the foundation of his fortune.

On that day, success was dependent on speed, as it still is. Yet, many legacy banks are still responding too slowly to a changing marketplace. That's either because they lack fast enough 'pigeons' (technology) or because they're shackled by an arthritic mindset that traps them in the past.

It's this inherent sluggishness that makes the legacy banks sitting ducks for the disruptive fintechs that have shoulder-charged their way into a party to which they have not been invited. Their appearance has put immense pressure on many banks that have until now stood the test of time, and some will fall. Others will be irrevocably transformed, either through chance or choice.

TOO BLEAK A PICTURE?

Of course, as we've already noted, if you lead a legacy bank you may not agree with our rather pessimistic conclusion. You wouldn't be alone — some smart, reputable people won't buy into our central premise at all, or think they have sufficient time to make a gradual shift in response to it.

We don't believe that will be possible. From our in-depth research, we feel certain that the contrarians are hastening the demise of fine old banks that are hurtling toward the precipice.

An apt comparison might be what happened to traditional news media 10-15 years, as we touched on earlier. The sector was taken by surprise as, seemingly overnight, the vast majority of advertising went digital. That left the pages of newspapers and magazines devoid of ads, which were their bread and butter.

Similarly, in banking, new technology has brought about a fundamental change in business and revenue models, delivering a beating to those who've hung on to their complex portfolios, staid old offerings and sclerotic infrastructures.

And if you think we're just witnessing the start of a shift to digital transformation, think again. The harsh reality is that leading banks and disruptors are already into their second or even third phase of digitization.

NEW ENTRANTS SHAKE THE TREE

In this topsy-turvy new environment, the non-banks and fintechs are already way ahead of the curve, because they're the ones who set out to disrupt it all in the first place. Their start-up mentality also means they're more focused, aligned, nimble and aggressive, and therefore well placed to exploit the weaknesses of legacy providers.

Some traditional institutions will be better equipped than others to cope. Corporate and investment banks are least likely to have to readjust, because of their deep pockets and the fact that they're relationship-driven. For the universal or retail bank, though, it's a very different picture. We'll say it again: in this game, trying to be all things to all people will nearly always end in disaster.

Even before the financial crisis of '08, large monolithic banks weren't creating value. The stock price of a giant like Bank of America has hardly moved in 14 years.[268] And this isn't confined to a single geography. It's a global phenomenon that's replicated in Europe, South America and the Middle East, and even in China and Southeast Asia, despite their local economies having grown rapidly. Only a handful of legacy banks managed to overcome the harsh capital market discounts and increase their value. The rest – especially those in the west – have lost many times their value over the last two decades.

And things are only going to get worse for those who are ill-prepared for what's happening. The ultra-low interest rate environment means there is no margin to earn the income necessary for transformation, while in parallel, banking fees are being challenged by political and regulatory bodies. Unfortunately for them, banks will soon face a deluge of NPLs as a post-pandemic recession bites.

IS THERE A WAY BACK?

In their defense, legacy banks have two weapons they can call upon. The first is their huge financial resources, which are second only to Big Tech. The second is a client base that remains relatively sticky, as traditional banks are still trusted to look after people's money. However, they're seeing more and more of their customers defecting to non-banks that better serve their needs.

Another ray of hope for legacy banks is that fintechs are swimming with a lot of other sharks. For instance, the market for payment companies is seriously overcrowded, with many players starved of capital and staring down empty balance sheets. Inevitably, this will create a bloodbath from which many non-banks won't emerge.

Does this mean that the legacy banks have a lifeline after all, and aren't necessarily doomed to fail? Yes, it does.

Does it mean that the legacy banks are capable of turning around their losing position? Again, that's right… but only if they follow the ambidextrous model we've set out here.

Though the way ahead appears murky, for those bankers who are brave, creative, have a clear picture of their industry's point of arrival and are willing to reshape their organization accordingly, there's a unique opportunity to place themselves front and center in the emerging new financial ecosystem.

Unfortunately, those with undifferentiated, run-of-the-mill strategies, who continue to spread their resources too widely across geographies, business lines, capabilities and customer segments, will remain vulnerable to more focused competitors and continue to post sub-optimal returns that disappoint the markets.

For these guys, there is only one fate. They will fall prey to the predators prowling Wall Street, looking for cheap acquisitions they can asset-strip to the bone.

SMALLER SHARE, BIGGER PIE

If this weren't enough, technology is accelerating the erosion of boundaries between traditional banking and other sectors. As we've seen, such convergence is enabling outsiders to jump into financial services. This is particularly happening where they have strong horizontal capabilities – Apple and Google are obvious examples. While we don't see these Big Tech players taking over the world, we do see them having an increasing role to play in providing the technological backbone of the industry.

This will further reconfigure the banking landscape and lead to the creation of new financial products and services, driven by the need to stand out and in anticipation of changing consumer demands. Embedded finance, marketplaces and can't-live-without super apps that help people enjoy a more 'frictionless' life are all areas where the fintechs have eased ahead. Each time this happens, they steal a little more of the traditional banks' pie.

The good news is that the pie is likely to get bigger as the addressable banking market expands. Before the pandemic, the number of transactions was on the rise,[269] and levels of consumer credit were growing, thanks to developments such as *buy now, pay later* products. As the marketplace becomes more complex and new segments emerge in response, the customers of banks and non-banks alike will be looking for new solutions to their problems.

Unfortunately for them, many legacy banks won't be around to benefit. They will have become someone else's dinner, except for those in a very select club where only the biggest can play. In their rarefied universe, technology will have an impact, but not to the same degree. Although they will embrace tech developments like blockchain, this will be more at the margins, rather than part of a fundamental reinvention of their business or revenue models.

Most banks will need to retrench, but this should not be seen as a retreat. Rather, it could present an opportunity to release resources that can be reinvested in the creation of the new business model that's needed. We have a good example of this with DBS in India, which switched resources to a digital-only bank model with absolutely no physical presence. As we detailed earlier, this is a successful model that DBS is considering expanding into Southeast Asia.

While banks do have some strategic latitude in choosing their future path, there are overarching forces they'll all be governed by. For one, banking will largely move online, with a narrower range of hyper-personalized offerings being sold through newly evolved ecosystems like marketplaces. Banks will also need to move toward higher-value products and services aimed at previously ignored segments, like SMEs. There is no more mileage in low-margin areas like check clearing, card issuing and custody management, which have been killed off as categories by new entrants.

On the other side of the divide, we predict that because of their market capitalization, the better non-banks, such as Stripe, will increasingly buy legacy banks and just strip them of what they need. The choicest cuts will be the client relationship and customer franchise components. We already have an example of this with LendingClub buying the Boston-based digital bank Radius, which it turned into LendingClub Bank.

And so, after everything, whom might we predict coming out on top in the long-term: legacy banks or the fintechs? Despite all the opprobrium we've heaped on them, we believe that on balance banks might just have the edge, although this will depend on how well they answer a vital set of questions.

— QUESTION ONE —
DO YOU HAVE A CLEAR POINT OF
ARRIVAL FOR THE INDUSTRY?

This is, in many ways, the biggest and most important question of all: when you look into the future, what do you see?

If you don't have a clear industry point of arrival in mind, you'll just find yourself reacting to the latest competitive threat without knowing whether it's an indicator of structural change or just a one-off. In other words, if you aren't disrupting, you're the one who is being disrupted, and it's not difficult to see where that disruption is coming from. Just take a look at what's happening to the global fintech market, which was worth $127.66 billion in 2018. By 2022, its value is expected to reach $309.98 billion as new entrants pile in.

And with them come different, destabilizing ways of doing business, such as 'triangular strategies' that allow them leveraging assets and channels banks don't have. Or, there's embedded finance, which along with the rise of e-commerce across many markets and channels offers the opportunity for exponential growth. For instance, in the US, the size of the embedded finance market is forecast to equal that of Big Tech – in other words, about half the value of today's global banking market.

As the traditional value chain is dissolved by these disruptors, it's being replaced by a much wider financial ecosystem consisting of many niches. This is creating a world where, at least for now, capital-intensive models still co-exist alongside the capital-light.

In this hybrid business environment, the old-school British banking model that has for so long underpinned financial services is looking increasingly irrelevant and creaky. If retail banks are to maintain any kind of position in the market, they will need to turn to a balance-sheet-light model that revolves around selling third-party products rather than recycling deposits into new loans.

And for that, they will need a very different set of capabilities.

Of course, as with any transformation, there will be inevitable peaks and troughs, but we do believe this fintech disruption will continue long-term… and we aren't the only ones. If we take market cap as a good proxy for financial resilience – which it is, like it or not – we can see that the markets are more interested in looking forward, at future value, rather than yesterday's balance sheet.

What's happening to banks is, of course, part of a much bigger economic shift in the marketplace. As Anne Bennett, CEO of the National Australian Bank, says: "The largest movie house owns no cinemas, the world's largest taxi company owns no taxis, and increasingly, large phone companies own no telco infrastructure. What then is the future asset for banks?"

Her answer?

"Experience."

But that's of little use if it's being applied in the wrong direction, fighting long-lost battles.

This makes understanding what the industry's point of arrival will be a key question. It's a question that requires some imaginative, and perhaps painful, thinking.

While that arrival point will be different for every bank, given the uniqueness of each, a common requirement is that it should be far, far away from where the bank is now. If it isn't, the senior leadership team just haven't been thinking big enough. And, if that's the case, they probably won't be able to answer the next question.

— QUESTION TWO —
HAVE YOU PICKED THE RIGHT
BATTLES TO FIGHT?

If you recognize that things have changed, and that it's no longer possible to be all things to all people, where are the battlegrounds where you have an advantage or can gain by acquiring new capabilities that'll help you stand out?

A legacy bank hoping to compete against fintechs and non-banks can no longer afford to dilute its resources by pursuing a 'hedging your bets here and there' strategy. Putting your eggs in different baskets may work for an investor, but not a legacy bank. This is the surest way to fail, because it can only yield sub-optimal results and ensure that you keep investing in areas you should have abandoned long ago. Consequently, banks will have some hard business decisions to make regarding whether to serve or exit the existing market.

Instead, you need to lead from the front by focusing on market segments where you can leverage core competencies and embrace new opportunities being created by things like open banking and embedded finance.

As we've said repeatedly, a total bank transformation should never be viewed as a side project for your IT department or something that can be solved with an off-the-shelf, one-size-fits-all solution. This is not work at the margins; it's about finding ways to move the dial by a factor of ten.

It means shedding long-established activities; re-evaluating the levels of risk you're willing to accept; restructuring systems and processes; investing without quibble in the new technology that's needed; and appointing the right kind of leader, who will accept and embrace the ambidextrous model we've detailed here. This will be the only way to differentiate yourself in an increasingly commoditized marketplace, where there's a narrowing of market share and a shrinking of spreads between low- and high-priced services.

Are you ready to do that? And, how will you know if have you an effective strategy in place for doing what needs to be done?

The simplest way to evaluate a bank's corporate strategy of course is to just ask, 'Does it work?' The glib answer is that all depends on what you mean by 'working.'

Using performance metrics will get you only so far. They just tell half the story, since they depend on both the chosen strategy and how well it's been implemented. This means you need to consider other assessment indicators, like the degree of consensus among executives about the corporate goals and policies to be pursued. Or, consider the extent to which you don't have to redirect resources, shelve planned programs or embark on 'meat axe' cost-cutting programs, all of which are obvious signs of strategic planning failure.

All this should be obvious to a bank's leaders, but all too often we see scarce and precious resources deployed on a large scale without any well thought-out point or purpose. Without a clear strategy to follow, it's no exaggeration to say a bank could be heading for bankruptcy.

And let us be clear, digital is neither a strategy nor a business model in itself, but a means to enhance and implement a business model.

— QUESTION THREE —
ARE YOU BEING SUFFICIENTLY DECISIVE AND FAST?

How quickly a legacy financial institution can realistically transform itself is one of its biggest challenges. The change you require must be undertaken now; there is no time for procrastination. It's change or be changed. Survive or be killed.

The time has come for decisiveness, for bold action, for the ruthless implementation of your strategic choices. There is no point in waiting things out, in the hope that this is just some kind of 'ripple in the Matrix.' It is not. What banks are experiencing is a complete shift of the tectonic plates.

Some, like CBA, have benefited from a long runway to achieve their current position. Today, financial institutions don't have that luxury. CBA had 10 years to change, while those at a bank's helm these days must think of doing what's needed in just three!

Is that an exaggeration? Blatant scaremongering? We think not.

Just look at electric vehicles. Five years ago, people thought it would be decades before we'd reach any meaningful inflection point in the market. In Norway, 95% of new vehicle registrations are now for electric cars. The company with the clearest view of the auto industry's point of arrival is Tesla, which long ago saw an 'electric integrated world' of batteries and solar panels and decided how it was going to be part of it. That's the very definition of vision.

Whose fault is it that banks find themselves having to move so fast? Is this a crisis of their own making – a self-inflicted wound? Who else do they have to blame? Surely not the regulators. Aren't they the ones who've been sheltering legacy banks from a full-frontal onslaught by the fintechs?

The reality is that legacy banks should have used their time under this protective regulatory umbrella to prepare for a day when it's not there. 'Transform or be left behind' should have been their mantra, since well before the 2008 financial crisis. It wasn't, because those fat and happy old institutions thought they could keep fending off the inevitable until tomorrow. Well, guys, tomorrow has come, you're out from under the umbrella and it's still raining. Now, banks need to deploy the life rafts.

So where are we in this particular storm?

Well, we have certainly left the first stage of digital transformation behind and are now entering a new chapter. It's a place where convergence is blurring the lines between sectors, leading to the creation of new marketplaces and making the need for speed ever more imperative.

— QUESTION FOUR —
DO YOU HAVE THE RIGHT PERSON IN CHARGE, TO DO WHAT'S NEEDED?

This question is absolutely central to a legacy bank's survival and future success. The bold decisions that are required right now mean that CEOs cannot sidestep the imperatives or hide behind their teams as they go through this transition.

If a bank is to reposition itself, it needs a CEO with the creativity, bravery and vision to bring about real transformation. That's because preparing for banking's point of arrival – whatever you see it as – will require revamping the entire organization, including all front- and back-office processes. It will require trimming labor and IT costs, reducing time to market, improving agility and bringing about greater operational efficiencies. That's a tall order in the best of times, but particularly so given the choppy waters churned up by the pandemic.

There are few, if any, incumbent leaders who've ever had to deal with anything like this. One thing is certain: it can't be accomplished by a chief executive who's bound by old ways of doing business. What's needed is an ambidextrous leader who can deliver significant growth and productivity improvements in the short term, while simultaneously redesigning a bank's business model and moving it to a new place. The likes of BBVA, JP Morgan and Goldman Sachs have risen to the challenge and definitively done so.

This means banking leaders must have in mind a 'transformative vision' that encompasses the desired point of arrival and a path for getting there that doesn't destroy the bank en route. This is quite different from being 'forward-looking,' which involves doing little more than identifying a few industry trends and sketching out some possible options in response.

The truly ambidextrous CEO must also be adept at peering through the blizzard of largely irrelevant information, slicing into the complexity of others' opinions and driving their decisions forward even when they're based on incomplete information.

This is not some superficial PR exercise or an attempt to appease concerned board members. A serious player is needed in the wheelhouse. Do you have one?

— QUESTION FIVE —
DOES THE BOARD ALSO UNDERSTAND WHAT NEEDS TO BE DONE?

Does the board of directors – which appoints the CEO – fully understand how radically the disruptors are disaggregating banking's traditional value chain? Are your board members up to the job?

Do they completely appreciate that legacy models are no longer economically plausible, and that investing in a multitude of businesses to see which one will flourish is no longer a viable option? Do they see that that's a luxury bet they can no longer afford to make?

If they don't 'get it,' and think that we are still in a business-as-usual mode, they will just end up appointing someone to run the business who thinks like them. That's a recipe for disaster.

Unfortunately, if they go down this tired old route, their collective, blindered view of the industry's future will ensure that their bank remains firmly stuck in the past, and they'll hire someone with all the wrong skills and capabilities.

They will not recruit the ambidextrous leader who's needed, defaulting instead to a 'status quo CEO' who by definition has experience making a universal bank perform poorly. That's precisely the last person they need in charge right now.

How do you stop this from happening? Refresh the board by bringing in a more diverse mix of open-minded individuals, representing a range of different gender, race and experience profiles. They must also be tech-savvy, with knowledge – or at least a strong awareness – of such things as artificial intelligence, machine learning, RPA and augmented reality.

And then, to ensure their knowledge stays fresh, the board needs not just someone who 'does IT,' but a true technology advocate. This would be a board member who's not only technically competent, but also an excellent communicator, who can explain simply and clearly the ongoing need for wholesale digital transformation.

If the default position of your board is to look for reasons *not* to spend on tech, then there is cause to worry.

Going digital is about far more than just having an app or customer interface that offers balance and payment features. It means having the courage to scrap the obsolete cost and revenue models that banks have clung to for so long, replacing them with an entirely new value proposition.

So, if you're the kind of executive who has an assistant print out emails for you to read, we urge you to become more enlightened. Open your eyes to how much banking is being changed by technology. Just look at your children, or your grandchildren, and see how comfortable they are with their smartphones, social media apps and online games. They're quickly becoming the ones to whom your bank must cater.

— QUESTION SIX —
ARE YOUR CORPORATE VALUES AND ORGANIZATIONAL CULTURE RIGHT FOR WHAT NEEDS TO BE DONE?

Bankers tend to flinch at the mention of anything that doesn't have hard financial edges to it. This is the traditional bankers' mindset.

Today's leaders have to think in terms of an organization's personality and culture, given how consumers are looking beyond the mere mechanism of a transaction to the look and feel of the company that sits behind it.

As we saw in the last chapter, if your culture isn't right, you're always going to lose out to the fintechs.

Corporate cultural change doesn't happen by accident. It will spring from an open, forward-thinking mindset instilled by the CEO.

Again, this is why landing an ambidextrous leader is absolutely crucial. It will be their job to convince everyone in the organization that the good old days of banking have gone. It's no longer about moving slowly and cautiously, never taking a risk and believing that it's better to do nothing instead of *something*. It's time to throw that dog-eared rulebook out of the window and start again, with a different way of thinking. That is the message that must be pushed into every corner of the organization.

Sadly, many bank executives do not yet understand the impact of something like digitization and how it affects every aspect of the business, from core functions to organizational structure and culture.

We have seen what happened at RBS, where despite the institution's massive resources it was incapable of creating a successful digital bank. It was hamstrung by old ways of thinking that were a total mismatch with the new model. Contrast that with the likes of N26 and Tandem, which broke on through and achieved great things with just pocket change. They did it with a mindset that was focused, fast-moving and aimed squarely at meeting their customers' needs in the best way possible.

Having the right culture in place is also fundamental to recruiting and retaining staff. This is even more important given post-pandemic, with many once-loyal employees reconsidering their options. This has led to what some are calling the 'Great Resignation.'[270] In April 2021, for instance, nearly

4 million Americans quit their jobs – the highest monthly figure ever recorded by the US Bureau of Labor Statistics.

Nearly two-thirds of employees now list corporate culture among the most important reasons for staying with their current employer… or, conversely, for leaving them.[271] In fact, culture is often cited as the single best predictor of employee satisfaction, more so than compensation or work-life balance.[272]

However, the cultural values and day-to-day behaviors of banks are often out of sync with those they want to recruit and retain. All too often, they fail to respect their employees, which is truly unfortunate, because being shown respect is the thing people want most from those they work for.

Is your bank a respectful organization? If it isn't, it needs to become one, especially if you're embarking on a fundamental reorganization. Lack of common respect is universally loathed in the workplace, not just because of its association with layoffs and job instability. It's also associated with change that is often ill-conceived, pursued in haste, implemented inconsistently and vaguely communicated, so that there's no real clarity about how it fits into an organization's longer-term strategy.

There is also the question of how a bank's culture takes into account the growing interest in Environmental, Social, and Corporate Governance (ESG) considerations, which reflects a firm's collective consciousness beyond the purely commercial. This is something that matters to growing numbers of consumers and investors, so banks must be switched on to this change. Are you?

— QUESTION SEVEN —
ARE YOU INVESTING IN THE RIGHT TECHNOLOGY?

As we've previously discussed, technological obsolescence is rife in today's banking environment. Many regulators have woken up to that fact, even if all banks haven't. Those not paying attention to approaching end-of-life hardware and software situations will find themselves in front of a funding abyss, as they scramble to replace their tired old IT infrastructure with something more fit for purpose.

The effective adoption and use of next-generation technology is the road to greater customer engagement, faster product development, better operational management, and improved compliance, efficiency and growth. It will also enrich the customer experience through stellar, hyper-personalized service.

Shifting to new technology will obviously necessitate the writing off of old systems and software, but this is a price that must be accepted. Fortunately, the cost of IT continues to fall and the adoption of cloud-based services can dramatically cut infrastructure costs.

Banks must also become technology-agnostic by using architectures for front-, middle- and back-office processes the allow for easy integration with third-party solutions and facilitate the migration away from legacy IT solutions.

For some banks, this is a bigger mountain to climb than for others. We were vividly we reminded of that during the writing this final chapter. What happened? A very large international bank, a household name, asked for confirmation of a transaction to be sent by fax! Really!

We're talking about technology that is at least a decade out of date. How many offices still actually possess fax machines, let alone private individuals? Rather than asking for a secure means of communication – such as a PDF in which information is embedded – the bank was happy with a document into which one could copy and paste anything, sent from an unverified phone number that could have belonged to anyone, anywhere. Ridiculous.

Technology is the key to the future because it enables a bank of any size or description to solve its biggest, most complex issues. Gartner Research Vice President Brian Burke calls technological innovation a "key enabler of competitive differentiation" and "the catalyst for transforming many industries."[273] From increasing productivity and cutting costs to reaching previously inaccessible market segments and enriching the customer experience, technology makes it all possible.

Of course, given the pace of change that technology brings to every sector, predicting the future of any industry is a highly speculative venture. Who knows how other emerging technologies will impact the banking sector over the next decade? Just because there's no clear or immediate picture of how this might happen, there are no guarantees that they can't or won't have an influence.

And with such breakthrough technologies continually appearing, staying at the forefront of a banking segment is going to challenge even the most innovative financial institutions. Banks will have to work increasingly hard to carve out a niche through innovation, and then protect it with an unrelenting commitment to high levels of service and efficiency improvement. In other words, identifying emerging technologies and then using them to lever an advantage must become a continually repeating process.

Whatever you think will be banking's future point of arrival, it seems sensible to adopt the motto of the Scouts and 'be prepared' for a financial landscape that's going to keep on pitching and shifting.

This is no longer about adapting old tools and products with a new wrapper, but a complete rethinking of the bank and how it operates.

Going head-to-head with competitors who offer a lower-cost product when you have slow, obsolete systems and processes is an impossible task. Legacy banks simply can't compete, because their outdated software doesn't allow it, and the historic web of cross-subsidies – where profitable products prop up the unprofitable – just can't be disentangled.

— QUESTION EIGHT —
ARE YOU PUTTING THE CUSTOMER AT THE FOREFRONT OF EVERYTHING?

For banks, the customer should now be everything. This means any digital transformation must be firmly and fundamentally anchored in the customer value they provide. You can slice, dice and measure anything you want, but this is really the only KPI in town.

Of course, if banks really want to serve their customers, then they need to move away from thinking of them in terms of their demographics and purchase histories, which can be quite misleading about their future needs.

Instead, they need to employ technology to acquire a much greater understanding of those they do business with, and then use this to personalize every interaction with them.

State of the art 'chatbots' and other computer-supported conversation tools are really now a minimum requirement. If you can apply AI to recognize each customer, and then accurately predict the purpose of their every conversation, so much the better. If this helps you become a seamless problem solver who can offer 'one-call resolution,' you'll save your customers time and effort, and that will go a long way in making you the winner of their hearts and minds.

With open banking meaning that disruptive third parties can now access customer data held with another financial institution, banks have no choice but to focus on becoming high-level, data-first organizations themselves, so they can monetize their wealth of customer knowledge. Again, this comes down to investing in the right technology and top-notch analysis.

This creates opportunities, but generally only for those who are early movers, as they're the ones who tend to capture the market and then hold onto their customers. Life is then harder for those who come afterwards.

Have you started the move to becoming a customer-first organization, in more than name only?

— QUESTION NINE —
WHAT STEPS ARE YOU TAKING TO BECOME THE INNOVATIVE ORGANIZATION YOU NEED TO BE?

Running parallel with improvements in short-term performance is the need for effective innovation. This is a bank's engine of change and the fundamental driver of its transformation.

So, have you adopted the agile approach of a non-bank? Create quickly. Seek fast feedback. Double down on your winners. Kill your losers. Then, rinse and repeat. If you haven't, you should do so now. As we've seen, the breakthrough incubator is a great vehicle for encouraging experimentation without compromising the wider organization.

Of course, this means you must always be prepared to accept a higher degree of failure, but the rewards can be worth it. Orange Bank is proof of what's possible: it's able to bring out six to eight product innovations in a month, which is double what a legacy institution could deliver in a year.

Innovation is the engine of growth. According to a PWC study, leading innovators can grow at a rate 16% greater than the least innovative in sectors that include financial services.

So, if senior leaders haven't put a credible innovation strategy in place, a bank will have a hard time delivering the products and services of tomorrow that their customers will be searching for. This isn't possible, of course, if you're content to simply play follow-the-leader and hope for the best.

And as we have said elsewhere, you cannot ever be innovative enough, because the idea that once seemed ahead of its time can become mainstream in a year. Or less!

— QUESTION TEN —
ARE YOU WILLING TO SET ASIDE YOUR CORPORATE EGO?

Only the biggest banks can now realistically expect to go it alone. This means that if traditional banks are to deliver exceptional value to their customers – as they must – they have to be willing to work in partnership with the fintechs, who have the digital knowledge and experience they can tap into to plug any gaps in their offering.

In fact, most banks must be prepared to become part of a much wider ecosystem that's geared toward serving the broader needs of the customer. By doing so, they will be able to turn defense into attack and better protect their position.

In such an environment, it isn't generally possible for a financial brand to stand out as it did before. However, banks can to some extent mitigate this loss of visibility by ensuring that they play a proactive role in shaping any platform they are part of. Santander, for instance, has done this by launching 'Trade Hub,' a proprietary platform that encompasses non-financial services. For many financial institutions, the coming together with third parties to provide sector-specific solutions will be the only way to a long-term future.

But, are you and your bank ready to do this? Are you willing to become less visible? Or, are you going to continue fighting your corner alone?

— QUESTION ELEVEN —
ARE YOU READY, WILLING AND ABLE TO
MOVE TO WHERE YOU NEED TO BE?

This really is the billion-dollar question.

Legacy banks must become lean, mean fighting machines, running capital-light business models like their digital rivals. The only way they can do that is by becoming ambidextrous organizations, capable of balancing immediate survival requirements with a longer-term transformation. For many, this is likely to pose an even greater threat than disruptive newcomers.

If you don't think you need to shift, everything else is irrelevant. As Winston Churchill famously said, "Those that fail to learn from history are doomed to repeat it."[274]

You just need to see far enough ahead.

When we asked some CEOs what they saw as the banking industry's point of arrival, many said that there wasn't one. They meant that it is constantly shifting, so 'take aim, fire and miss' is pretty much the standard process. It's how far you miss that matters.

So, once you've reinvented yourself, you need to do it again and again, through a constant cycle of deconstruction and reconfiguration. It's analogous to the Buddhist notion of an endless cycle of reincarnation – continual rebirth is the foundational doctrine.

As we see it, the point of arrival may shift, but it tends to stay within a certain bandwidth for extended periods – perhaps 10–15 years – before breaking out of these boundaries, probably because of technological change. It then settles into another position, ready for the process to repeat. We can think of universal banking as one of these phases, the rise of the fintechs another, and marketplaces probably the next.

The more astute CEOs will be thinking in terms of these cycles so they can be winners not just in 5–10 years, but 20 or more years down the road.

Having a clear picture of the industry's point of arrival doesn't mean you have to be able to see every step you must take along the way. It would be a pointless waste of time to even try, since the only two certainties now facing any business are constant instability and the shortening of timeframes for doing anything.

We're sure that Jeff Bezos, when he began Amazon in his garage,[275] he had no idea of where his company would be in 25 years, or the degree of disruption it would cause. How could he have conceived of Amazon collapsing the established value chain by providing buyers with an unbeatable combination of lower prices, great convenience and fast delivery? He just began with a disruptive model in mind and took it from there.

After that, it was a matter of being prepared to continually adapt and seize new opportunities as they arose. That's why Amazon.com is no longer just a seller of books, as it was when its first sale – Douglas Hofstadter's book, *Fluid Concepts and Creative Analogies: Computer Models of the Fundamental Mechanisms of Thought* – went out of the door.

But as we've seen, there are no guarantees. Even with the will, smarts and resources, digital transformations can fail. Sometimes this is because of slow and uncertain decision-making that doesn't deliver on a vision. Or, there may be insufficient commitment to bringing in the right people. Or, perhaps, an inability to create an entrepreneurial spirit within the organization or change the staid old banking culture fast enough.

We have written this book not to provide a prescription for the ills of banking, but to help stimulate a discussion about the changing nature of the industry and the choices that bankers face. We've hopefully done so in a way that provides a new depth of understanding.

We have explained why we believe leaders of legacy banks have no choice but to grasp the nettle and begin the difficult task of creating an ambidextrous organization that can generate short-term results for investors while simultaneously freeing up capital to retool the entire business for long-term transformation.

The path any bank takes will depend on how its leaders view the future – banking's point of arrival – and how they answer questions like those above.

In the end, the winners will be those banks that can overcome the inertia that legacy institutions have traditionally been incapable of surmounting.

So, that's it.

Bank executives ... now it's over to you.

ENDNOTES

1. "From the Archives: The ATM is 50," Barclays, last modified 27 June 2017, https://home.barclays/news/2017/06/from-the-archives-the-atm-is-50.

2. Will Kenton, "Big Bang," Investopedia, last modified 25 June 2019, https://www.investopedia.com/terms/b/bigbang.asp.

3. "FTSEurofirst 300 (FTEU3)," Investing.com, accessed 12 October 2021, https://uk.investing.com/indices/ftse-eurotop-300-historical-data.

4. "Implementing Basel III in Europe," European Banking Authority, accessed 12 October 2021, https://www.eba.europa.eu/regulation-and-policy/implementing-basel-iii-europe.

5. "Analysing Differences in Bank Profitability: Europe Versus the US," SEFO, accessed 12 October 2021, https://www.sefofuncas.com/Spains-financial-sector-Challenges-and-risks/Analysing-differences-in-bank-profitability-Europe-versus-the-US.

6. Kenneth Rapoza, "Goodbye, Dow 30,000! Hello, Dow 10,000?" Forbes, last modified 22 March 2020, https://www.forbes.com/sites/kenrapoza/2020/03/22/goodbye-dow-30000-hello-dow-10000.

7. Eustance Huang and Thomas Franck, "US 30-Year Treasury Yield Falls to New Historic Low," CNBC, last modified 15 August 2019, https://www.cnbc.com/2019/08/15/us-30-year-treasury-yield-falls-below-2percent-for-the-first-time.html.

8. Tobias Adrian and Fabio Natalucci, "Financial Conditions Have Eased, but Insolvencies Loom Large," IMF Blog, last modified 25 June 2020, https://blogs.imf.org/2020/06/25/financial-conditions-have-eased-but-insolvencies-loom-large.

9. Marc Jones, "Global Debt Shattering Records – IIF," Reuters, last modified 13 January 2020, https://www.reuters.com/article/uk-global-debt-iif-idUKKBN1ZC1VS.

10. Aaron O'Neill, "China: National Debt from 2016 to 2026," Statista, last modified 2 June 2021, https://www.statista.com/statistics/531423/national-debt-of-china.

11. Marc Jones, "Global Debt Shattering Records – IIF," Reuters, last modified 13 January 2020, https://www.reuters.com/article/uk-global-debt-iif-idUKKBN1ZC1VS.

12. Daniel Boffey and Jennifer Rankin, "EU Leaders Seal Deal on Spending and €750bn Covid-19 Recovery Plans," The Guardian, last modified 21 July 2020, https://www.theguardian.com/world/2020/jul/20/macron-seeks-end-acrimony-eu-summit-enters-fourth-day.

13. Dawn Allcot, "Should You Follow the Rich and Invest in ETFs?" Go Banking Rates, last modified 4 May 2021, https://www.gobankingrates.com/investing/strategy/follow-the-rich-and-invest-in-etfs.

14. Michael Deely, "Profitability Analysis: Is Your Bank's Bottom Line Bleeding?" Big Sky Associates, accessed 22 October 2021, https://www.bigskyassociates.com/blog/profitability-analysis-is-your-bank%E2%80%99s-bottom-line-bleeding.

15. Marc Jones, "S&P Global Expects Coronavirus to Cost Banks $2.1 Trillion," Reuters, last modified 9 July 2020, https://www.reuters.com/article/us-health-coronavirus-banks-creditlosses-idUSKBN24A2B2.

16. Marc Jones, "European Banks Face More than 400 Billion Euros in COVID Loan Losses," Reuters, last modified 21 July 2020, https://www.reuters.com/article/uk-health-coronavirus-europe-banks-idUSKCN24M164.

17. Amie Tsang, "Europe Fines 5 Banks $1.2 Billion for Their Roles in Foreign Exchange Cartels," New York Times, last modified 16 May 2019, https://www.nytimes.com/2019/05/16/business/european-commission-foreign-exchange-banks-fine.html.

18. "Credit Suisse Pleads Guilty to Helping 'Tax Cheats,'" BBC News, last modified 20 May 2014, https://www.bbc.co.uk/news/business-27478532.

19. "Settlements and Fines," Sanctions AML, accessed 12 October 2021, https://sanctionsaml.com/settlements-and-fines.

20. Huw Macartney and Paola Calcagno, "All Bark and No Bite: The Political Economy of Bank Fines in Anglo-America," *Review of International Political Economy* 26 (2019): 630–665.

21. Jill Treanor, "Deutsche Bank and Credit Suisse Agree Multi-Billion-Dollar Settlements with US," The Guardian, last modified 23 December 2016, https://www.theguardian.com/business/2016/dec/23/deutsche-bank-credit-suisse-us-mortgage-securities-barclays.

22. "Deutsche Bank Agrees to Pay $7.2 Billion for Misleading Investors in Its Sale of Residential Mortgage-Backed Securities," Department of Justice, last modified 17 January 2017, https://www.justice.gov/opa/pr/deutsche-bank-agrees-pay-72-billion-misleading-investors-its-sale-residential-mortgage-backed.

23. Nate Raymond, "BNP Paribas Sentenced in $8.9 Billion Accord over Sanctions Violations," Reuters, last modified 1 May 2015, https://www.reuters.com/article/us-bnp-paribas-settlement-sentencing-idUSKBN0NM41K20150501.

24. "Bank of America Reaches $8.5 Billion Settlement on Mortgage-Securities Claims," Huffpost, last modified 6 December 2017, https://www.huffpost.com/entry/bank-of-america-nears-85b-mortgage-settlement_n_886412.

25. "JP Morgan in Record $13bn Settlement with US Authorities," BBC News, last modified 20 November 2013, https://www.bbc.co.uk/news/business-25009683.

26. "Bank of America to Pay $16.65 Billion in Historic Justice Department Settlement for Financial Fraud Leading Up to and During the Financial Crisis," Department of Justice, last modified 21 August 2014, https://www.justice.gov/opa/pr/bank-america-pay-1665-billion-historic-justice-department-settlement-financial-fraud-leading.

27. "Number of Banks Decreasing," Eurostat, accessed 12 October 2021, https://ec.europa.eu/eurostat/cache/digpub/european_economy/bloc-3d.html.

28. F. Norrestad, "Number of FDIC-Insured Commercial Banks in the United States from 2000 to 2019," Statista, last modified 30 November 2020, https://www.statista.com/statistics/184536/number-of-fdic-insured-us-commercial-bank-institutions.

29. "FSB Reports on Global Trends and Risks in Non-bank Financial Intermediation," Financial Stability Board, last modified 16 December 2020, https://www.fsb.org/2020/12/fsb-reports-on-global-trends-and-risks-in-non-bank-financial-intermediation.

30. Karim R Lakhani and Marco Iansiti, Competing in the Age of AI: Strategy and Leadership When Algorithms and Networks Run the World (Boston: Harvard Business Review Press, 2020).

31. "Emerging Markets Respond to Retrenchment of Overseas Banking Operations," Oxford Business Group, accessed 12 October 2021, https://oxfordbusinessgroup.com/overview/swing-balance-following-retrenchment-overseas-operations-numerous-major-banks-how-are-4.

32. Anil D'Silva and David Henry, "Citi Pulls Out of Consumer Banking in 11 Countries, Profit Jumps," Reuters, last modified 14 October 2014, https://www.reuters.com/article/us-citigroup-results-idUSKCN0I31AF20141014.

33. "HSBC speeds up exit from emerging markets," Financial Times, accessed 22 October 2021, https://www.ft.com/content/85642fcc-e50d-11e4-bb4b-00144feab7de.

34. "About HSBC," HSBC, accessed 12 October 2021, https://www.about.hsbc.co.uk.

35. Arjun Kharpal and Antonia Matthews, "Deutsche Bank to Shed 35,000 Jobs, Exit 10 Countries," CNBC, last modified 29 October 2015, https://www.cnbc.com/2015/10/29/deutsche-bank-reports-q3-net-loss-of-60b-euros-barclays-h1-pre-tax-profit-398b.html.

36. "Britain's Barclays to Sell Spanish Assets to Caixabank," Reuters, last modified 31 August 2014, https://www.reuters.com/article/us-barclays-spain-caixabank-idUSKBN0GV0UX20140831.

37. Mark Shapland, "Barclays Sells Its Italian Banking Business to Mediobanca for a £258m Loss," This Is Money, last modified 30 August 2016, https://www.thisismoney.co.uk/money/markets/article-3765212/Barclays-sells-Italian-banking-business-Mediobanca-258m-loss.html.

38. "Barclays' Sale of Portuguese Ops at Discount Likely to Impact Exits in Italy, France," Forbes, accessed 12 October 2021, https://www.forbes.com/sites/greatspeculations/2015/09/04/barclays-sale-of-portuguese-ops-at-discount-likely-to-impact-exits-in-italy-france.

39. "Barclays to Sell Egypt Operations in $500m Deal," Financial Times, accessed 12 October 2021, https://www.ft.com/content/aac2d4be-8a4b-11e6-8aa5-f79f5696c731.

40. "Emerging Markets Respond to Retrenchment of Overseas Banking Operations," Oxford Business Group, accessed 12 October 2021, https://oxfordbusinessgroup.com/overview/swing-balance-following-retrenchment-overseas-operations-numerous-major-banks-how-are-4.

41. Alan Katz, "The Cost of Dirty Money," Bloomberg, last modified 28 January 2019, https://www.bloomberg.com/graphics/2019-dirty-money.

42. "Emerging Markets Respond to Retrenchment of Overseas Operations by Major Banks," Oxford Business Group, accessed 12 October 2021, https://oxfordbusinessgroup.com/overview/swing-balance-following-retrenchment-overseas-operations-numerous-major-banks-how-are-7.

43. Daniel Kurt, "The 10 Biggest Latin American Banks," Investopedia, last modified 21 September 2021, https://www.investopedia.com/articles/investing/111314/10-biggest-latin-american-banks.asp.

44. Arthur E Wilmarth Jr, *The Dark Side of Universal Banking: Financial Conglomerates and the Origins of the Subprime Financial Crisis*, GW Law Faculty, 2009, accessed 12 October 2021, https://core.ac.uk/download/pdf/232645623.pdf.

45. Malcolm Soctt, Paul Jackson and Jin Wu, "A $9 Trillion Binge Turns Central Banks into the Market's Biggest Whales," Bloomberg, last modified 7 July 2021, https://www.bloomberg.com/graphics/2021-central-banks-binge.

46. "Global Finance Names the World's 50 Safest Banks 2020," Global Finance, accessed 12 October 2021, https://d2tyltutevw8th.cloudfront.net/media/document/press-release-worlds-safest-banks-2020-1602792478.pdf.

47. Bill Streeter, "Gen Z Prefers Banks to Big Techs, but Shuns Branches," The Financial Brand, accessed 12 October 2021, https://thefinancialbrand.com/100375/gen-z-banks-big-techs-p2p-branches-payments. https://thefinancialbrand.com/100375/gen-z-banks-big-techs-p2p-branches-payments/.

48. "Gen Z Are the Bank Customers of the Near Future," Fintech Futures, last modified 25 December 2019, https://www.fintechfutures.com/2019/12/gen-z-are-the-bank-customers-of-the-near-future.

49. "Generation Z Is Goal-Oriented and Motivated to Pursue Enjoyable Careers but Uncertain about How to Manage Finances," Northwestern Mutual, accessed 12 October 2021, https://news.northwesternmutual.com/2019-08-13-Generation-Z-Is-Goal-Oriented-And-Motivated-To-Pursue-Enjoyable-Careers-But-Uncertain-About-How-To-Manage-Finances.

50. "90 Percent of Gen Z Tired of How Negative and Divided Our Country Is around Important Issues, According to Research by Porter Novelli/Cone," PR Newswire, last modified 23 October 2019, https://www.prnewswire.com/news-releases/90-percent-of-gen-z-tired-of-how-negative-and-divided-our-country-is-around-important-issues-according-to-research-by-porter-novellicone-300943452.html.

51. "What Do You Know about MBNA?" MBNA, accessed 12 October 2021, https://www.mbna.co.uk/about-us.html.

52. "ING Group," Companies History, accessed 12 October 2021, https://www.companieshistory.com/ing-group.

53. Alistair Osbourne, "The History of Egg: A Shattering Experience," The Telegraph, last modified 1 March 2011, https://www.telegraph.co.uk/finance/newsbysector/banksandfinance/8354336/The-history-of-Egg-a-shattering-experience.html.

54. Miranda Marquit, "Too Big to Fail Banks: Where Are They Now?" Investopedia, last modified 27 April 2021, https://www.investopedia.com/insights/too-big-fail-banks-where-are-they-now.

55. "How RegTech Innovations Are Taking the Complexity out of Compliance," Waracle, last modified 25 October 2019, https://waracle.com/blog/fintech/how-regtech-innovations-are-taking-the-complexity-out-of-compliance.

56. Clyde Wayne Crews Jr, *Ten Thousand Commandments: An Annual Snapshot of the Federal Regulatory State*, Competitive Enterprise Institute, 2018, accessed 12 October 2021, https://cei.org/sites/default/files/Ten_Thousand_Commandments_2018.pdf.

57. "How European Banks Are Using Regtech Solutions," Go Medici, last modified 6 June 2018, https://gomedici.com/how-european-banks-are-using-regtech-solutions.

58. Peter Thal Larsen, "Breakingviews: Wirecard Collapse Is Real-Life Fintech Stress Test," Reuters, last modified 25 June 2020, https://www.reuters.com/article/us-wirecard-accounts-breakingviews-idUSKBN23W1T7.

59. "BaFin Bosses Forced Out over Handling of Wirecard Scandal," Financial Times, accessed 12 October 2021, https://www.ft.com/content/4f948457-678e-485c-92f7-2837064a5010.

60. Kate Rooney, "Fintech's Fast Pass to Traditional Banking Is Now Cut Off," CNBC, last modified 24 October 2019, https://www.cnbc.com/2019/10/24/fintechs-fast-pass-to-traditional-banking-is-now-cut-off.html.

61. "UK CEOs Have Less Time than Ever to Make Their Mark," PWC, last modified 15 May 2017, https://www.pwc.co.uk/press-room/press-releases/uk-ceos-have-less-time-than-ever-to-make-an-impact.html.

62. Matt Egan, "Jamie Dimon Says JPMorgan Has Begun to Prepare for Potential US Default," CNN Business, last modified 28 September 2021, https://edition.cnn.com/2021/09/28/business/jamie-dimon-jpmorgan-us-default/index.html.

63. Marie Kemplay, "Top 1000 World Banks 2021," The Banker, accessed 12 October 2021, https://top1000worldbanks.com.

64. Joanna England, "What Makes a Fintech Startup a Success?" Fintech Magazine (March 2021), https://issuu.com/fintechmagazine/docs/fintech_magazine_march2021.

65. "Digital Banking Market Report," Research Dive, 2020, https://www.researchdive.com/53/digital-banking-market.

66. Ellen Daniel, "Over a Quarter of Brits Now Have a Digital-Only Bank Account," Verdict, last modified 14 January 2021, https://www.verdict.co.uk/digital-only-bank-finder

67. "Digital Banking Market Report," Research Dive, 2020, https://www.researchdive.com/53/digital-banking-market.

68. "Digital Banking in Asia Sees Prime Time," Fintech News Singapore, last modified 1 March 2021, https://fintechnews.sg/48975/virtual-banking/digital-banking-in-asia-prime-time.

69. "Online Banking Penetration in the European Union (EU28) from 2007 to 2017," Statista, last modified 5 July 2021, https://www.statista.com/statistics/380803/online-banking-penetration-in-the-eu.

70. Laxman Pai, "Global Fintech Investment Reaches $105bn with Robinhood Raising Most in H2," Oplaesque, last modified 2 March 2021, https://www.opalesque.com/684344/Global_fintech_investment_reaches_with_Robinhood_raising434.html.

71. Neobanks 2021: Shifting from Growth to Profitability? Exton Consulting, 2021, accessed 12 October 2021, https://extonconsulting.com/wp-content/uploads/2021/01/Report-Neobanks-2021.pdf.

72. "The 10 Most Innovative Finance Companies of 2021," Fast Company, last modified 3 September 2021, https://www.fastcompany.com/90600205/finance-most-innovative-companies-2021.

73. "Fintech & Banking: Collaboration for Disruption," Axis Corporate and Efma, 2016, accessed 21 October 2021, https://axiscorporate.com/wp-content/uploads/Report-fintech-and-banking-ENGLISH_VD.pdf.

74. "New Normal: Digital Banking Shift could Accelerate," Bloomberg, last modified 13 August 2020, https://www.bloomberg.com/professional/blog/new-normal-digital-banking-shift-could-accelerate.

75. "Neo Banks: Performance and New Ideas," Finnovate Research, 2018, accessed 12 October 2021, https://irp-cdn.multiscreensite.com/91156662/files/uploaded/NeoBanks%20Performance%20and%20New%20Ideas%20Finnovate_v7_10_11_2018.pdf.

76. Ben Winck, "Jack Ma's Ant Group Aims to Raise $34.5 Billion in Largest IPO of All Time," Business Insider, last modified 26 October 2020, https://markets.businessinsider.com/news/stocks/ant-group-ipo-billion-largest-ever-jack-ma-alibaba-raise-2020-10.

77. Louise Lucas, "Ant Financial Valued at $150bn in Offering," Financial Times, last modified 21 May 2018, https://www.ft.com/content/d45c5090-5c3e-11e8-ad91-e01af256df68.

78. "Goldman Sachs Market Cap 2006–2021," Macrotrends, accessed 12 October 2021, https://www.macrotrends.net/stocks/charts/GS/goldman-sachs/market-cap.

79. "Morgan Stanley Market Cap 2006–2021," Macrotrends, accessed 12 October 2021, https://www.macrotrends.net/stocks/charts/MS/morgan-stanley/market-cap.

80. Duncan Lam, "The Ant IPO: Why It Failed, and Why It Matters," Asia Careers Society, last modified 13 December 2020, https://www.lsesu-acs.com/post/the-ant-ipo-why-it-failed-and-why-it-matters.

81. "AliPay History," AuthoriPay, accessed 21 October 2021, https://authoripay.co.uk/alipay.

82. Louise Lucas, "Ant Financial's $150bn Valuation Belies Glaring Risks for Investors," Financial Times, last modified 17 April 2018, https://www.ft.com/content/f556ca56-413f-11e8-93cf-67ac3a6482fd.

83. "Chime Overview," PitchBook, accessed 12 October 2021, https://pitchbook.com/profiles/company/97267-96.

84. "North Korea Is Exploring Fintech and Blockchain," Fintech News Hong Kong, last modified 13 September 2018, https://fintechnews.hk/6847/fintechkorea/north-korea-fintech-blockchain.

85. "N26 Ranks #1 on Forbes' List of the World's Best Banks," N26, last modified 14 April 2021, https://n26.com/en-fr/blog/n26-the-worlds-best-bank-by-forbes.

86. "Homepage," MyBank, last accessed 13 November 2021, https://mybank.eu/en.

87. "Homepage," Starling Bank, last accessed 13 November 2021, https://www.starlingbank.com.

88. "Homepage," Revolut, last accessed 13 November 2021, https://www.revolut.com/en-US.

89. "Homepage," Ally, last accessed 13 November 2021, https://www.ally.com.

90. "Personal," Axos Bank, last accessed 13 November 2021, https://www.axosbank.com/Personal.

91. "Homepage," Moven, last accessed 13 November 2021, https://moven.com.

92. "Number of Customers at Select Online Only European Banks as of 2021" (Statista), last modified 8 July 2020, https://www.statista.com/statistics/941342/europe-largest-online-banks.

93. "Fiscal 2018 Annual Report," Starbucks, 2018, accessed 12 October 2021, https://s22.q4cdn.com/869488222/files/doc_financials/annual/2018/2018-Annual-Report.pdf.

94. David Curry, "PayPal Revenue and Usage Statistics (2021)," Business of Apps, last modified 17 October 2021, https://www.businessofapps.com/data/paypal-statistics.

95. "PSD2: A Game Changing Regulation", PWC, accessed 12 October 2021, https://www.pwc.co.uk/industries/banking-capital-markets/insights/psd2-a-game-changing-regulation.html.

96. Ryan Browne, "Revolut, Europe's $5.5 Billion Digital Bank, Quietly Broke Even in November," CNBC, last modified 8 December 2020, https://www.cnbc.com/2020/12/08/digital-bank-revolut-breaks-even-in-november.html.

97. Noor Zainab Hussain, "PayPal Profit Tops Estimates as Pandemic Drives Online Spending to Record Levels," Reuters, last modified 3 February 2021, https://www.reuters.com/article/us-paypal-results-idUSKBN2A332O.

98. "Market Capitalization of Square (SQ)," Companies Market Cap, accessed 12 October 2021, https://companiesmarketcap.com/square/marketcap.

99. "Market Capitalization of Deutsche Bank (DB)," Companies Market Cap, accessed 12 October 2021, https://companiesmarketcap.com/deutsche-bank/marketcap.

100. "BNP Paribas SA Market Cap 2006–2021: BNPQY," Macrotrends, accessed 12 October 2021, https://www.macrotrends.net/stocks/charts/BNPQY/bnp-paribas-sa/market-cap.

101. Emily Bary, "PayPal Valued at Over $300 Billion for the First Time," MarketWatch, last modified 4 February 2021, https://www.marketwatch.com/story/paypal-valued-at-over-300-billion-for-the-first-time-11612463466.

102. "Citigroup Market Cap 2006–2021: C," Macrotrends, accessed 12 October 2021, https://www.macrotrends.net/stocks/charts/C/citigroup/market-cap.

103. "Wells Fargo Market Cap 2006–2021: WFC," Macrotrends, accessed 12 October 2021, https://www.macrotrends.net/stocks/charts/WFC/wells-fargo/market-cap.

104. Jeff Cox, "Google Is Getting into Banking with the Search Giant Set to Offer Checking Accounts Next Year," CNBC, last modified 13 November 2019, https://www.cnbc.com/2019/11/13/google-reportedly-offering-checking-accounts-next-year.html.

105. Alexandria White, "Is the Apple Card Worth the Hype?" CNBC, last modified 15 September 2021, https://www.cnbc.com/select/apple-card-review.

106. Ron Shevlin, "Google Plex: The Mobile Banking App Every Bank Wants," Forbes, last modified 30 November 2020, https://www.forbes.com/sites/ronshevlin/2020/11/30/google-plex-the-mobile-banking-app-every-bank-wants.

107. "Retailers Try Payment Apps to Sidestep $90bn in Third-Party Swipe Fees," Emirates Business, last modified 8 December 2018, https://emirates-business.ae/retailers-try-payment-apps-to-sidestep-90bn-in-third-party-swipe-fees.

108. Rachel Green, "Tech Companies in Financial Services: How Apple, Amazon, and Google Are Taking Financial Services by Storm," Business Insider, last modified 30 May 2019, https://www.businessinsider.com/tech-companies-in-financial-services.

109. Ryan Browne, "Big Tech Will Push Deeper into Finance this Year – but Avoid the 'Headache' of Being a Bank," CNBC, last modified 3 January 2020, https://www.cnbc.com/2020/01/03/big-tech-will-push-into-finance-in-2020-while-avoiding-bank-regulation.html.

110. "Our History: An Ally through the Years," Ally, accessed 12 October 2021, https://www.ally.com/about/history.

111. Hugh Son, "LendingClub Buys Radius Bank for $185 Million in First Fintech Takeover of a Regulated US Bank," CNBC, last modified 18 February 2020, https://www.cnbc.com/2020/02/18/lendingclub-buys-radius-bank-in-first-fintech-takeover-of-a-bank.html.

112. "Raisin Completes Takeover of MHB-Bank," Finextra, last modified 28 August 2019, https://www.finextra.com/pressarticle/79604/raisin-completes-takeover-of-mhb-bank.

113. "Green Dot Completes Its Acquisition of Bonneville Bank," Businesswire, last modified 8 December 2011, https://www.businesswire.com/news/home/20111208006460/en/Green-Dot-Completes-its-Acquisition-of-Bonneville-Bank.https://internationalbanker.com/banking/the-digital-imperative-for-banking-in-the-new-normal-by-ciko-thomas-group-managing-executive-retail-business-banking-rbb/.

114. "Revolution or Evolution? The Starling Report – Predictions and Challenges for UK Fintech in 2017," Starling Bank, accessed 12 October 2021, https://explainthemarket.com/wp-content/uploads/2019/02/Starling-Bank-FinTech-2017.pdf.

115. "Trends in Mortgage Origination and Servicing: Nonbanks in the Post-crisis Period," FDIC Quarterly 13, accessed 12 October 2021, https://www.fdic.gov/analysis/quarterly-banking-profile/fdic-quarterly/2019-vol13-4/fdic-v13n4-3q2019-article3.pdf.

116. Mark Shilling, Gary Shaw and Jim Berry, "The Path Ahead: Navigating financial services sector performance post-COVID-19," Deloitte, last modified 10 September 2020, https://www2.deloitte.com/us/en/insights/economy/covid-19/covid-19-financial-services-sector-challenges.html.

117. Ciko Thomas, "The Digital Imperative for Banking in the New Normal," International Banker, last modified 15 June 2020, https://internationalbanker.com/banking/the-digital-imperative-for-banking-in-the-new-normal-by-ciko-thomas-group-managing-executive-retail-business-banking-rbb.

118. "The Slowdown in Euro Area Productivity in a Global Context," *ECB Economic Bulletin* 3 (2017), accessed 21 October 2021, https://www.ecb.europa.eu/pub/pdf/other/ebart201703_01.en.pdf.

119. Alison Griswold, "Amazon Is Unapologetically Spending Money on One-Day Shipping," Quartz, last modified 26 July 2019, https://qz.com/1675621/amazon-profit-falls-on-investment-in-one-day-prime-delivery.

120. Douglas A Ready, Carol Cohen, David Kiron and Benjamin Pring, "The New Leadership Playbook for the Digital Age," (*MIT Sloan Management Review*), last modified 21 January 2020, https://sloanreview.mit.edu/projects/the-new-leadership-playbook-for-the-digital-age.

121. Meredith Somers, "Strategic Leadership for the Digital Economy" (MIT Management Sloan School), last modified 5 May 2021, https://mitsloan.mit.edu/ideas-made-to-matter/strategic-leadership-digital-economy.

122. Douglas A. Ready, Carol Cohen, David Kiron and Benjamin Pring, "The New Leadership Playbook for the Digital Age" MIT Sloan Management Review, last modified 21 January 2020, https://sloanreview.mit.edu/projects/the-new-leadership-playbook-for-the-digital-age.

123. Jeremy Grant, "Transforming a Traditional Bank into an Agile Market Leader," Strategy+Business, last modified 19 December 2018, https://www.strategy-business.com/article/Transforming-a-Traditional-Bank-into-an-Agile-Market-Leader.

124. Melanie C Nolan and Nicole Murillo, "The Board's Role in Digital Transformation," Corporate Board Member, accessed 12 October 2021, https://boardmember.com/the-boards-role-in-digital-transformation.

125. "EU Births: Decline Continues, but Not from Foreign-Born Women," Eurostat, last modified 23 March 2021, https://ec.europa.eu/eurostat/web/products-eurostat-news/-/ddn-20210323-2.

126. Caroline Castrillon, "Why More Women Are Turning to Entrepreneurship," Forbes, last modified 4 February 2019, https://www.forbes.com/sites/carolinecastrillon/2019/02/04/why-more-women-are-turning-to-entrepreneurship.

127. Kai Nicol-Schwarz, "A Third of UK Unicorns Founded by Ethnic Minorities," Sifted, last modified 19 March 2021, https://sifted.eu/articles/ethnic-minority-founders-uk.

128. David Rock, Heidi Grant and Jacqui Grey, "Diverse Teams Feel Less Comfortable – and That's Why They Perform Better," Harvard Business Review, last modified 22 September 2016, https://hbr.org/2016/09/diverse-teams-feel-less-comfortable-and-thats-why-they-perform-better.

129. "BNP Paribas Today Launches Hello Bank! The First 100% Digital Mobile Bank in Europe," BNP Paribas, last modified 16 May 2013, https://group.bnpparibas/en/press-release/bank-mobile.

130. "Our History," Commank, accessed 12 October 2021, https://www.commbank.com.au/about-us/our-company/history.html.

131. Brian Westlake, "Commonwealth Bank Achieves Digital Primacy in the Australian Banking Market," HBS Digital Initiative, last modified 11 March 2020, https://digital.hbs.edu/platform-digit/submission/commonwealth-bank-achieves-digital-primacy-in-the-australian-banking-market.

132. "Ping An Ranked the World's Most Valuable Insurance Brand for Fifth Year in a Row," PR Newswire, last modified 29 April 2021, https://www.prnewswire.com/news-releases/ping-an-ranked-the-worlds-most-valuable-insurance-brand-for-fifth-year-in-a-row-301280128.html.

133. Michael Bucy, Stephen Hall and Doug Yakola, "Transformation with a Capital *T*," McKinsey & Company, last modified 7 November 2016, https://www.mckinsey.com/business-functions/rts/our-insights/transformation-with-a-capital-t.

134. Noam Wasserman, "The Founder's Dilemma," (Harvard Business Review, last modified February 2008, https://hbr.org/2008/02/the-founders-dilemma.

135. Kilian Berz and Deborah Lovich, "RBC's Dave McKay on a Future-Focused Culture," Boston Consulting Group, last modified 12 December 2019, https://www.bcg.com/publications/2019/rbc-dave-mckay-future-focused-culture.

136. Martin Arnold, "RBS Becomes a Shadow of Its Former Self," Financial Times, last modified 13 January 2015, https://www.ft.com/content/a2f39e78-9b1c-11e4-882d-00144feabdc0.

137. "RBS Bailout 'Unlikely to Be Recouped'," BBC, last modified 12 September 2018, https://www.bbc.co.uk/news/business-45500384.

138. Quoted in "The Sorry History of the Near-Destruction of Investment Banking at RBS," Business Insider, last modified 6 March 2015, https://www.businessinsider.com/why-rbs-failed-as-an-investment-bank-2015-3.

139. Wallace Young, "Banks Are Becoming More Efficient – Is that Good or Bad?" Community Banking Connections, accessed 12 October 2021, https://communitybankingconnections.org/articles/2017/i2/banks-are-becoming-more-efficient.

140. Michael Deely, "Why A Value-Added Analysis Is Essential For Lean Banking Operations," Big Sky Associates, accessed 22 October 2021, https://www.bigskyassociates.com/blog/why-a-value-added-analysis-is-essential-for-lean-banking-operations.

141. "Lean Forward or Fall Back: How Applying Lean Principles Can Improve the Finance Function," PWC, 2012, accessed 12 October 2021, https://www.pwc.com/us/en/financial-services/publications/viewpoints/assets/fs-viewpoint-finance-function-lean-principles.pdf.

142. Doanh Do, "11 Steps to Building a Continuous Improvement Culture," The Lean Way, last modified 15 August 2017, https://theleanway.net/11-Steps-to-Building-a-Continuous-Improvement-Culture.

143. Sarah Butcher, "Here's How Much Banks Spend on Tech vs. Amazon and Google," Efinancial Careers, last modified 17 June 2021, https://www.efinancialcareers.com/news/finance/banks-tech-spending-vs-google-and-amazon.

144. "Artificial Intelligence and the Banking Industry's $1 Trillion Opportunity," The Financial Brand, accessed 12 October 2021, https://thefinancialbrand.com/72653/artificial-intelligence-trends-banking-industry.

145. Patrick Jenkins, "Citigroup CEO Says Machines Could Cut Thousands of Call Centre Jobs," Financial Times, last modified 18 February 2019, https://www.ft.com/content/b04d502a-329c-11e9-bb0c-42459962a812.

146. "Discover the Help Desk Software Built for Small Businesses," Salesforce, accessed 12 October 2021, https://www.salesforce.com/solutions/small-business-solutions/help-desk-software.

147. "Homepage," Zendesk, last accessed 13 November 2021, https://www.zendesk.com.

148. Toma Kulbyte, "37 Customer Experience Statistics You Need to Know for 2022," Superoffice, last modified 24 June 2021, https://www.superoffice.com/blog/customer-experience-statistics.

149. "EBA Report Identifies Key Challenges in the Roll Out of Big Data and Advanced Analytics," European Banking Authority, last modified 13 January 2020, https://www.eba.europa.eu/eba-report-identifies-key-challenges-roll-out-big-data-and-advanced-analytics.

150. Stephen Watts, "What Is Spaghetti Code (And Why You Should Avoid it)," BMC Blogs, last modified 17 June 2020, https://www.bmc.com/blogs/spaghetti-code.

151. David Cassel, "COBOL Is Everywhere: Who Will Maintain it?" The New Stack, last modified 6 May 2017, https://thenewstack.io/cobol-everywhere-will-maintain.

152. Philippe A De Backer, Juan Gonzalez and Rocio Castedo, "Financial Services: Banking on Change – Transformation or Failure?" Arthur D Little Global, accessed 12 October 2021, https://www.adlittle.com/en/BankingTransformation.

153. "Banks Must Empower SME Clients with More Than a Repackaged Retail Account," Fintech Futures, last modified 8 October 2020, https://www.fintechfutures.com/2020/10/banks-must-empower-sme-clients-with-more-than-a-repackaged-retail-account.

154. Steve Denning, "Making Sense of Shareholder Value: 'The World's Dumbest Idea,'" Forbes, last modified 17 July 2017, https://www.forbes.com/sites/stevedenning/2017/07/17/making-sense-of-shareholder-value-the-worlds-dumbest-idea.

155. Alfred Rappaport, "Selecting Strategies that Create Shareholder Value," Harvard Business Review, accessed 12 October 2021, https://hbr.org/1981/05/selecting-strategies-that-create-shareholder-value.

156. Peter Drucker, *The Practice of Management* (New York: Harper Business, 1954).

157. Aran Ali, "The Soaring Value of Intangible Assets in the S&P 500" (Visual Capitalist), last modified 12 November 2020, https://www.visualcapitalist.com/the-soaring-value-of-intangible-assets-in-the-sp-500.

158. "The Creator Economy: Paul Saffo" (Long Now Foundation), last modified 22 April 2020, https://www.youtube.com/watch?v=lGQe9oaHXf1.

159. Emily Bauer, "All About Customer Acquisition Cost (CAC)" (Propeller), last modified 27 March 2017, https://www.propellercrm.com/blog/customer-acquisition-cost.

160. "Consumer Culture," 5WPR, accessed 21 October 2021, https://www.5wpr.com/new/research/consumer-culture-report.

161. Steve Martin, "Philosophy/Religion/College/Language," in *A Wild and Crazy Guy* (1978), accessed 12 October 2021, https://genius.com/Steve-martin-philosophy-religion-college-language-annotated.

162. Jim Marous, "Banking Industry Not Meeting Basic Consumer Expectations," The Financial Brand, accessed 12 October 2021, https://thefinancialbrand.com/52101/banking-consumer-service-expectation-study.

163. "Number of banking & credit cards services customer complaints in the United Kingdom (UK) in the first half of 2020, by company," Statista, accessed 22 October 2021, https://www.statista.com/statistics/418820/customer-complaints-regarding-banking-products-in-uk/.

164. Vala Afshar, "50 Important Customer Experience Stats for Business Leaders," Huffpost, last modified 6 December 2017, https://www.huffpost.com/entry/50-important-customer-exp_b_8295772.

165. Katherine Denham, "Monzo Top and Tesco Bottom of Customer Service Tables," The Times, last modified 24 January 2021, https://www.thetimes.co.uk/article/monzo-top-and-tesco-bottom-of-customer-service-tables-0wj2ntjxv.

166. Alex, "UXDA Methodology: Does Your Mindset Fit the Value-Driven Digital Age," UX Digital Advantage, accessed 12 October 2021, https://www.theuxda.com/blog/5-banking-trends-that-will-define-future-of-banking.

167. Julija A, "Customer Experience Statistics for Cultivating Happy Clients," Smallbizgenius, last modified 24 March 2021, https://www.smallbizgenius.net/by-the-numbers/customer-experience-statistics.

168. "US Digital Ad Spending Will Surpass Traditional in 2019," Emarketer, last modified 20 February 2019, https://www.emarketer.com/newsroom/index.php/us-digital-ad-spending-will-surpass-traditional-in-2019.

169. "How Has Covid Affected Household Savings?" Bank of England, last modified 25 November 2020, https://www.bankofengland.co.uk/bank-overground/2020/how-has-covid-affected-household-savings.

170. Bethan Staton, "UK Households Save a Fifth of Disposable Income in First Quarter," Financial Times, last modified 30 June 2021, https://www.ft.com/content/b0ff38be-1b16-42dc-9e42-14463ce07f1f.

171. Leor Melamedov, "Report Reveals How Banks Have Managed New Loans over the COVID-19 Period," Lightico, accessed 12 October 2021, https://www.lightico.com/blog/covid-19-bank-lending-report.

172. "Gen Z Are the Bank Customers of the Near Future," Fintech Futures, last modified 25 December 2019, https://www.fintechfutures.com/2019/12/gen-z-are-the-bank-customers-of-the-near-future.

173. "Insurance Customers Would Consider Buying Insurance from Internet Giants, According to Accenture's Global Research," Accenture, last modified 6 February 2014, https://newsroom.accenture.com/subjects/research-surveys/insurance-customers-would-consider-buying-insurance-from-internet-giants-according-to-accentures-global-research.htm.

174. Radhika Kajarekar, "Amazon, Flipkart Eyes Insurance Sector Even as Govt. Investigates Their FDI Violation In India," Trak, last modified 20 March 2019, https://trak.in/tags/business/2019/03/20/amazon-flipkart-eyes-insurance-sector-even-as-govt-investigates-their-fdi-violation-in-india.

175. Eugene Kim, "Alibaba CEO Jack Ma: 'We Earned the Trust of People Today'," Business Insider, last modified 20 September 2014, https://www.businessinsider.com/alibaba-jack-ma-says-he-earned-the-trust-2014-9.

176. "Fidor Bank," Fidor Solutions, accessed 12 October 2021, https://www.fidor.com/work/fidor-bank-2.

177. "Eric Schmidt – ADMS Keynote & Audience Q&A: 'Innovation'," TheADMS2010, last modified 12 March 2010, https://www.youtube.com/watch?v=9GMjtOSvMDs.

178. Jon Fortt, "Top 5 Moments from Eric Schmidt's Talk in Abu Dhabi," Fortune, last modified 11 March 2010, https://fortune.com/2010/03/11/top-5-moments-from-eric-schmidts-talk-in-abu-dhabi.

179. Simon Cadbury, "Why and How Banks Should Innovate," ieDigital, last modified 6 September 2016, https://www.iedigital.com/research/how-can-financial-services-innovate-digitally-within-the-constraints-of-their-legacy-infrastructure-2.

180. Wayne Busch and Juan Pedro Moreno, "Banks' New Competitors: Starbucks, Google, and Alibaba," Harvard Business Review, last modified 20 February 2014, https://hbr.org/2014/02/banks-new-competitors-starbucks-google-and-alibaba.

181. S O'Dea, "Number of Smartphone Users in the United States from 2018 to 2025," Statista, last modified 19 March 2021, https://www.statista.com/statistics/201182/forecast-of-smartphone-users-in-the-us.

182. "For Challenger Digital Banks, It's Game On," PYMNTS, last modified 20 July 2017, https://www.pymnts.com/news/digital-banking/2017/challenger-atom-bank-video-games.

183. "The State of the Financial Services Industry 2020," Oliver Wyman, accessed 12 October 2021, https://www.oliverwyman.com/content/dam/oliver-wyman/v2/publications/2020/January/Oliver-Wyman-State-of-the-Financial-Services-Industry-2020.pdf.

184. Matt Levine, "Expensive Research and Cheap Hedge Funds," Bloomberg, last modified February 2017, https://www.bloomberg.com/opinion/articles/2017-02-28/expensive-research-and-cheap-hedge-funds.

185. Freek Vermeulen, "How Capitec Became South Africa's Biggest Bank," Harvard Business Review, last modified 10 October 2018, https://hbr.org/2018/10/how-capitec-became-south-africas-biggest-bank.

186. "Digital Transformation Investments to Top $6.8 Trillion Globally as Businesses & Governments Prepare for the Next Normal," IDC, last modified 8 December 2020, https://www.idc.com/getdoc.jsp?containerId=prMETA47037520.

187. "We, the Post-digital People," Accenture, accessed 12 October 2021, https://www.accenture.com/us-en/insights/technology/_acnmedia/Thought-Leadership-Assets/PDF-2/Accenture-Technology-Vision-2020-Full-Report.pdf.

188. "Only 17 Percent of Banks Have Deployed Digital at Scale – Finds Infosys Finacle and Efma 'Innovation in Retail Banking' Report," Infosys, last modified 17 October 2019, https://www.infosys.com/newsroom/press-releases/2019/finacle-innovation-retail-banking-report2019.html.

189. Francisco Gonzalez, "Transforming an Analog Company into a Digital Company: The Case of BBVA," Open Mind and BBVA, accessed 12 October 2021, https://www.bbvaopenmind.com/wp-content/uploads/2015/01/BBVA-OpenMind-Transforming-an-Analog-Company-into-a-Digital-Company-The-Case-of-BBVA-Francisco-Gonzalez.pdf.pdf.

190. "Banking in the Near Future: Optimising Risk Management and Resilience in the Digital Age," The Times, last modified 25 April 2021, https://www.thetimes.co.uk/static/banking-in-the-future-risk-management-resilience-raconteur.

191. "Gartner Executive Guidance: Speed Up Your Digital Business Transformation," Gartner, accessed 12 October 2021, https://www.gartner.com/en/executive-guidance/business-model-change.

192. "Banking in the Near Future: Optimising Risk Management and Resilience in the Digital Age," The Times, last modified 25 April 2021, https://www.thetimes.co.uk/static/banking-in-the-future-risk-management-resilience-raconteur.

193. "DBS among Top 10 Business Transformations of the Decade: Harvard Business Review," DBS Bank, accessed 12 October 2021, https://www.dbs.com/newsroom/DBS_among_top_10_business_transformations_of_the_decade__Harvard_Business_Review_19.

194. "Industry Convergence: The Digital Industrial Revolution," Gartner, accessed 12 October 2021, https://www.gartner.com/en/documents/2684516/industry-convergence-the-digital-industrial-revolution.

195. "E-commerce," Microsoft, accessed 21 October 2021, https://azure.microsoft.com/en-us/solutions/ecommerce.https://www.fitsense.io/

196. "Amazon Loans More than $3 Billion to Over 20,000 Small Businesses," Businesswire, last modified 8 June 2017, https://www.businesswire.com/news/home/20170608005415/en/Amazon-Loans-More-Than-3-Billion-to-Over-20000-Small-Businesses.

197. "ThinkAg Releases 'Ag-Tech in India: Investment Landscape Report 2021'," ThinkAg and MSC Consulting, last modified 16 July 2021, http://www.agrospectrumindia.com/news/26/2854/thinkag-releases-ag-tech-in-india-investment-landscape-report-2021-.html.

198. "Agrihive," Facebook, last accessed 13 November 2021, https://www.facebook.com/agrihive.

199. "Homepage," Farm Drive, last accessed 13 November 2021, https://farmdrive.co.ke.

200. "Homepage," Croppro, last accessed 13 November 2021, https://www.croppro.ca.

201. "Homepage," Fitsense, last accessed 13 November 2021, https://www.fitsense.io.

202. "Homepage," Exante, last accessed 13 November 2021, https://exante.eu.

203. "Homepage," Docdoc, last accessed 13 November 2021, https://docdoc.ru.

204. "In-Depth Report: B2B E-Commerce 2019," Statista, accessed 12 October 2021, https://www.statista.com/study/44442/statista-report-b2b-e-commerce.

205. Jérôme de Guigné, "B2B in eCommerce: The new El Dorado?" Amazon Expert Medium, last modified 6 February 2020, https://amazon-expert.medium.com/b2b-in-ecommerce-the-new-eldorado-7c493c1900df.

206. "Business-to-Business E-commerce Market Size, Share & Trends Analysis Report by Deployment Model (Intermediary-oriented, Supplier-oriented), by Application, by Region, and Segment Forecasts, 2021–2028," Grand View Research, last modified June 2021, https://www.grandviewresearch.com/industry-analysis/business-to-business-b2b-e-commerce-market.

207. "Homepage," Payability, last accessed 13 November 2021, https://www.payability.com.

208. "The Power of Small: Unlocking the Potential of SMES," International Labour Organization, last modified October 2019, https://www.ilo.org/infostories/en-GB/Stories/Employment/SMEs.

209. Chira Barua, Balazs Gati, András Havas, Tara Lajumoke, Miklos Radnai and Zubin Taraporevala, "How Banks Can Use Ecosystems to Win in the SME Market," McKinsey & Company, last modified 10 June 2019, https://www.mckinsey.com/industries/financial-services/our-insights/how-banks-can-use-ecosystems-to-win-in-the-sme-market.

210. "Unlocking £8.5 Billion in New Revenue from SME Customers," Accenture, accessed 12 October 2021, https://www.accenture.com/gb-en/insight-unlocking-new-revenue-sme-customers.

211. "The SME: Not Just Another Retail Banking Customer," Banking Gateway, last modified 24 January 2017, https://www.banking-gateway.com/features/featurethe-sme-not-just-another-retail-banking-customer1-5722331/index.html.

212. Elizabeth Glagowski, "Customer Value Drives Growth at Nordea Bank," TTEC, accessed 12 October 2021, https://www.ttec.com/articles/customer-value-drives-growth-nordea-bank.

213. "The SME: Not Just Another Retail Banking Customer," Banking Gateway, last modified 24 January 2017, https://www.banking-gateway.com/features/featurethe-sme-not-just-another-retail-banking-customer1-5722331/index.html.

214. "Financial Stability Review, November 2020," European Central Bank, accessed 12 October 2021, https://www.ecb.europa.eu/pub/financial-stability/fsr/html/ecb.fsr202011~b7be9ae1f1.en.html.

215. "Best Infrastructure as a Service (IaaS) Providers," G2, accessed 21 October 2021, https://www.g2.com/categories/infrastructure-as-a-service-iaas.

216. Steven Arons, "Deutsche Bank CEO's Last-Ditch Plan to Save Best of His Business," Bloomberg, last modified 22 November 2019, https://www.bloomberg.com/news/features/2019-11-22/deutsche-bank-ceo-s-plan-to-shrink-the-lender-back-to-glory.

217. Rich Horwath, "What CEOs Think about Strategy," Strategic Thinking Institute, last modified 8 July 2015, https://www.strategyskills.com/what-ceos-think-about-strategy.

218. "Banking in the Near Future: Optimising Risk Management and Resilience in the Digital Age," The Times, last modified 25 April 2021, https://www.thetimes.co.uk/static/banking-in-the-future-risk-management-resilience-raconteur.

219. "Number of Regulated Open Banking Account Providers and Third Party Providers (TPPs) in the United Kingdom (UK) from February 2021 to August," Statista, accessed 12 October 2021, https://www.statista.com/statistics/1211911/number-of-regulated-open-banking-account-and-third-party-providers-united-kingdom.

220. "Top Four Money Management Apps Crowned Open Up Challenge Winners," Open Banking, accessed 12 October 2021, https://www.openbanking.org.uk/news/top-four-money-management-apps-crowned-open-up-challenge-winners.

221. "Banking in the Near Future: Optimising Risk Management and Resilience in the Digital Age," The Times, last modified 25 April 2021, https://www.thetimes.co.uk/static/banking-in-the-future-risk-management-resilience-raconteur.

222. Haibo Lui, Jurgen Mihm and Manuel E. Sosa, "Where Do Stars Come From? The Role of Star vs. Nonstar Collaborators in Creative Settings," *Organization Science* 29 (2018), https://pubsonline.informs.org/doi/full/10.1287/orsc.2018.1223.

223. "BBVA Buys Simple for $117m," Finextra, last modified 20 February 2014, https://www.finextra.com/newsarticle/25757/bbva-buys-simple-for-117m.

224. "BBVA Strengthens Its Commitment to U.K.'s Atom Bank," BBVA, accessed 12 October 2021, https://www.bbva.com/en/bbva-strengthens-commitment-u-k-s-atom-bank.

225. "BBVA Acquires Finnish Banking Startup Holvi," BBVA, accessed 12 October 2021, https://www.bbva.com/en/bbva-acquires-finnish-banking-start-holvi.

226. "Groupe BPCE Agrees to Buy Fidor," Finextra, last modified 28 July 2016, https://www.finextra.com/newsarticle/29238/groupe-bpce-agrees-to-buy-fidor.

227. Scott Carey, "What Is PaaS? A Simpler Way to Build Software Applications," InfoWorld, last modified 6 July 2021, https://www.infoworld.com/article/3223434/what-is-paas-a-simpler-way-to-build-software-applications.html.

228. Mark Wilson, "Tom Wolfe in 1972: 'Logos are Strictly a Vanity Industry'," Fast Company, accessed 12 October 2021, https://www.fastcompany.com/90172836/tom-wolfe-in-1972-logos-are-strictly-a-vanity-industry.

229. Quoted in "The Code Behind the Vaccine, Best of 2020 Design, Vitalik Buterin's Endnotes and Bezos' Thinking Process," *D&T* 34, accessed 21 October 2021, https://howtogetalogo.com/designer-advice-on-logo-design. https://www.efma.com/storage/study/1-195ype-summary-1618904332Zm6mY.pdf

230. Mary Ann Glynn and Rikki Abzug, "Institutionalizing Identity: Symbolic Isomorphism and Organizational Names," *Academy of Management Journal* 45 (2002): 267–280.

231. "Arthur D. Little's Global Innovation Excellence Survey," Arthur D Little Global, last modified February 2013, https://www.adlittle.com/en/insights/viewpoints/arthur-d-little%E2%80%99s-global-innovation-excellence-survey.

232. "Understanding the Innovator's Dilemma," Wired, accessed 12 October 2021, https://www.wired.com/insights/2014/12/understanding-the-innovators-dilemma.

233. Rocky Agrawal, "Tim Cook Is Absolutely Right: Apple Must Embrace Cannibalism," Quartz, last modified 25 January 2013, https://qz.com/47728/tim-cook-is-absolutely-right-apple-must-embrace-cannibalism.

234. "Innovation in Retail Banking," Efma and Infosys, accessed 12 October 2021, https://www.efma.com/storage/study/1-195ype-summary-1618904332Zm6mY.pdf.

235. "Homepage," Klickex, last accessed 13 November 2021, https://klickex.org.

236. Aimee Groth, "Companies that Put Tons of Money into R&D Aren't More Innovative than Those that Don't," Business Insider, last modified 24 October 2011, https://www.businessinsider.com/booz-and-cos-innovation-study-2011-10.

237. Alyson Shontell, "Jamie Dimon: Silicon Valley Startups Are Coming to Eat Wall Street's Lunch," Business Insider, last modified 10 April 2015, https://www.businessinsider.com/jamie-dimon-shareholder-letter-and-silicon-valley-2015-4.

238. Jim Marous, "Culture Is Key to Digital Transformation in Banking, not Technology," The Financial Brand, accessed 12 October 2021, https://thefinancialbrand.com/85412/digital-banking-culture-transformation-trends.

239. "Bank of America Sets Record for Patents in 2020 with Majority of Employees Working from Home," Yahoo! Finance, last modified 18 February 2021, https://finance.yahoo.com/news/bank-america-sets-record-patents-140000033.html.

240. "Homepage," Inovabra, last accessed 13 November 2021, https://www.inovabra.com.br.

241. "ICBC Officially Launches Innovative Culture," ICBC, accessed 12 October 2021, https://www.icbc.com.cn/icbc/en/newsupdates/icbc%20news/ICBCOfficiallyLaunchesInnovativeCulture.htm.

242. "Building an Agile Process Flow: A Comprehensive Guide," Kanbanize, accessed 12 October 2021, https://kanbanize.com/agile/project-management/workflow.

243. Rhoda Davidson and Bettina Büchel, "The Art of Piloting New Initiatives," *MIT Sloan Management Review* 53 (2011), accessed 12 October 2021, http://aproaingenieria.com/intranet/uploads//the-art-of-piloting-new-initiatives.pdf.

244. Blake Masters, "Peter Thiel's CS183: Startup – Class 11 Notes Essay," Blake Masters Tumblr, last modified 11 May 2012, https://blakemasters.tumblr.com/post/22866240816/peter-thiels-cs183-startup-class-11-notes.

245. Tanaya Macheel, "The Big Question: Should Fintech Startups Buy Banks?" Tearsheet, last modified 13 April 2017, https://tearsheet.co/modern-banking-experience/the-big-question-should-fintech-startups-buy-banks.

246. Ellen Daniel, "Digital Bank Bo Closes: Inside RBS's Failed Challenge to the Challenger Banks," Verdict, last modified 5 May 2020, https://www.verdict.co.uk/bo-digital-bank-rbs-natwest.

247. "The Innovation Game: Why and How Businesses Are Investing in Innovation Centers," Capgemini Consulting and Altimeter, last modified 11 May 2016, https://www.slideshare.net/rbouter/the-innovation-game-why-and-how-business-are-investing-in-innovation-centers.

248. "Barclays Accelerator Powered by Techstars," Barclays, accessed 12 October 2021, https://home.barclays/who-we-are/innovation/barclays-accelerator.

249. "Deutsche Bank Innovation Network," Deutsche Bank, accessed 12 October 2021, https://www.db.com/what-we-do/focus-topics/innovation-network.

250. "Digital Innovation: A Driving Force for Positive Transformation," Societe Generale, accessed 12 October 2021, https://www.societegenerale.com/en/societe-generale-group/strategy/innovation-and-digital.

251. "The Start-Up Spirit within the Company," BNP Paribas, accessed 12 October 2021, https://group.bnpparibas/en/hottopics/intrapreneurship.

252. "Goldman Sachs Accelerate," Goldman Sachs, accessed 12 October 2021, https://www.goldmansachs.com/what-we-do/asset-management/gs-accelerate.

253. "Stronger Together: Citi Partners with Fintechs to Co-create New Innovation across Payments, Trade and Receivables," Citi, accessed 12 October 2021, https://www.citigroup.com/tts/solutions/receivables/assets/docs/Stronger-Together-Citi-Fintechs.pdf.

254. "In-Residence," J. P. Morgan, accessed 12 October 2021, https://www.jpmorgan.com/insights/technology/in-residence.

255. Erica Volini, Jeff Schwartz, Kraig Eaton, David Mallon, Yves Van Durme, Maren Hauptmann, Rob Scott and Shannon Poynton, "The Social Enterprise in a World Disrupted," Deloitte Insights, last modified 9 December 2020, https://www2.deloitte.com/us/en/insights/focus/human-capital-trends/2021/social-enterprise-survive-to-thrive.html.

256. "16+ Millennials in the Workplace Statistics for 2021," TeamStage, accessed 12 October 2021, https://teamstage.io/millennials-in-the-workplace-statistics.

257. Virginia Matthews, "Mapping a Through Route to Culture Change," Raconteur, last modified 13 April 2021, https://www.raconteur.net/hr/corporate-culture/mapping-a-through-route-to-culture-change.

258. "New Survey: Company Mission & Culture Matter More than Salary," Glassdoor, last modified 10 July 2019, https://www.glassdoor.com/blog/mission-culture-survey.

259. "TEKsystems 2021 State of Digital Transformation Report: How to Succeed in the Face of Disruption," teksystems.com, last modified 8 March 2021, https://www.teksystems.com/en/insights/newsroom/2021/state-of-dx-2021-press-release.

260. "USAA CEO Joe Robles Reveals Why Culture Has Given the Company a Huge Competitive Edge in a New Thought Leadership Video by Culture Shaping Firm Senn Delaney," Cision PR Web, last modified 9 October 2012, https://www.prweb.com/releases/2012senndelaneyceovideos/usaaceojoerobles/prweb9991117.htm.

261. Komal Nadeem, "Insurance Ratings Actions: A.M. Best Affirms USAA, QBE Insurance," S&P Global Market Intelligence, last modified 11 March 2021, https://www.spglobal.com/marketintelligence/en/news-insights/latest-news-headlines/insurance-ratings-actions-a-m-best-affirms-usaa-qbe-insurance-63133702.

262. Zainab Oyegoke, "Culturally Diverse Teams Are More Creative," CIPD, last modified 29 April 2021, https://www.cipd.co.uk/news-views/news-articles/managing-multicultural-teams.

263. Jeanne Meister, "Cisco HR Breakathon: Reimagining the Employee Experience," Forbes, last modified 10 March 2016, https://www.forbes.com/sites/jeannemeister/2016/03/10/the-cisco-hr-breakathon.

264. Erica Volini, Pascal Occean, Micheal Stephan and Brett Walsh, "Digital HR: Platforms, People, and Work," Deloitte Insights, last modified 28 February 2017, https://www2.deloitte.com/us/en/insights/focus/human-capital-trends/2017/digital-transformation-in-hr.html.

265. "How Happy Employees Lead to Happy Customers," Glassdoor, last modified 7 August 2019, https://www.glassdoor.com/blog/glassdoor-reviews-customer-satisfaction.

266. "Critical Thinking Tips for HR Managers and Leaders," Changeboard, last modified 19 July 2019, https://www.changeboard.com/article-details/16955/critical-thinking-tips-for-hr-managers-and-leaders.

267. "Old Money: Battle of Waterloo – Making a Killing," Global Capital, last modified 9 June 2015, https://www.globalcapital.com/article/ry3hgfjfbv79/old-money-battle-of-waterloo-making-a-killing.

268. "Bank of America – 35 Year Stock Price History: BAC," Macrotrends, accessed 12 October 2021, https://www.macrotrends.net/stocks/charts/BAC/bank-of-america/stock-price-history.

269. "The 2019 Federal Reserve Payments Study," Federal Reserve, accessed 12 October 2021, https://www.federalreserve.gov/paymentsystems/2019-December-The-Federal-Reserve-Payments-Study.htm.

270. I Ivanova, "People Are Quitting Their Jobs at Record Rates: That's a Good Thing for the Economy," CBS News, last modified 21 June 2021, https://www.cbsnews.com/news/workers-quitting-jobs-record-rate-economy.

271. "Mission & Culture Survey 2019," Glassdoor, accessed 21 October 2021, https://www.glassdoor.com/about-us/app/uploads/sites/2/2019/07/Mission-Culture-Survey-Supplement.pdf.

272. Amanda Stansell, "Which Workplace Factors Drive Employee Satisfaction around the World?" Glassdoor Economic Research, last modified 11 July 2019, https://www.glassdoor.com/research/employee-satisfaction-drivers.

273. "Gartner Identifies Key Emerging Technologies Spurring Innovation through Trust, Growth and Change," Gartner, last modified 23 August 2021, https://www.gartner.com/en/newsroom/press-releases/2021-08-23-gartner-identifies-key-emerging-technologies-spurring-innovation-through-trust-growth-and-change.

274. Quoted in "Folger Library – Churchill's Shakespeare," International Churchill Society, accessed 12 October 2021, https://winstonchurchill.org/resources/in-the-media/churchill-in-the-news/folger-library-churchills-shakespeare.

275. Urian B, "Amazon Turns 27: Here's How the Company Started from a Garage and Turned into a $1.77 Trillion Titan!" Tech Times, last modified 6 July 2021, https://www.techtimes.com/articles/262472/20210706/amazon-turns-27-heres-how-the-company-started-from-a-garage-and-turned-into-a-1-77-trillion-titan.htm.

ABOUT THE AUTHORS

Ignacio Garcia Alves focuses on linking strategy, innovation and transformation for technology-intensive and converging industries. With 30 years of experience, Ignacio brings out the best of his creative thinking and strategic problem-solving skills in advising CEOs from around the world.

Ignacio has been Chairman and Chief Executive Officer of Arthur D Little since 2011, and is member of several prestigious international business forums and boards.

Ignacio holds a MSc Electrical Engineering from Delft University of Technology and a MSc Management from ESCP Europe.

Philippe De Backer draws from his extensive experience as a global leader in financial services to share a provocative view on the disruption in banking and emerging business models, which are reshaping the sector and many industries as traditional business boundaries are blurring.

Philippe leads Arthur D. Little Global Financial Services Practice and has, over the last 25 years, worked with leading banks in multiple geographies, as well as recent capital market experience on Wall Street.

An MBA graduate from Tuck School at Dartmouth, Philippe De Backer is widely published and an investor.

Juan Gonzalez has worked extensively on the impact of technological change on the information flows that shape organizations and their interactions with their environment.

Juan leads the Arthur D Little Financial Services practice in Spain. He has advised financial institutions and technology companies on strategy and transformation for more than 25 years.

He is an IEEE Senior Member and MBA graduate from the Wharton School.